Following Directions

American University Studies

Series IV
English Language and Literature
Vol. 3

PETER LANG
New York · Berne · Frankfurt am Main

Edward Trostle Jones

Following Directions
A Study of Peter Brook

PETER LANG
New York · Berne · Frankfurt am Main

Library of Congress Cataloging in Publication Data

Jones, Edward Trostle.
Following Directions.

(American University Studies. Series IV, English
Language and Literature, ISSN 0724-1453; vol. 3)
Bibliography: p.
Includes index.
1. Brook, Peter. 2. Theatrical Producers and
Directors – Great Britain – Biography. I. Title.
II. Series.
PN2598.B69J66 1985 792′.0233′0924 [B] 84-47528
ISBN 0-8204-0116-1

CIP-Kurztitelaufnahme der Deutschen Bibliothek

Jones, Edward Trostle:
Following Directions: a Study of Peter Brook /
Edward Trostle Jones. New York; Berne;
Frankfurt am Main: Lang, 1985.
(American University Studies: Ser. 4, Engl.
Language and Literature; Vol. 3)
ISBN 0-8204-0116-1
NE: American University Studies / 04

The interviews with Peter Brook, from *Parabola: The Magazine of Myth and Tradition,*
courtesy of Larraine Kisly, Editor and Publisher.

Peter Brook, from *The Empty Space.* Copyright © 1968 by Peter Brook. Reprinted with
the permission of Atheneum Publishers.

Printed by Lang Druck, Inc., Liebefeld/Berne (Switzerland)

TABLE OF CONTENTS

ACKNOWLEDGMENTS

To many I owe a debt of gratitude for helping me to complete this study of Peter Brook. My earliest, dearest, and profoundest thanks are due my parents, Edward G. and Naomi T. Jones, who took me at a young age to the theatre where I saw among others my first Brook productions and who have over the years subsidized much of my subsequent theatre-going and research.

Besides correspondents and interviewees cited within my text to whom I am most grateful, I thank also Irene Worth, Paul Scofield, and other theatrical figures who graciously took time to answer questions I posed to them in letters. Responsibility for errors is, of course, wholly mine. I thank my former editor, Warren French, for his early encouragement of this study; I am sorry we could not finish it together.

The National Endowment for the Humanities -- and through it the American taxpayers -- underwrote my participation in two Summer Seminars for College Teachers which aided me greatly. As my text often indicates, I am much indebted to Professor Philip Rieff in whose seminar, "Art and Society: Primary and Secondary Images of Sacred Order," given at the University of Pennsylvania in 1979, I began my investigation of Peter Brook. The exciting theatrical atmosphere of New York City as made available to me by Professor Thomas Bishop in his seminar, "Avant-garde Theatre in Europe and the United States," at New York University in 1982 helped me to complete my inquiry. I thank the apostolic number of my colleagues in these seminars as well.

The administration of York College of Pennsylvania generously supported my efforts in several ways. I appreciated course load reductions for two semesters granted to me by my department chairman, Richard P. Batteiger, and the Dean of Academic Affairs, William A. DeMeester. Moreover, I thank President Robert V. Iosue and the Board of Trustees for awarding me a sabbatical leave in fall

7

of 1980 which permitted me to research in England. Friends in Britain, the Robert O'Dells, the John Waggoners, and the David Naylors, offered kind hospitality and help.

The staffs of the Schmidt Library of York College of Pennsylvania, of the British Film Institute, of the Nuffield Library, Shakespeare Centre at Stratford-upon-Avon, of the Lincoln Center Library of the Performing Arts, and of the International Theatre Institute in New York extended themselves most graciously for me, and I thank them collectively.

Lastly, my heartfelt thanks to my wife, Ruth, in whose company theatre and life remain a pleasure.

INTRODUCTION

The object of this study is the career in theatre and in film of the distinguished British director, Peter Brook – a rich terrain, to be sure, both in quantity and quality, but not one with especially dramatic beginning, middle, turning point, or, fortunately terminus. Moreover, Brook's career does not readily assume an especially distinctive pattern nor does it manifest a clear presiding myth. A proper recognition of the significance of Brook's career involves understanding the conventional relationship between what the director has done and the values an audience assigns to it. Thus this study relies on description of Brook's productions in isolation as well as together and on evaluation which is demonstrated by the extent of acceptance offered Brook's stagings by his audience witnessing them.

Since many of the details here presented are based on archival material and published remembrances from spectators in attendance at particular productions, audience perspectives loom large as a means of assessing Brook's position and influence in twentieth-century Western theatre. To a lesser degree some interpretation will be offered of the evolving tensions and resolutions between the director and the works he elected to stage, often derived from Brook's own published comments. Admittedly, there are built-in difficulties in conceiving a book on directing largely as a research project. Even with interviews and fairly extensive correspondence with participants, intimate knowledge of individual productions is not always possible. Indeed, in the case of this study, often the published public record was selected for inclusion at the expense of the personal anecdote for analytical and critical purposes.

Peter Brook has been written about in the English-speaking world more than any other stage director of the past twenty-five years, but in that extensive literature there is remarkable agreement about his importance and contribution to the modern theatre. The present study attempts to be both descriptive and critical as a work of assembly, interpretation, and finally evaluation of Brook's career. It is not a synthesis of all previous commentary, as if that were possible, but it does survey a great deal of received opinion, though often selectively and subjectively. Peter Brook has been extremely prolific, and his invention has been largely uninterrupted. There has been hardly a theatrical season since he was a young man of twenty-one when he has not brought out something new in the nature of theatre. We might say of Brook what Berlioz said of the young Saint-Saëns after he heard the latter's first symphony composed at about age eighteen, "Very good, but the young man lacks inexperience!" Given his auspicious beginning, Brook might have burned himself out, as directors often do; but he kept after new challenges, never satisfied to duplicate past achievements.

Brook's almost saint-like service to world theatre and the quantity and quality of his inter-action with so many of his contemporaries in the theatre arts make him a patron to something much larger than his own career. Never the self-serving director, Brook as a personality does not dominate center stage; that place is reserved for his notion of a theatre community to which everyone who works with him contributes and looks toward. Brook has not been the disciple of "modernism," creating an art without precedent; rather he has defined the "modern" direction of classical theatre and its tradition, somewhat analogous to the late George Balanchine's work in ballet.

Rather than through observance of strict chronology, the following pages examine Peter Brook's career according to media, thematic, generic, and structural groupings of theatre and film productions in the hope thereby of illuminating underlying conceptual unities which contribute to the creation of a director's oeuvre, if that term from literature may be adapted to this context. Effort is made to isolate some governing patterns informing and uniting the epigenetic and artistic development of Peter Brook even while it must be admitted that with Brook the chief expectation is often the unexpected. Nevertheless some backward illumination through critical hindsight does serve to show Brook's career as evidence of his coming to terms with his place in a volatile time theatrically and culturally. His career has been dramatic, but it would not be fair to say that every production has advanced a vast imaginative design. Still a figure or two in the carpet may appear as a retrospective of Brook's career unfolds. Like most directors, Brook is more interested in his latest work than in exhuming the past as a study such as this one must do. The productions and films discussed in the following chapters should make sense taken together, offering themes, topics, attitudes, which leave an impression of the state of theatre and culture, if only momentarily, upon Brook during the time covered and upon the reader now who desires to understand something of Brook's career.

Very little of Brook's biography figures in this study. In terms of his adult life the biographical facts are remarkably conventional. He married the beautiful and talented actress, Natasha Parry, who is like himself of Russian extraction, on November 11, 1951. Their marriage which continues at present has produced two children, a daughter, Irina Demetria, born on April 5, 1962 in Paris and christened in the Russian Orthodox Church, and a son, Simon, born on the 27th of September 1966. Natasha Parry Brook is a permanent member of the company attached to her husband's International Centre for Theatre Research and, therefore, often accompanies him professionally as well as personally on his frequent theatrical field-experiences throughout the world. On New Year's Day 1965, Peter Brook was named Commander of the Order of the British Empire at the annual New Year Honours. Admirers occasionally speculate as to reasons why he has not been subsequently knighted considering his contribution to the prestige of the British theatre. That Brook has chosen to work primarily in France for more than a decade may have inspired some hard feelings or at least disappointment about him in Britain. Despite the prominence of a number of contemporary English stage directors at the moment, there is no figure in London or Stratford to match Brook's authority in world theatre. Perhaps at home he has paid a price for that stature. No other British director, for example, serves in France as Officier de l'Ordre des Arts et des Lettres.

Because Brook appears very conversant on thinkers and their theories, it is possible to give the impression that he is principally an intellectual director and a great reader of serious texts. Actually Brook works much more instinctively than intellectually and claims he reads rather little; or at least he does not read critical analyses of dramatists in order to figure out how to stage them. One of the most forthright of Brook's descriptions of himself and his profession Jack Kroll published in *Newsweek* in 1980:

> I don't think of myself as a theater artist. I'm not particularly interested in theater or art as such. I'm a traveler, an explorer whom life has thrust into this field. I'm like a volcanologist who goes from volcano to volcano, looking for the biggest eruption. I've got themes I want to explore and experiments I want to make and places I want to see. It's all part of a process I hope is getting richer and richer in human material -- and human discovery.[1]

How appropriate that Peter Brook whose productions of Shakespeare in the last half of the twentieth century have generated the most excitement for the Bard sees himself as part of a new age of exploration astriding the globe geographically as Shakespeare did theatrically, and it is drama and theatre which Brook carries with him into the unknown in his search for those metaphorical volcanoes, which punningly might be seen as "peak-experiences." Brook has discovered during his years in the theatre from commercial director to writer/creator more recently that a poet's or dramatist's intuition may be more available to a peasant in the Third World than to a philosopher or a sophisticated Western theatre-goer. The theatrical experience of Peter Brook has been a journey, a test (of self, of assumptions and suppositions about others), a ritual passage, an exposure to peril, and an acceptance of a just and noble fear which will take up arms at the approach of insolence.[2] Such grandiloquence must be tested against the end of this study, not its beginning. The boy-wonder of London's West End matured into the explorer whose grip on the theatre is almost phenomenological, experiential, rather than traditionally dramatic, the stage director who recognizes only too well the corrupt emptiness of most theatrical versions of reality.

Early and late in his career Brook perceived a failure of moral vision and the breakdown of ideals not only in the theatre but also of a society in transition, i.e., the loss of what psychologists and sociologists call "beliefs systems" -- those commonly-held convictions which traditionally guide individual and group deeds as well as

12

aspirations. That Brook experienced such anxiety in the midst of his own highly successful career journey suggests the depth of his moral sensitivity. Unlike so many struggling directors, particularly in the United States, Peter Brook has enjoyed financial success and security from the beginning of his work in the theatre, but he repays that privileged position by accepting his obligation to advance theatre for others less well-blessed. His concern for purpose in the theatre has contributed to Brook's openness to the range of experiments and movements which have come and gone during his career. If he robbed many a nest along the way with his eclecticism, Brook usually arranged for each egg to hatch out something which was his own.

Among the avant-garde, Brook generally seems more the follower than the pioneer, touching base with major innovations and theories from the "poor theatre" to post-modern indeterminancy and retribalization through ritual; but his capacity to integrate [sometime discard] the experiments of others into something that works for a more mainstream end is distinctive and valuable. He avoids the miserable satisfaction of being consistent, and therefore eludes any neat system of synchronization, critically or otherwise. The direction Brook took in theatre more than a decade ago -- from a national phase to an inter-cultural phase -- has emerged as the genuine advance in the theatrical theory and practice of the eighties. Again Brook has helped to popularize something which in the work of others, such as Jerzy Grotowski's Theatre of Sources, remains rather more arcane. Some detractors of Brook may think of him as a kind of transcultural travel agent, but the present study argues that Brook better deserves the description to be applied to him specifically from the following excellent generalizations made by Richard Schechner:

> Most essentially, intercultural exchange takes a teacher: someone who knows the body of performance of the culture being translated. The translator of culture is not a mere agent, as a translator of words might be, but an actual culture-bearer. This is why performing other cultures becomes so important. Not just reading them, not just visiting them, or importing them – but actually doing them. So that "them" and "us" is elided, or laid experientially side-by-side.[3]

Brook the undergraduate language major at Oxford has learned to conjugate a good deal more than French in the intervening years, as he becomes a precursor of those who can practice other cultures, using this knowledge to enhance understanding of their own.

Brook's aim is nothing less than to re-direct the work and purpose of the theatre in, paradoxically, both an old and permanently revolutionary way. The material he is electing to stage increasingly is old -- the *Mahabharata* being a good deal earlier than his touchstone, Shakespeare; however, his methods seem startlingly postmodern in the sense of the perfomance not transmitting narrative action so much as what Richard Schechner calls "multiplex signals," composed of bits and pieces of information to be processed by performers and audience alike. If, as Schechner prophesizes, we shall see in theatre the coming of a postmodern traditional art and with it the return of a necessary, healing stability,[4] this study nominates Peter Brook as the non-political candidate to bring it about. Here, almost as surprise, Brook works on the cutting edge of change, perhaps because he had a head start instinctively. Brook is able to shift temporal channels with the best of the postmodernists, but he also demonstrates an inherent conservatism in his respect for the history of theatre being the history of dramatic literature. While Schechner claims that Brook continues to encourage performance texts,[5] I think, on the contrary, as in his projected work on the *Mahabharata*, his desire is to create a new work of dramatic literature which is the effect of seeing the French texts of the productions done by the ICTR. The director becomes playwright, and the text he produces may be done by others who have not been privy to the performance embodiment of it under his direction. Unlike so many so-called performance texts from other avant-garde directors and groups, Brook's "plays" are almost always based on actual texts -- be it an anthropological study published as *The Mountain People*, the libretto of Bizet's *Carmen*, or an Indian epic. For all his interest in performance, Peter Brook still venerates dramatic literature; he does not really overthrow authors as some twentieth-century directors have appeared to do before performers struck a coup against them, as for example in the solo performance art of a Stuart Sherman or the monologues of Spalding Gray. Once more there is a measure of

14

contradiction in Brook's approach to postmodern performance and his respect for texts of dramatic literature, yet the very multicentricity of experience is a principal postmodern trait.

This study tries usually to avoid excessive reliance on current code or buzz words like "postmodern." While the phrase seems apt in its application to Peter Brook's work at the end of the seventies and start of the eighties, it must be acknowledged that the director's interest in indeterminancy, things-space-time, ritual and re-tribalization -- concepts which now are placed under the rubric of post-modernism -- has been evolving long before the label became popular. Perhaps the greatest advantage of postmodernism as a contemporary intellectual movement is its breadth sufficient to include nearly all facets of Brook's eclecticism -- the "ism" to which he seems born, but the phrase itself may be little more than a convenience.

Peter Brook is an inheritor in the arts who revealed early and late in his career a knack for healing the rift between the modernist avant-garde and the theatrical mainstream; whether this success represented a conscious decision on his part I hesitate to say. I doubt strongly that he proceeded along these lines identifying himself therefore as a postmodernist. In motive and purpose Brook must be seen, though, as part of the therapeutic but again without necessarily his acceptance of the term. This study surveys the impressive career of the world-class director, Peter Brook, to reaffirm some of the ways he has exalted the theatre in our time with his uncompromising honesty, formalist grace, intellectual daring, and penetrating knowledge of the interrelationship of all humanity. For Brook in the beginning was the deed conceived as a performance. In his theatre the conventions of the stage come out newly minted and formed to be powerful elements rather than ornaments or mere gestures, yet the tradition of Shakespearean drama serves as the base for renewal. Here we collect, collate, and analyze recurring facts and details of Brook's career; but in considering his history we must not forget that a major characteristic of Brook's greatest productions is their ability to continue to spark the imagination long after the performance has ended, letting them live, so to speak, in the present tense for those people lucky enough to have experienced them in the theatre.

Because he has remained his own man in the midst of buffets
– many of which he has accepted gladly -- from one avant-gardism
after another, Peter Brook lets us at this point in his prolific career
pause, though not for long, and see how far theatre has come since
he began working in the decade of the forties. Furthermore, as a
director very much of his and our time, Brook brings us to a position
in world theatre and thought where consolidation is possible. Without theoretical polemics and explanations, Brook offers theatrical
action which synthesizes disparate movements in avant-garde aesthetics that have been jostling each other for the last twenty years. If
he is successful, the direction for theatre in the remainder of the
twentieth century may be delineated.

NOTES FOR INTRODUCTION

The policy followed in this study is to place all subsequent references to a text cited after the initial note in parentheses within the
body of the exposition.

1 Quoted in Jack Kroll, "Peter Brook's Volcanoes," *Newsweek*, May 19, 1980,
  pp. 101-102.

2 For some of these ideas I am indebted to the late Professor Victor Turner of
  the University of Virginia who graciously sent me an unpublished manu-
  script, "The Anthropology of Experience," from which I have drawn.

3 Richard Schechner, "Intercultural Performance: An Introduction by Guest
  Editor," *The Drama Review*, 26 (Summer, 1982), 3-4.

4 Richard Schechner, "The End of Humanism," in *The End of Humanism:
  Writings on Performance* (New York: Performing Arts Journal Publications,
  1982), pp. 95-106.

5 Ibid., "The Decline and Fall of the (American) Avant-Garde," p. 33.

Chapter One

THE CURTAIN RISES: BROOK'S EARLY YEARS

One of the few British stage directors who confirmed almost from the start of his long career that the twentieth century had become theatrically the age of the director is Peter Brook who has never performed as an actor like his English predecessors, the venerable actor-managers, but who embodies as completely as any figure in the theater today those talents associated with that distinctive entity of the modern theater known as the director. Brook's success arises from his genius for eclecticism, dependent on the strength of his individual response. Yet he has the ability to communicate that response to others so that performers and audiences alike participate in it; and, significantly, this power of theatrical communication for Brook is not limited to the English-speaking world. Peter Brook has made directing a global undertaking, not piecemeal in the manner of the reliable but curiously local British journeyman directors who stage show after show in a given season. Brook's vision of the theater is holistic, and his practice, as we shall examine in this study, is to get as many components of the theater and the world beyond the theater to interact so that the whole may well be greater than the sum of the separate parts.

Of perhaps more than passing interest in understanding his distinguished career is the Russian descent of Peter Brook, notwithstanding his archetypal English-sounding name. His parents, Simon Brook and Ida (Janson) Brook, were Russian students who met and married in Belgium where both were studying chemistry and the physical sciences at the University of Liège. They emigrated as refugees to England in 1914. Before long as pharmaceutical chemists the Brooks established a successful drug company, best-known for manufacturing a popular over-the-counter laxative named Brooklax. Born at their family home in Bedford Park, Chiswick, a first son in 1920, Alexis, now a practicing psychiatrist, and Peter Stephen Paul Brook on 21 March 1925.

Brook's parents were loving and rather indulgent, encouraging their son in his early artistic pursuits. An often-repeated story recalls Brook's father presenting his six-year old son with a toy theater complete with curtain, trap door, and working lights. On this stage with scenery and costumes cut out by him and his brother, Peter produced an interminable *Hamlet* of six hours duration for the delight of his family. J. C. Trewin in his biography of Brook records how with childish audacity, and maybe a little prescience, Brook as a youngster compiled a notebook inscribed *"Hamlet* by P. Brook and W. Shakespeare."[1] Similarly, before age ten, Peter Brook had his own 9,5 mm movie camera. The circumstances of Brook's youth and the pharmaceutical origin of his family's wealth are somewhat reminiscent of the upbringing of another notable British figure in the performing arts from an earlier generation -- Sir Thomas Beechum, Baronet, whose parents surpassed the generous encouragement of the Brooks by supplying their son with an entire symphony orchestra before whom he could practice conducting!

Brook's first public school was Westminster, but as a result of a serious glandular disease before his adolescence, he was sent to Switzerland for recuperation where he was tutored. Upon his return to England he entered Gresham's from which he departed during the early days of the Second World War for schools in Norfolk and Cornwall. Although he was asked to remain, Brook left his secondary schools at age sixteen to join a unit which made commercial and industrial films for Gaumont-British Films in suburban London. There he worked in many facets of film-making including scriptwriting, editing, and directing.

At his father's urging, Brook, now seventeen, entered Magdalen College of Oxford University in 1942 from which he received his degree in English literature and foreign languages in 1945. Because he was barred from joining the Oxford University Dramatic Society as a result of an insufficient period of residency, Brook turned his attention to reviving the Oxford University Film Society. It was with this organization that the undergraduate director made his first film, a version of Laurence Sterne's *A Sentimental Journey through France and Italy by Mr. Yorick* (1768), written, directed, and produced by Peter Brook on a budget of 250 pounds. Brook was able

18

to use Rex Whistler's sets borrowed from John Gielgud's production of Congreve's *Love for Love* which had successfully filled the Haymarket Theatre in 1943. The cast comprised undergraduate friends and classmates of Brook including the future film and theater director, John Schlesinger. Brook's choice of text has a compelling consistency to his own later career, as the subsequent peripatetic director, with his base of operations in France, would become a truly great and indefatigable traveller. The film itself was apparently seen by very few people and has become quite unavailable, probably through the director's design. Nevertheless, enough shared attitudes exist between Sterne and Brook to tease us into speculations of affinity between them as experimenters in the cultivation of visual responsiveness and as retrievers of objects to trigger memory. Much of Brook's characteristic conception of modern theater as a process of seeking rather than as a product found may owe as large a debt to Sterne as to more recent experimentalists and theorists.

After departing from Oxford, Brook again worked as a director and writer for the Crown Film Unit with whom he continued to produce shorts and advertising films. At Oxford in 1942, Brook had directed an amateur cast in Christopher Marlowe's *Dr. Faustus* which played briefly at the Torch Theatre, London. In 1945 Brook seized the opportunity to direct *The Infernal Machine* by Jean Cocteau at the Chanticleer Theatre Club in London and followed it with stagings of Rudolf Besier's *The Barretts of Wimpole Street* at 'Q' Theatre, Kew Bridge, London and Shaw's *Pygmalion* for the Entertainments National Service Association which took it on tour. During one of the dress rehearsals of this latter production, William Armstrong, director of the Liverpool Repertory Theatre, was sufficiently impressed by the young director to recommend Brook to Sir Barry Jackson who, in turn, invited the recent Oxford graduate to join the Birmingham Repertory Theatre where as part of the 1945-46 season Brook staged Shaw's *Man and Superman,* Shakespeare's *King John*, and Ibsen's *The Lady from the Sea*, all enhanced by the presence of an equally talented young actor, Paul Scofield. This initial association with Sir Barry Jackson led to Brook's first season at Stratford-on-Avon, discussed in a later chapter which deals expressly with the director's work on Shakespeare.

Also in 1946 Brook became associated with the Company of Four's tenure at the Lyric Theatre, Hammersmith, one of the most important so-called "fringe" theaters whose financial losses during this period were covered by the non-profit-making side of H. M. Tennent, Ltd., London's most successful producers with whom Brook would later be connected for almost all of his "commercial" enterprises. Peter Glenville's production, critically judged distinguished, of William Saroyan's *The Time of Your Life* had, for example, proven so expensive that virtually no money was available for the next production which happened to be Brook's staging of Alec Guiness's adaptation of Dostoyevsky's *The Brothers Karamazov* which starred Guiness. This production was assembled and presented for a mere 75 pounds. It received rave notices, but the audiences were small. Kitty Black who as translator collaborated with Peter Brook during this period of his early career recalls that "the whole team at the Lyric adored Peter and would have gone through fire and water if he wanted such a procedure in any of his future productions."[2] Without the benefit of an expensive set designed by Tania Moiseiwitch such as was provided for Peter Glenville's staging of Saroyan's play, Brook's production was notable for the economy of means and the clarity of ideas in his production, perhaps by necessity avoiding everything superfluous in expressing his conception.

In July of the same year Brook joined Guiness again to present Jean-Paul Sartre's *Huis Clos*, translated then in Kitty Black's version as *Vicious Circle*, but better-known later in English as *No Exit*, at the Arts Theatre Club. Interestingly, this production was the first play by Sartre to be produced in England. The cast included, besides Alec Guiness, Betty Ann Davies and Beatrix Lehmann with Donald Pleasance in the small role of the attendant to the doomed trio in hell. While some critics objected to the play's material of implied lesbianism and the like, most praised Brook's production as clever. Ronald Barker of *Plays and Players* observed prophetically as Brook's career turned out that "the power of the play was matched by a production which shattered the ordinary theatre-goer looking for a pleasant evening's entertainment in the theatre."[3] Moreover, Barker found in Brook's staging an imaginative vitality which had been absent from the British theatre during the war years. Brook, like his beloved Shakespeare, did seem to arrive on the London theater scene at a propitious moment.

As he often would do later in his career, once Brook embarked on staging a particular dramatist he continued with other works beyond his initial engagement with that playwright. Consequently, returning to the Lyric, Hammersmith, Brook collaborated for the third and last time in 1946 with Alec Guiness in a double-bill of two more Sartre plays, *Men Without Shadows* [*Morts sans Sépulture*] and *The Respectable Prostitute* [*La Putain Respectueuse*] in translations by Kitty Black. In the first play Brook altered Sartre's dramatic structure by eliminating the scene break between scenes three and four, an action which the director deemed necessary dramatically even as he dreaded having to say so to Sartre who journeyed to London for the opening. As it happened, no unpleasantness on this score ensued, but the plays were judged box-office failures in the pattern of the year's repeated Lyric, Hammersmith disasters.

From the outset of his career, Brook as a director did not inspire nervousness or limiting self-consciousness. He operated at a level of candor beyond embarrassment. As his earliest productions attest, Brook never suffered from that insularity which British culture alternately celebrates and laments; seemingly instinctively Brook assumed the holistic nature of human endeavors and creativity -- not for him the twoness or threeness of dramatic culture, but its oneness. The great significance of Brook's habit of mind in this regard becomes manifest fully in his more recent years, but it is provocatively potential in his earliest phase.

The Empty Space as summation and harbinger

Brook's theoretical and critical volume, *The Empty Space* (1968), provides his own lucid summation of the formative years of his career and prefigures the subsequent direction he has taken in the recent past. As prophecy and quasi-autobiography, *The Empty Space* exists as a seminal work of backward and forward illumination on Brook's theoretical assumptions as well as of his applied theatrical practice. Lively and candid in his self-appraisal, Peter Brook seeks

21

throughout this book which is based on lectures given originally at the University of Birmingham dispensations to what he calls "The Deadly Theatre," as he strives to help the theatre but indirectly other performance media as well fulfill a ritualistic and cognitive function. Brook demonstrates a scholarly appreciation of theatre history and of dramatic theory coupled with dramatic criticism, all buttressed or sometimes corrected by the authority of his artistic skills applied in stage productions.

We shall have occasion often in this study to refer to *The Empty Space*, since it is the most comprehensive record of Brook's working ideas, but it is worth quoting an early passage from the book as a springboard to later assessment:

> I can take any empty space and call it a bare stage. A man walks across this empty space whilst someone else is watching him, and this is all that is needed for an act of theatre to be engaged. . . .
>
> I will try to split the word [theatre] four ways and distinguish four different meanings -- and so will talk about a Deadly Theatre, a Holy Theatre, a Rough Theatre and an Immediate Theatre. Sometimes these four theatres really exist, standing side by side, in the West End of London, or in New York off Times Square. Sometimes they are hundreds of miles apart, the Holy in Warsaw and the Rough in Prague, and sometimes they are metaphoric: two of them mixing together within one evening, within one act. Sometimes within one single moment, the four of them, Holy, Rough, Immediate and Deadly intertwine.[4]

As the foregoing passage suggests, Peter Brook functions here as both critic and artist, and he sets himself against those who would consider theatre a wholly secularized pursuit.

The failure of the Deadly Theatre, as Brook sees it, is that it does not entertain adequately, quite apart from its not elevating or instructing. He compares this species of theatre to a prostitute who provides little genuine pleasure for the payment received. He inveighs less against the commercial theatre which often demonstrates considerable and undeniable appeal but against the so-called "classic" theatre with its ossified formulae and traditions:

> Of course nowhere does the Deadly Theatre install itself so securely, so comfortably and so slyly as in the works of

William Shakespeare. . . . We see his plays done by good actors
in what seems like the proper way – they look lively and colour-
ful, there is music and everyone is all dressed up, just as they
are supposed to be in the best of classical theatres. Yet secretly
we find it excruciatingly boring – and in our hearts we either
blame Shakespeare, or theatre as such, or even ourselves. *(The
Empty Space*, p. 10)

The director implicates the deadly spectator as causal contributor
to such theatrical fare, arguing that such a theatre-goer wants nothing
new to distract him from what is familiar and infinitely repetitious.
Indeed, Brook accuses almost every constituency of the theatre for
its complicity in the tedium which arises unchecked from Deadly
Theatre, especially a triad of critic, playwright, and director, to
assign responsibility beyond the audience. Brook challenges the
typical assumption on the part of the director that one should let a
play speak for itself: "If you just let a play speak, it may not make a
sound." (*The Empty Space*, p. 35) To the not wholly rhetorical
questions Brook raises at the end of his comments on the Deadly
Theatre -- "Why theatre at all? What for?" -- his second essay on the
Holy Theatre supplies a personal testament, which may be better
than answers, in a predicate of the ideal theatre where the invisible
becomes visible, the experience on the stage transcending for the
audience its experience in life.

Brook's conception of the Holy Theatre has provoked the most
controversy and generated the most misunderstanding of his categories. He expresses his debt to earlier theorists and directors like
Meyerhold and, in particular, Artaud, and finds the nearest approach
to the possibilities he envisions in the more recent work of Jerzy
Grotowski. The Artaudian formulation exerts the greatest persuasive
force upon Brook: "A Theatre working like the plague, by intoxica-
tion, by infection, by analogy, by magic; a theatre in which the play,
the event itself, stands in place of a text." (*The Empty Space*, p. 44)
Brook correctly recognizes in his working through of Artaud, that
rendering of the invisible, what in Durkheimian terminology might
be called further the interdictory, must take place in the repressive
mode, as the price one unconsciously pays for getting around the
interdicts. Brook shrewdly asks: "But is this revealing, is this contact

with our own repressions creative, therapeutic? Is it really holy -- or is Artaud in his passion dragging us back to a nether world, away from striving, away from light. . . (*The Empty Space*, p. 49) Because it is the unconscious which can best be equated with sacred order, as the repressive is to be identified with culture itself, Brook's creativity in its selfconscious theatrical application more frequently results in the therapeutic than in the holy, as the director himself almost admits. Brook laments the loss of consecrated acts in the contemporary theatre, but his conception of the Holy Theatre probably misjudges human resistances to the sacred. Therefore the therapeutic is often substituted for the sacred. In reality, what Brook diagnoses as the unresolved dilemma of Julian and Judith Becks' Living Theatre may likewise describe his own problems in developing the Holy Theatre: "Searching for holiness without tradition, without source, it [The Living Theatre] is compelled to turn to many traditions, many sources -- yoga, Zen, psychoanalysis, books, hearsay, discovery, inspiration -- a rich but dangerous eclecticism." (*The Empty Space*, p. 57) Therapeutic order-hopping, as we shall observe, pervades much of Peter Brook's work, even though as a director he seems aware that therapy distracts us from the soul-making journey which the noble aim of the Holy Theatre would map out. Admirable for his restraint and tact in not offering a facile blueprint for change and improvement, Brook makes the Holy Theatre a desideratum worthy in its vision, despite some difficulty in relating means to ends, of the best mysterious power that the institution of the theatre can manifest. The Holy Theatre retains the potential for authentic action and responsibility in the moral realm--the ritual enactment of sacred drama.

In his first two categories, Brook gives us the theoretical best and the actual worst of contemporary theatre practice -- both the Holy and the Deadly Theatre. His remaining categories represent the compromised amalgam which theatre usually is. The Rough Theatre, for example, stands as performance closest to the people, whether as puppet or shadow show or as fully staged drama as Shakespeare was presented in the Elizabethan Age. Brook finds its distinguishing characteristic the deliberate and even artful absence of style:

> The Rough Theatre doesn't pick and choose; if the audience is restive, then it is obviously more important to holler at the trouble-makers – or improvise a gag – than to try to preserve the unity of style of the scene. In the luxury of the high-class theatre, everything can be all of a piece: in the rough theatre a bucket will be banged for a battle, flour used to show faces white with fear. The arsenal is limitless: the aside, the placard, the topical reference, the local jokes, the exploiting of accidents, the songs, the dances, the tempo, the noise, the relying on contrasts, the shorthand of exaggeration, the false noses, the stock types, the stuffed bellies. The popular theatre, freed of unity of style, actually speaks a very sophisticated and stylish language: a popular audience usually has no difficulty in accepting inconsistencies of accent and dress, or in darting between mime and dialogue, realism and suggestion. (*The Empty Space*, p. 60)

Consequently, in light of the foregoing, Brook celebrates the "dirt" that gives roughness its edge in his paen to the popular theatre which he finds blessedly anti-authoritarian, anti-traditional, anti-pomp, and anti-pretense. Not surprisingly, he singles out Brecht for particular praise in this theatrical category, and he casts a favorable aside on Jean Genet as a more recent practitioner of the Rough Theatre. Finally, though, Brook returns to his beloved Shakespeare of the Elizabethan playhouse as the embodiment of both the Rough and Holy Theatre, of squalor and sacredness. Brook uses Shakespeare as a gauge to measure the health of the theatre, since approaches to this greatest of dramatists may fall anywhere from deadliness to holiness, with intermediate visitations to Brook's other categories, the Rough and Immediate Theatres along the way. The peculiar challenge of the Rough Theatre, as Brook sees it, is to capture the attention of its audience and compel its belief without resorting to meretricious tricks and covert manipulation. The roughness must be equated with honesty.

From the standpoint of much of his own work in the theatre, Brook's final category has perhaps the most interest autobiographically, since it bears closest witness to his own evolving theatrical practice and experience. The Immediate Theatre takes as a given that the practical problems of the theatre are likewise most often artistic ones as well. It is to Brook's aesthetic credit that he rarely separates the two in evaluating a solution to some problem of staging. Increasingly we come to appreciate Brook's reliance on improvisation in a number of theatrical decisions -- not only relative to acting – especially after absorbing the humor and embarrassment he shares with the reader relative to his first rehearsal of *Love's Labour's Lost* at Stratford in 1945 when he arrived, in youthful emulation possibly of Max Reinhardt's great *regiebuch* for each production, with a fat promptbook inscribing all the action which quickly reduced his actors to the cardboard cutouts of his model. On the basis of such experience Brook asserts his subsequent and enduring *modus operandi:*

> However much home-work he [the director] does, he cannot fully understand a play by himself. Whatever ideas he brings on the first day must evolve continually, thanks to the process he is going through with the actors, so that in the third week he will find that he is understanding everything differently. . . .
> In fact, the director who comes to the first rehearsal with his script prepared with the moves and business, etc., noted down, is a real deadly theatre man. (*The Empty Space*, p. 96)

Brook's aim in this last section seeks nothing less than endorsement of a necessary theatre keyed to the immediate realities of life and art, "one in which there is only a practical difference between actor and audience, not a fundamental one." (*The Empty Space*, p. 122) Significantly enough, his example of "a true image of necessary theatre going" is a psychodrama session in an asylum, which leaves the audience/participants changed somehow from what they were when they entered the session. Brook's therapeutic analogy of the necessary theatre may be little more than a latter-day version of Aristotelian catharsis to purge the more violent emotions of pity and fear. As Brook's career progressed he reduced his interest in psychology in favor of anthropology and a species of theatrical interculturalism, through the incorporation of Eastern and Western thoughts and techniques. The director's eclecticism seldoms suggests one favored aesthetic, though he does move toward a more selective eclecticism at times in his career.

The categories of theatre in *The Empty Space* hint that Brook has been from his earliest years a pupil of his own experience and other people's theories -- a habit which this study takes to be his most English trait. His endorsement of eclecticism represents the twentieth-century's substitute for the particular styles which flourished in and contented the audience for nineteenth-century theatre. Apart from any one theory of performance or any single style, Brook admits the empirical pleasure we have all experienced in the theatre which transcends all categorizing:

> Those are the moments of achievement which do occur, suddenly, anywhere: the performances, the occasions when collectively a total experience, a total theatre of play and spectator makes nonsense of any divisions like Deadly, Rough and Holy. At these rare moments, the theatre of joy, of catharsis, of celebration, the theatre of exploration, the theatre of shared meaning, the living theatre are one. But once gone, the moment is gone and it cannot be recaptured slavishly by imitation -- the deadly creeps back, the search begins again. (*The Empty Space*, p. 123)

Always the seeker and explorer in theatre and in life, Peter Brook's ideal for the theatre most nearly resembles that of the great Russian director, Meyerhold, until recently badly neglected in theatre history, as his legend is demystified by accurate data. Curiously, Brook has written and spoken less about Meyerhold as an influence on him than of Artaud and Brecht, but this Russian antecedent seems particularly apposite for Brook's search for a theatrical language, simple, laconic and economic in means which might lead to complex associations and extravagant ends for actors and audiences. Indeed Brook conceptions of the actor as shaman and the audience as true believers which have figured in the experiments of the more recent years increasingly assume a Meyerholdian character. Like the great Russian director, Brook has been less interested in psychological realism than in celebrating the stage qua stage to elicit visceral response from both actors and audience. Theatricality, unabashedly revealed, supersedes concerns of inner motivation in Meyerhold and Brook.

Even from his earliest period of success, Brook's conception of the production often became the star performance, usually representing a union of theoretical thinking with practical application and frequently bridging the gap between the fringe theatre and the commercial enterprise. It is understood that genius produces a large body of work that appears to comment on itself and on its own methods in a rich and complex way, resulting in the creation of an *oeuvre* as Brook has done on the principles articulated in *The Empty Space*. His productions sometimes appear as an act of devotion [and sometimes a criticism] directed at the forms of theatre that he has inherited, used, and often transcended -- a gesture at once of gratitude and of competition. On the other hand, taking advantage of serendipity, his own best ideas and inspiration may arise unbidden from the unconscious depths. Either way the vitality and creativity of the production nearly matches the imagination and achievement of the playwright himself, which may be the test of any "conceptual" director. Brook keeps taking risks perhaps because he becomes easily bored with success. But more basic to this risk-taking is Brook's constant quest for intellectual and spiritual connection which will restore the art of theatre to a place of centrality in contemporary life comparable to what the Shakespearean theatre enjoyed in the Renaissance.

In rather guru-like fashion, Peter Brook has brought actors and audiences willingly to submit to his guidance and that of the dramatist interpreted through the director's vision as he helps us to select stored experiences, images, perceptions which, in turn, can be shaped in accord with the design of the play produced. He has dreamed and shaped valued theatrical memories for two generations of playgoers and performers. Brook takes the risk of filling the empty space with new visions which yet reflect continuity with received theatrical craft, lore, and tradition. While he argues for the eclectic enlargement of possibilities in stage productions, Brook nevertheless recognizes that it is the special nature of the theatre to focus and narrow down life to a kind of distillation or quintessence. Herein lies the basis for the ritual enactment of sacred drama and recovery of the theatre's moral energy to which Brook humbly and poignantly aspires.

NOTES FOR CHAPTER ONE

1 J. C. Trewin, *Peter Brook: A Biography* (London: MacDonald, 1971). p. 89.
2 Letter from Kitty Black to the author, 2 July 1981.
3 Ronald Barker, "Enfant Terrible," *Plays and Players*, April, 1954, p. 6.
4 Peter Brook, *The Empty Space* (New York: Avon, 1969), p. 9.

Chapter Two

ECLECTIC EFFLORESCENCE: OPERAS, CLASSICS, AND COMMERCIALS

His career well-launched, Peter Brook set off in a number of directions, seemingly inimical to one another, yet linked by his imaginative energy and high standards of theatrical freshness. During an approximately eight year period, divided somewhat unequally between the end of the forties and the first five years of the fifties, with one or two further excursions beyond this chronology in the realm of the traditionally considered commercial theater, Brook gained great recognition before electing to pursue an entirely opposite approach to the performing arts once and for all. For ease of treatment, this period of Brook's career has been classified into three categories representing opera, classical plays, and commercial ventures.

I. Nights at the Opera

Notwithstanding the precedent of stage directors entering the opera house to produce isolated operas early in the twentieth century -- from David Belasco to geniuses like Max Reinhardt, Vsehold Meyerhold, and Constantin Stanislavsky, few remained within the lyric precincts for long. Fresh from the controversy surrounding his production of *Romeo and Juliet* (1947), discussed elsewhere, Peter Brook essayed the Royal Opera House, Covent Garden as its first Director of Productions (1947-50), as office Brook himself created and named. His function was to fix responsibility for artistic unity in production, supervising and coordinating the work of numerous directors and designers besides assuming stage direction for three operas during the first year of his tenure. Of particular concern to Brook and the management of Covent Garden was the fact that opera directors generally seemed concerned primarily about opening night, and the quality of their productions steadily declined from

31

that date without the intervention of someone responsible for maintaining the production subsequently.

At the beginning of his post Brook compared practices of English opera production with contemporary British staging of Shakespeare to the disparagement of the former:

> High standards in opera are not and must not be a luxury for the first night audience. . . . We must acknowledge that operatic production here is where Shakespearean production was fifty years ago. . . . There is a great deal to be done; the working out of a style, the integration of the producer's interpretation and the musical conception, the treatment of the chorus, the style of the movement and the acting, particularly the elaboration of a style of acting suitable to a big theatre.[1]

Brook's contribution to a re-evaluation of acting standards for opera was considerable. Likewise his candor in diagnosing the harmful effect of under-rehearsed singers who fly around the world to drop in for a performance somewhere without any recognition of the rudiments of acting or elementary grace of movement, while hardly endearing Brook to operatic superstars, presaged much recent opinion within world opera houses. Brook's corrective required distinctively produced operas which could not be staged interchangeably with any other company in the world. Good stage direction, in his view, was a prerequisite for successful realization of an operatic work on stage, and singers had to be obliged to put in hours of rehearsal in order for that end to be achieved.

Brook staged his first opera at Covent Garden in May of 1948 with Mussorgsky's *Boris Godunov*, featuring the noted Bulgarian bass, Paolo Silveri, who proved rather resistant to the new ideas the Director of Production brought to this Russian opera. The lighting for *Boris* was often singled out for praise, as was Brook's handling of the crowds in the opera. Visually the production was described as sumptuous. Some additional devices such as recorded bells, a procession of ghosts, and sliding doors in the Kremlin failed to impress or delight, and mutterings were heard from the critics about Brook's inattention to the text.

Backtracking a little, Brook's next two productions were fairly traditional but successful stagings of *La Boheme* and *The Marriage of*

32

Figaro in which he demonstrated the importance of the director's assuming responsibility for everything seen on stage so that one style and interpretation prevailed. Then Brook turned to a newly commissioned opera, *The Olympians*, with music by Arthur Bliss and a libretto by J. B. Priestley. With this production, critics and opera buffs claimed that Brook had exceeded "his place."[2] Parenthetically, the noted director Frank Corsaro has recently remarked that for the audacious stage director in opera that place in usually on his knees -- "I have often been forced," Corsaro writes, "to operate from that position, in the service or (depending on your point of view) disservice of opera."[3] The young Peter Brook stood in the advance guard of the conflict between old and innovative staging of opera a good ten years before the large influx of prominent stage directors into the opera house led to Andrew Porter's term of "malinscenation" in staging which amounts to malpractice, the separation of music and drama in a conspicuously poor or misconceived approach.

Unabashed, Brook went on to defeat finally with his next production, a new staging of Richard Strauss's *Salome* with sets and costumes designed by Salvador Dali which were intended, in the bold words of the director, to "reflect both the cold fantastic imagery of Wilde's text and the hot eroticism of Strauss's music."[4] Fortunately, some of Dali's more extraordinary effects could not be implemented such as equipping Salome's brassiere with fireworks which would go off at the end of her Dance of the Seven Veils, flying a hippopotamus overhead for a surrealistic fillip, or flooding the stage with blood so that the head of John the Baptist could float by. Nonetheless, a characteristic bit of surrealism was retained in that the frame of the harp which was played for Salome's dance was a painted giraffe's neck.[5] The Daliesque play of light and darkness in the production finally won its supporters, but critics complained about Brook's "deliberate reversal of stage directions,"[6] and disregard of the composer's original intentions.

Harold Rosenthal in his history, *Two Centuries of Opera at Covent Garden*, summarized the debacle of opening night in November, 1949 when Karl Rankl, the conductor of *Salome*, refused to take a curtain call, although the Bulgarian soprano, Ljuba Welitch, Brook's Salome, took eleven calls, and when Brook appeared for his bow he was booed off the stage.[7] With the British love of scandal, the press copy about Brook's *Salome* guaranteed sold-out houses for the remaining performances of the production; nevertheless, Brook's association with Covent Garden came to abrupt end early in 1950 concurrent with the final performances of *Salome*. Some years later, Brook told Charles Marowitz: "After two years of slogging I came to the conclusion that opera as an artistic form was dead."[8] Certainly Brook had been frustrated in his efforts to plan, organize, and monitor the large collaborative enterprise which defines grand opera to achieve a unified style as a result of the calm, logical, and decisive manner of the Director of Productions. In theory, Brook's purpose was valid enough, but with his youthful confidence he did not count on the controversy and resistance which overtook him. The institution of opera he found even less willing to change than the institution of the theater – to which he returned with alacrity and some sense of relief.

Apart from what he learned personally about lighting and stage design in meeting the challenge of operatic production, Brook's greatest legacy to the quality of opera performances in the years following his service at Covent Garden lay in the example of excellence he sought in singing actors who could sing beautifully, move well, and act expressively to supersede former stand-up-and-sing virtuosi. Brook recognized that singers did not gravitate to opera because they wanted to act, yet he helped motivate singers to acquire freer and more expressive movements on stage. Opera in the post-Brook years at Covent Garden and elsewhere in the western world has become more truly lyric theater, as Peter Brook early on had tried to make it. The parade of stage directors continues in temporary residence in the world's opera houses in witness to some felt need for better theater within musical drama.

In 1953 Brook staged Gounod's *Faust* at the Metropolitan Opera House in New York, on invitation from manager Rudolph Bing. This time Brook chose an unconventional interpretation without taint of the drastically experimental. His chief alteration was to bring the decor and costumes into conformity with the early nineteenth-century idiom of the composer's music rather than adhere to the medievalism which traditionally was the focus in stagings of *Faust*. Mephistopheles, therefore, was transformed into an elegant, caped, and monocled baron of Napoleonic Europe.[9] The production was well-received. Neither willful nor self-serving, as his detractors in London sometimes claimed of his work with Covent Garden, Brook demonstrated at the Met that opera could be creative theater without twisting old operas into new interpretations or inventing scenarios that had scant connection with either the music or the drama. Brook returned to Russian opera for his last staging at the Met in 1957 with Tchaikovsky's *Eugene Onegin* almost as a catharsis of his earlier hopes and ambitions in the operatic mode. Brook was not to take up opera again until a revival of *Carmen* in Paris late in 1981 which will be discussed briefly in a later chapter.

II. *Dark of the Moon* (1949): Critical Success and Commercial Management

In 1949 Peter Brook allied himself with Hugh Beaumont, managing director and often inspired impresario, of H. M. Tennent, Ltd., the largest and most consistently successful producer in London's West End, under whose management Brook would remain until his break with the traditional commercial theater years later. Brook's first play, under his new management, was the British production of *Dark of the Moon* (1949) by Howard Richardson and William Berney, which had been a New York success four years earlier under the aegis of the Messrs. Shubert, the American counterpart of the successful H. M. Tennent, Ltd. This rather operatic "Legend with Music," derived from the Smoky Mountain folk ballad of Barbara Allen, first attracted the attention of Brook and his assistant, Kitty Black, when they had seen it at the Royal Academy of Dramatic Arts. *Dark of the Moon* proved to be Brook's first unqualified success in the theater, apart from Shakespeare, and helped to launch his career. In retrospect, the choice of this play, combining an equal measure of local color and universal strangeness, and the nature of Brook's details go a long way to make *Dark of the Moon* a repository of distinctive Brook practices. Unlike the American critical reception of *Dark of the Moon* wherein the play was discussed as a work of dramatic literature, the London press tended to hail Brook's direction, saying, in effect, how brilliant of Peter Brook to produce such theatrical excitement out of what was essentially a simple folk tale of little consequence. Square dancing and American country/western music were just coming into vogue in Britain at this time.

After an extensive out of town tryout tour, Brook's production opened on March 9, 1949 at the Lyric Theatre, Hammersmith, and moved to the West End for a respectable run at the somewhat too small Ambassadors Theatre on April 12. With the exception of William Sylvester who played John the Witch Boy and Craddock Monroe as Preacher Haggler, both American actors, the cast was all British, though most of the character parts were performed by Welsh, Scottish, and Irish actors whose temperaments seemed more suitable to those roles than those of very English actors. In order to obtain credible Appalachian dialect and accents for the company, Brook had Howard Richardson, co-author of *Dark of the Moon*, record some of the dialogue and songs for the cast to work from. The results were spectacular. Shelia Burrell's highly-praised Barbara Allen evidenced as much Appalachian authenticity as William Sylvester's John. Later Howard Richardson commented on the effect Brook achieved with the cast's accent: "They succeeded to such an extent that I felt I was back in Black Mountain, North Carolina, my home town. Going backstage after the performance and hearing the cast talking in flawless Noel Coward/public school diction, I felt like saying to them, 'Aw, come off it. Who are you foolin'? You're all Tar Hells just like me.' "[10] To be sure, such attention to verbal and non-verbal nuance would become a Brook trademark in later years. The production's sets were also designed by Brook, although executed by Hubert Gurschner and W. Stanley Moore, and in every aspect *Dark of the Moon* sustained the warp of authenticity and enchantment.

The deceptively simple story of a witch boy who temporarily gains humanity in order to marry Barbara Allen, the girl he has impregnated, only to lose that humanity along with his wife, child, and, finally, any memory of all of them elicited Brook's own theatrical conjuring for a production which seemed more supernatural and exotic in its presentation of American folk material in London than

36

it might have in New York. But Brook's boldness of conception and superb pantomimic choreography were stunning and original. For example, at the end of the play when John has been restored to being a witch, Brook added the devastating touch of having John kick his unrecognized and forgotten wife off the rock, where she has been lying in an almost romantic position of peaceful death. Her body then sprawled on the stage, her knees spread apart and raised, with her dress pulled up. This gruesome image recalled the earlier rape scene where Marvin Hudgens took Barbara Allen violently, with the encouragement and approval of the townspeople at a revival meeting as an aggressive way to renew her place in and subjugation to the Christian community. The mountain folk celebrate the grace of the heavenly Lamb, but Brook highlighted the actuality of rape which is disguised in their paean. This particular scene, which had been suppressed in the New York production after much criticism on the road about it, was restored in Brook's *Dark of the Moon* to memorable dramatic effect. Brilliant in themselves, these sequences anticipate the images of cruelty and pain which occupy so many stages, figuratively and literally, in Brook's subsequent career.

Brook early manifested considerable talent for working with large casts to achieve a genuinely ensemble performance. The revival meeting and the public dance in *Dark of the Moon* engendered for the London audience a participatory response that bordered on the ritualistic. Preacher Haggler's "congregation" extended well beyond the boundaries of the proscenium arch, and at least one critic was moved to speak of Brook's production as a "supernatural experience," all from a twenty-four year old director, a "boy. . . with a genius for production that escapes many an established director old enough to be his grandfather."[11] As anyone who is familiar with *Dark of the Moon* in performance can testify, on the basis of almost any competent production, amateur or professional, the play quite easily invites this kind of identification and empathetic response, which is not to derogate the confirmed excellence of Brook's exciting staging. Perhaps the supposed simplicity of the folk material in *Dark of the Moon* permitted the London critics to accept and commend in Brook's direction what formerly some of them had considered "production tricks" as now the inspired means necessary to create a poetic atmosphere and to connect anything nicely to everything, from the movements of the constellations to the rituals of eating in the Smoky Mountains of the United States. While Brook himself has never acknowledged the centrality of *Dark of the Moon* in his career, it probably should be accorded a larger significance than it has previously enjoyed for its combination of holy and rough elements in his theatrical crucible as well as for its place in the ascendancy of his reputation as a director. While *Dark of the Moon* was not a runaway commercial hit, it surely substantiated Hugh Beaumont's faith in the young director as the Stratford *Love's Labour's Lost* had earlier in 1946 confirmed Barry Jackson's foresight in turning a major production over to Peter Brook.

Later in his career Brook would study Artaud and openly strive to implement some of the latter's theoretical positions in performance. If *Dark of the Moon* was not informed by the sophisticated theorizing of some subsequent Brook productions, the director, nevertheless, instinctively used effects that were often immediate and painful in an incipiently Artaudian fashion. His address to danger was greater and more visceral in Brook's production of the play than in other productions of *Dark of the Moon* by directors as diverse as Guthrie McClintic, Jose Quintero, and Vinette Carroll. Author of the play, Howard Richardson, ranks the Brook production as the best by far of the numerous presentations he has seen.

From the moment the curtain went up in Brook's production and the audience beheld a somewhat stylized and iconic black mountain-top in North Carolina, the drama was born in the sky. The visualization was complemented by the ear's response to the terror of witch-cries interrupting the silence. From physical effects, Brook retrieved and projected ritual through music and rhythmic forms, finding metaphor deeply rooted in the Smoky Mountain world of ordinary, but to London audiences extraordinary, beliefs and sensory experience. In some respects, Brook's production of *Dark of the Moon* anticipated his later interest in anthropology, folklore, and shamanism. The eagle, off stage, toward which John the Witch Boy runs at the end of *Dark of the Moon*, becomes perhaps emblematic of the magic force Brook seeks identification with throughout his long career. Fabling and bird-lore will exert mounting appeal to Peter

Brook in the following decades as a means of dramatizing the elemental realm between commonplace thoughts and the buried life of deepest instincts. Everyone associated with Brook's *Dark of the Moon*, according to Kitty Black, recalls it with pride and great emotion,[12] but it has the further importance of beginning for him a period of long cultivation of mythic concerns and the search for an appropriate aesthetic to go with them.

III. Brook and Anouilh: The French Connection

A playwright the Francophilic Peter Brook earnestly staged in a series of productions until his interest and his audience's delight waned was Jean Anouilh with whom the director was most often associated in England with adaptations by Christopher Fry. Because Anouilh occupied a position in the French theater somewhere between the avant-garde and the commercial "boulevard" success, he is a particularly interesting dramatist for Brook's own pilgrimage from the popular theater to the experimental, from the commonplace of all the world's a stage to a genuine understanding of the relationship of theater and life. Anouilh's theatricalism which calls attention to itself so frequently in his plays invites comparison with Shakespeare's own kind of self-reference, and this analogy may help explain Brook's enthusiasm for the twentieth-century French dramatist for a time, paralleling his anterior and more enduring commitment to Shakespeare.

Still possibly "moon-struck," Brook's first Anouilh production was Christopher Fry's adaptations, called a "charade with music," *Ring Round the Moon* (1950), the English version of *L'invitation au château* (1947) which had been a great success in Paris, the earliest of what became known in the Anouilh canon as *pièces brillantes*. A highly stylized and romantic work, *Ring Round the Moon* traces two couples, one innocent and sweet, the other detached and cynical, through a number of misunderstandings and an enormously complicated plot before a happy ending may be tenuously won. Anouilh directs the audience's attention frequently to the artificiality of the play, represented most conspicuously by the presence of two young male characters, supposedly twins, played by the same actor -- a device which was old when Feydeau used it. In Brook's production, the actor for these roles was again Paul Scofield who charmed his audience by exiting as one character and reappearing immediately as the other. At the end of the play when all the characters are on stage, one of twins sends word asking to be excused from attendance for reasons that will be understood. Brook brought to his staging of the Anouilh/Fry comedy of manners the distinctive blend of exuberance and delicacy of timing seen earlier in the somewhat similar *Love's Labour's Lost*. Scofield was ably supported in this production by Claire Bloom and Margaret Rutherford.

A year later Brook staged the English version of Anouilh's *Colombe* (1951), adapted by Denis Cannan with whom Brook would often collaborate subsequently. This bittersweet comedy of ideas set in the Paris Theater of 1900 tells of a struggling young concert pianist who must give up his wife when she enters the theatrical world of artifice quite unlike his own. At this point in his career Brook was drawn to stylish French confections with some admixture of intellectual ingredients. Julien, the pianist, enters military service and turns his wife over to the care of his mother, Mme. Alexandra, a reigning stage luminary. In Brook's production the women were portrayed respectively by Joyce Redman and Yvonne Arnaud. A playwright who has written various star vehicles for Mme. Alexandra, includes a small role in his next play for Columbe which catapults her to fame and a rather more pliant social and moral life than she enjoyed in her puritannical past as a bride. Unable to cope with the perhaps justifiable suspicions of her husband, Columbe is persuaded to make her separation from him permanent at the end of the play. Brook had his own problems with the monotonic quality of this domestic dilemma, but the high-spirited caricatures of backstage life which Anouilh boldly penciled in received incisive presentation and bravura performances. From the long-suffering secretary to the star, from unctuous theater manager to aging matinee idol, Brook secured the dynamic effects for which he was becoming famous. In general, Brook's production was critically judged to be superior to Anouilh's play, but it was not a box-office success. Yet Brook's reputation for directing plays by the French dramatist continued to increase, achieving its greatest glory with the next Anouilh production.

40

Triumph for Brook with Anouilh came with Christopher Fry's translation of *L'Alouette* (1953), entitled *The Lark* (1955), another account of Joan of Arc which in England was often unfavorably compared to Shaw's *Saint Joan* but not to the detriment of Brook's production. While Brook's staging may have followed a little too scrupulously the French staging of the play, by the undisclosed Jean Anouilh, without actually matching it in any particular way, the English collaborators, Brook and Fry, paid compliment to the French original with their fidelity to it.[13] The Maid of Orleans was beguilingly portrayed by Dorothy Tutin, alumna of Brook's film of *The Beggar's Opera* (1953), with the distinguished English character-actor, Laurence Naismith, as Cauchon, Bishop of Beauvais, and Richard Johnson as Warwick.

As customary in his productions of the fifties Brook received praise for his skillful handling of crowds on stage in *The Lark*. In the trial scene, for example, Brook included the major characters with the extras, all comprising a company of actors about to go through their paces. Unobtrusively he related the story of Joan's girlhood by having her mother, father, and brother speak their lines from the middle of the encircling onlookers. Then, with equal casualness, they vanished into the throng. John Dexter would duplicate something of the same effect in his staging of *Equus* years later. Brook found Anouilh's innovative and inherently cinematic method of fluid presentation congenial to his own technical interests: the flash-backs, lap-dissolves, dual and split-time sequences, dialogue yielding to monologue and interior narration. Adapting the setting designed by Jean-Denis Malcle for the French production, Brook used movable sections of low fence railings which actors could lift and position to define various locales as the play's action proceeded.

Brook's last effort with Anouilh material took place somewhat later with *L'Hurluberlu ou le reactionnaire amoureux*, known in the English of Lucienne Hill's adaptation as *The Fighting Cock* (1959), which Brook staged in New York with Rex Harrison and Natasha Parry, Mrs. Peter Brook. As performed by Paul Meurisse as the General who would save his country but cannot manage his family, the play proved to be among the most popular of Anouilh's many works in its Paris production. Brook's approach to this comedy with tragedy in pursuit was not so fortunate. The formerly open admirer of Brook's work, Harold Clurman, who had directed his own unseccessful production of *Colombe* a few years before, assailed the director on this occasion: "The worst of *The Fighting Cock* is that the production has been meaninglessly stylized. . . . There is shouting and some cute stage business, but no atmosphere or idea is established."[14] On the other hand, Brooks Atkinson saw the production quite differently and far more favorably, especially praising Rex Harrison for the role of his career and Natasha Parry for "a beautifully composed performance that contains youth, sadness, restlessness, sympathy and valor."[15] The audience did not materialize, and the play closed with fewer than a hundred performances. Brook, despite good intentions and perhaps over-much effort, could not perform the necessary act of translation this time round of Anouilh's "conversation-piece" play. Slickness without the core of Anouilh's more deeply-felt truths too often dominated Brook's production. Trying to capture the tone and style of the Anouilh play, Brook built up his own sly allusions, but regrettably he found himself and his production cornered rather than enlarged by them.

IV. *The Little Hut* (1950; 1953): Thumbs Down across the Sea

In an even lighter vein than Anouilh, if still derived from France, Andre Roussin's play adapted by Nancy Mitford as *The Little Hut* captivated the West End in a Peter Brook production. The almost one-joke sex comedy of husband-wife-lover, all in evening clothes, marooned on a desert island, sharing the wife on alternate weeks until a supposed savage comes to join the ménage for a foursome seems unpromising for a successful production short of the most undiscriminating dinner theater. Brook's London production proved otherwise, perhaps thanks largely to the cast, most notably Robert Morley as the insouciant husband, with the able support of Joan Tetzel as the inconstant wife, and David Tomlinson as the humorously aggrieved lover.

Despite long runs in Paris and London, when *The Little Hut* migrated to New York in a production also directed by Peter Brook, it sunk swiftly and ignominiously. The hard-working New York cast could not succeed as the London cast had. Roland Culver assumed the former Morley role without the same panache; Colin Gordon was the lover, and the beautiful Anne Vernon, herself French, was the wife, now handicapped in presenting a convincing Mayfair manner. Later Brook would direct a distinguished film based on an island premise, *Lord of the Flies* (1963), but the sea-change of *The Little Hut* from London to New York was far from happy. Eric Bentley judged Brook's frenetic direction and Oliver Messel's over-wrought set as joint contributors to the debit side of the production as a result of their shared "note of self-congratulation, -- of pompous whimsy, ponderous cuteness -- which is the ruin of the evening."[16] Bentley concluded that Brook and Messel represented what he terms the new English aestheticism, which stridently endeavored to mean nothing. The vacuity of *The Little Hut* was manifest in the United States by and through the very means, alas too energetic and clever, which were meant to disguise the hollowness within. Brook was possibly too near his operatic phase at this time to encourage the minimal effects which were to work so well in his later productions. He worked so hard on the arch-telling, especially to American audiences, that *The Little Hut* lost its slight subtlety and amoral comic appeal. While Robert Morley correctly had worked somewhat against the material of the play in the London production, the New York cast worked too deligently with it to audience stupefaction.

V. *Venice Preserv'd* (1953): A Coronation Restoration

In the same year as *The Little Hut*, which happened to be the Coronation Year in which Elizabeth II became sovereign, H. M. Tennent, Ltd. produced Peter Brook's staging of the Restoration quasi-"heroic" tragedy of 1682 by Thomas Otway, *Venice Preserv'd, or A Plot Discovered* (1953). Notwithstanding Kenneth Tynan's classification of it among those long unopened play which Brook thrived on, Otway's masterpiece had been revived oftener than any other English non-Shakespearean tragedy, if seldom in the twentieth century. Many scholars consider *Venice Preserved*, written in blank verse, as the last expression of the Elizabethan tragic vein and the final reawakening of the Renaissance dramatic genius; modern theatergoers at the Lyric, Hammersmith, where Brook presented it with a talented and prestigious cast found Otway's play dramatically effective and theatrically exciting. The play is structured on a personal and psychological base with the tragedy emerging from the theme of friendship being stronger and higher than love in a struggle against corruption within the Venetian Senate. As a result of conflicting loyalties on the part of the play's three chief characters -- Jaffeir, performed by John Gielgud; Pierre, played by Paul Scofield, and Belvidera, performed by Eileen Herlie -- all meet their deaths in scenes of pathos and sentiment. The men die in a spectacular, hair-raising scaffold scene wherein Jaffeir stabs Pierre to fulfill the latter's request to be spared a felon's death on the rack and then kills himself, as atonement for his betrayal of Pierre which has led to this gory scene. Belvidera who is wife to Jaffeir had persuaded him to betray his friend Pierre in order to save her father's life; she, in turn, goes mad in a prolonged scene before her own demise. In the meantime the bloody ghost of Jaffeir makes a final appearance for a nice Senecan effect with the added fillip of the dying Belvidera lusting for this ghost of her husband.

Obviously the overwrought ingredients of Otway's *Venice Preserved* share similarities with elements in other plays of this period in Brook's career. For much of its theatrical history, following the sexual openness of the Restoration period, some bawdy scenes, originally written according to legend at the suggestion of Charles II himself, were purged from the play in performance. Not surprisingly, Peter Brook restored them. Samuel Johnson had commented on these scenes in question in his eighteenth-century assessment of *Venice Preserved* as "a tragedy which still continues to be one of the favourites of the public notwithstanding the want of morality in the original design, and the despicable scenes of vile comedy with which he [Otway] has diversified his tragic action."[17]

The scenes represent the amorous play between a prostitute, played expertly in Brook's production by Pamela Brown, and her masochistic old protector, Antonio, a Venetian senator whom Otway modeled satirically on the historical figure of his era, Anthony Ashley Cooper, the first Earl of Shaftesbury. In Brook's production Richard Wordsworth won plaudits for his portrayal of Antonio. The scenes are usually known as "Nicky Nacky," named for the sobriquet Antonio attaches to Aquilina. He desires her to abuse him as if he were an animal, especially a dog, in a provocative game of fantasy and reality characterized by erotic pain and humiliation which anticipates other de Sade excursions in Brook's career. Dramatically, these incidents relate to the theme of corruption in the Venetian Senate against which Jaffeir and Pierre conspire. Brook managed also to link up this material with the pervasive references to laceration imbeded in the play's imagery. In this regard, Brook's production looked forward to the interpretive direction taken by more recent scholars of the Restoration theater to the effect that Otway's play intentionally attacks the Restoration heroic ideal by emphasizing man's inability to control himself, especially in his animal and sexual nature. Derek W. Hughes, for example, comments on Otway's procedure in the play which Brook's production clearly mirrored: "Otway consistently uses imagery to illuminate his characters' psychology; they reveal their natures by translating human situations into animal ones and by expressing themselves in erotic imagery; in addition, financial imagery reveals an attitude towards relationships which cannot rise above the levels of prostitution and of sacrifice imagery in a primitive mentality."[18] Brook staged *Venice Preserved* appropriately to make graphic the play's association of eroticism and violence, a theme of abiding importance in some later Brook productions. As Derek Hughes further observes, in a perceptive remark which surely should win agreement or at least some amused interest from Peter Brook, the dramatist with whom Otway bears the greatest resemblance is neither of his well-known contemporaries John Dryden nor Nathaniel Lee but rather the twentieth-century Jean Genet!

Kenneth Tynan praised Brook's production and Leslie Hurry's decor for going straight to the play's atmospheric point -- "which is that, while reading it, you get the eerie sensation of being underground, trapped in a torch-lit vault." (*Curtains*, p. 51) In the scene where the two conspirators meet in a dark celler Brook's and Hurry's pictorial intelligence captured that quality concretely and expertly. Always the problem in producing Otway's *Venice Preserved* was deciding where the emphasis should be placed -- on the politics, the pathetic elements of feelings and sensibility, the quasi-heroic parts, the scurrilous comedy, or the sense of tragic meaning implied by the play's events. Brook succeeded in touching on all of these for a fusion of dramatic vision which, without making any gratuitous appeal to the twentieth century, found in the play itself interest less to the heart than to the nerves. Along with the Shakespeare plays of this period which Brook staged -- *Measure for Measure* (1950), *The Winter's Tale* (1951), *Titus Andronicus* (1955), and to a lesser extent, *Hamlet* (1955) -- the director displayed imaginative insight into classic plays with the restoration of *Venice Preserved* to the modern British theater.

VI. Some Failures and Near-Misses: The Uses of Adversity

Not every production Brook mounted proved successful, but the number of outright failures in his career is astonishingly small for such an active director. As if to confirm, at last, some measure of fallibility, Brook's early unbroken string of successes finally frayed a bit when his production of John Whiting's *A Penny for a Song* (1951) closed after three weeks in the early spring at the Haymarket Theatre. The cast was a strong one including Alan Webb, Virginia McKenna, and Ronald Squire, and Brook once more showed his acumen in being drawn to work by a promising playwright whose career had yet to flourish in his own country.

In terms of lack of commercial success 1954 stands as one of Brook's worst years. In April Brook staged Christopher Fry's *The Dark Is Light Enough* with Edith Evans, exquisite as the Countess Rosmarin Ostenburg. The play was greeted as a beautiful but dull star vehicle. Brook followed this production with a trifling comedy by Arthur Macrae, entitled *Both Ends Meet* (1954). Presented in June at the Apollo Theatre, London as typical West End summer fare, the play sported an attractive cast with Brenda Bruce, Alan Webb, Miles Malleson, and the playwright himself, Noel Coward-like, in a leading role, but, as the title suggests, closure came quickly, shortly after *Both Ends Meet* opened.

The remaining Brook tribulation of the year was the ill-fated New York production of *House of Flowers* (1954), a musical comedy with book by Truman Capote and music by Harold Arlen concerning a rivalry between two Caribbean island bordellos. The almost too lush sets and spectacular costumes were designed by Oliver Messel who had failed to please the New York critics with the earlier Brook production of *The Little Hut*. In *The Empty Space* Brook reminisces, rather disingenuously, about behind-the-scene elements of the commercial Broadway theater from his experience with this production:

> On the first day of rehearsal of *House of Flowers*, its composer Harold Arlen arrived wearing a blue cornflower, with champagne and presents for us all. As he hugged and kissed his way round the cast, Truman Capote who had written the libretto [curiously operatic description] whispered darkly to me, "it's love today. The lawyers 'll be in tomorrow." It was true. Pearl Bailey [the show's star] had served me with a 50,000 dollar writ before the show reached town. For a foreigner it was (in retrospect) all fun and exciting – everything is covered and excused by the term "show business" -- but in precise terms the brutal warmth directly relates to the lack of emotional finesse. In such conditions, there is rarely the quiet and security in which anyone may dare expose himself. I mean the true unspectacular intimacy that long work and true confidence in other people brings about – on Broadway, a crude gesture of self-exposure is easy to come by, but this has nothing to do with the subtle, sensitive interrelation between people confidently working together. (*The Empty Space*, p. 18)

Brook's turn to experimental workshop conditions as the basis for theatrical discovery later in his career may well have been inspired by the foregoing circumstances of staging a would-be blockbuster musical under the practices and expectations of the commercial Broadway theater.

An amusing sidelight of this production in light of Brook's subsequent devotion to exotic travel as a means of deepening the art of drama was a press release which boasted that Brook had visited Martinique and Haiti immediately prior to becoming director of *House of Flowers*; however, it did not specify bordello visitation as necessary preparation for the show.[19] As with the sexuality in *The Little*

Hut, little of its true power was acknowledged, seriously or comically, in *House of Flowers*. Thus the point of the musical was not very clear in Capote's fey book which suggested a bird-like or doll-like world removed from any possible reality of prostitution. Johnny Mercer was called in during rehearsals to re-write the lyrics for the show, and some improvement in them over the original ones may be assumed.

The talented black cast headed by the estimable Pearl Bailey as Mme. Fleur, the eponymous proprietress of the House of Flowers, also included Juanita Hall of *South Pacific* fame and the young Diahann Carroll in her Broadway debut. The original choreographer chosen for the show was none other than George Balanchine who was replaced by Herbert Ross, famous more recently as a successful movie director of stylish kitsch. The Haitian-inspired dances, performed brilliantly by Carmen de Lavallade, were unanimously praised for their beauty and apparent authenticity. Brook the later ritualist recycled the show's Voodoo ceremony which required only magic and a pool as the most enduring vestige of this otherwise rather forgettable musical. *House of Flowers* managed to hold its own on Broadway for five months from December 1954 until spring of 1955.

VII. Voilà – A Hit! *Irma la Douce* (1958;1960)

At last with another British adaptation of a French import, Brook achieved commercial success with a musical comedy, the Marguerite Monnot and Alexandre Breffort show, *Irma la Douce* (1958;1960), with English book and lyrics by Julian More, David Heneker, and Monty Norman. The three-year British run of the show was considerably longer than its New York tenure, but *Irma la Douce*, which opened in New York during fall of 1960, ran for a year and a half on Broadway and subsequently enjoyed much success on the road in the United States. Brook took an originally small and charming Parisian show, which was performed in a tiny "pocket" theater, and successively inflated its proportions first in London and, then, most grandiosely of all, in New York. For the Broadway version additional orchestrations were made in the form of dance music by John Kander, later to collaborate on *Cabaret,* and elaborate choreography by Onna White. Rolf Gerard's sets and costumes were less obtrusive than Oliver Messel's earlier contributions to Brook's work in the commercial theater, and his saucy Place Pigalle on Broadway obtained at least temporarily landmark status during the run of the show.

In a *New York Times* interview, prior to the Broadway debut of *Irma la Douce,* Brook claimed that his chief efforts in re-staging the musical were to perfect technical details which he submitted were more crucial in such a show than in classical theater:

> It's a refreshing change but a much more difficult job than a Shakespeare tragedy. If an actor flubs a line in *Hamlet* there are enough other immortal lines to carry him. But in a bubble like this [*Irma la Douce*] the thinking must be on the split second, every gesture and word right, or the whole thing is shattered.[20]

The refinement of blackouts, timing, gesture, and lighting effects was of the highest order in Brook's production of *Irma la Douce,* and his performers, a number of whom had extensive experience in Shakespeare and the classics, displayed versatility often bordering on virtuosity.

One highly unusual feature of the production was the appearance of only a single actress, the multifaceted gamine, Elizabeth Seal as Irma, re-creating her acclaimed London role. The rest of the fourteen-member cast was male, which approximates the kind of locution much favored in the anglicized *Irma.* Out of a company of seemingly immense depth and accomplishment, Keith Michell, as the leading man also recreating the role he played in the London production, and Clive Revill, as the rather Brechtian narrator/bartender, appeared especially notable. Brook's earlier work in filming *The Beggar's Opera* perhaps contributed to his interest in *Irma la Douce,* since the latter, too, is really a ballad opera, though nearer in style to the Brecht/Kurt Weill *Threepenny Opera* than to the John Gay original. The Paris underworld whose denizens enliven *Irma* speak a slang, or argot, which even in France required a glossary in the theater program. The English version retained much of the original French argot and used it to good effect throughout the musical.

49

Irma herself is the favorite prostitute, *poule*, of Montmartre, wildly admired and employed by the gang called the Sons of France. She falls in love with an impoverished law student, Nestor le Fripe, and continues working in her profession to pay for his studies. At this point Alexandre Breffort introduces intrigue worthy of Feydeau. Nestor desires to be Irma's only customer; to do so he disguises himself as a middle-aged protector, Monsieur Oscar, who will pay for her exclusive services. Irma is delighted by the arrangement, but the divided Nestor, exhausted by work in order to pay for Irma's services and further fatigued by the services themselves, experiences a psychological crisis. He becomes even more jealous of his alter-ego, Oscar, than he was of Irma's former customers and resolves to "kill" his rival. Executing this *crime passionel* results in Nestor's arrest and banishment to Devil's Island from which he finally escapes in a surrealistic ballet sequence. Irma, pregnant, give up her old profession, and Nestor returns to Paris to prove his innocence of the murder charge and to welcome his son born at Christmastime. The gangsters, Magi-like, present the infant with certain gifts necessary for survival in their milieu -- tommy guns, switch-blade knives, and a bullet-proof pram. Such details which mix the innocent with the sordid enrich Brook's production even as they blunt with sentimentality the Brecht/Weill edge of *Irma la Douce*. The argot itself, foreign and charming to the ear, further softens the reality of prostitutes, pimps, and gangsters to achieve a distancing effect rather different from Brecht's.

The haunting Parisian melodies of Marguerite Monnot were well-played in catchy orchestrations heavy with accordian and street-organ suggestions. Elizabeth Seal sang her ballads in a nasal way reminiscent of Edith Piaf. The company, under Brook's careful direction, shed their British articulation for a universalizing English diction which in its absence of distinct locale might somehow pass for never-never land Franglais. For example, Miss Seal did not in any way imitate French pronunciation, yet she seemed Gallic in speech and appearance. Brook's mysterious achievement in this linguistic regard anticipates his increasing experiments with language and speech in later predominantly non-commercial theatrical ventures.

Brook's work in the commercial theater often manifested excessive self-consciousness and archness -- technical problem-solving substituting for creativity. The exigencies of the Broadway theater, in particular, seemed to increase the director's tension and stridency when productions of his were transferred from London's West End to Broadway. The result may sometimes have appeared to be rather patronizing toward American audiences, though, I suspect, that effect was unintentional. His attention to splendid packaging for these commercial productions surpassed his recognition of other more important values necessary for genuine entertainment, factors which Brook rarely neglected outside his commercial ventures, as if he trapped himself in an exaggerated mythology of Broadway perfectionism and its concomitant religion of success. Peter Brook, as has been argued here, is a pragmatic director, and he came to recognize that his resistance to the culture of Broadway [and to a lesser extent, the West End] reduced his capacity to work effectively in the commercial theater. The idealization of rather tawdry pleasures in commercial comedies and musicals went more and more against the grain of Peter Brook in a way which can be clarified by developments later in his career. Nevertheless, there were hints present from Brook's earliest productions that he was too much attuned to the dangerous self in human nature ever to give himself over wholeheartedly to show business in its usual popular connotations. With *The Little Hut, House of Flowers,* and *Irma la Douce,* Brook tried almost too valiantly to fulfill the Broadway ideal of pleasure, but if his head was engaged in the enterprise, his heart seems not to have been.

NOTES FOR CHAPTER TWO

1 Peter Brook and Ossia Trilling, "The Prospect Before Us," *Theatre Newsletter,* December 13, 1947, pp. 4-5.

2 See, for example, Edward Lockspeiser, "Bliss Opera Staged at Covent Garden," *Musical America,* November 1, 1949, p. 6.

3 Frank Corsaro, " ' Malinscenation'? NO!," *Opera News*, March 7, 1981, p.9.

4 Peter Brook, "Richard Strauss' *Salome*," *Theatre Newsletter*, November 5, 1949, p. 3.

5 See *Time*, November 21, 1949, p. 81.

6 Dyneley Hussey, *The Musical Times*, December, 1949, pp. 448-9.

7 Harold Rosenthal, *Two Centuries of Opera at Covent Garden* (London: Putnam, 1958), p. 594.

8 Charles Marowitz, "From Prodigy to Professional as Written, Directed and Acted by Peter Brook," *The New York Times Magazine*, November 24, 1968, p. 96.

9 See *Current Biography* (New York: H. W. Wilson & Co., 1961), pp. 74-6.

10 For this remark and many of the specific details on the Brook production of *Dark of the Moon* I am indebted to correspondence with Howard Richardson, co-author of the play. This particular comment was part of a letter dated September 29, 1979.

11 Eric Johns, "Wonder Boy," *Theatre World*, June, 1949, pp. 35-6.

12 So testifies Kitty Black in a letter to me, July 2, 1981.

13 On Anouilh as his own often covert director, see John Harvey, *Anouilh: A Study in Theatrics* (New Haven and London: Yale University Press, 1964), p. 157.

14 Harold Clurman, *The Naked Image* (New York: Macmillan, 1966), p. 26.

15 Brooks Atkinson, Review of "The Fighting Cock," *New York Times*, December 20, 1959, X 3.

16 Eric Bentley, "Theater," *The New Republic*, October 26, 1953, pp. 20-1.

17 Samuel Johnson, *Lives of the Poets*, ed. G. B. Hill, Vol. I (Oxford: Clarendon Press, 1905), 246.

18 Derek W. Hughes, "A New Look at *Venice Preserv'd*," *Studies in English Literature*, 11 (Summer 1971), 437-57.

19 Press Release, *House of Flowers*, August 16, 1954.

20 Ira Henry Freeman, "Comprenez-vous, Irma?," *The New York Times*, September 25, 1960, P. X 3.

Chapter Three

PETER BROOK AND THE MODERN REPERTORY: SINGULAR AND BINARY

After the success of Brook's production of *Titus Andronicus* (1955) and the less luminous *Hamlet* of the same year, Peter Brook concentrated for the most part on contemporary plays for a number of seasons and showed unusual skill in staging some of the more durable dramatic works in the modern repertory. Rarely did Brook stage only a single play from a particular dramatist he found interesting enough to direct at all; it was far more common for him to produce two works, sometimes separated by a gap of a few years before turning to another playwright. In most instances, his second venture with the dramatist received less enthusiastic response than the maiden effort, though not invariably. A true watershed of Brook's work with modern drama was 1956 in which he covered an impressive range of plays.

I. The Brook/Scofield Season: Graham Greene and T. S. Eliot

Under Tennent Productions Peter Brook staged three consecutive productions from *Hamlet* (1955) to the Denis Cannan and Pierre Bost adaptation of Graham Green's novel, *The Power and the Glory* (1956), and T. S. Eliot's *The Family Reunion* (1956), starring Paul Scofield, which Kenneth Tynan termed "the Peter Brook-Paul Scofield season of sin and damnation." (*Curtains*, p. 132) Only the last of these achieved much critical or audience favor. The director frequently provided music and set designs for these productions, sometimes for the latter in collaboration with Georges Wakhevitch. The thematic common denominator of the three plays was Scofield's anguished attempt to come to terms with his father/Father, biological and/or divine, before his characters can find their way either in or out of the world.

While the theatre-going public did not frequent the production in large numbers, Brook and Scofield garnered much critical praise for the dramatization of Greene's 1940 novel, *The Power and the Glory*, vividly showing the metaphysical contest between good and evil, the temporal and the spiritual. As the deeply wretched and culpable priest who has yielded to temptation of both flesh and bottle, Scofield persuaded the audience that he could be the vessel of divinity through his vocation. Transforming himself in size, voice, and face to a shrunken shell, Scofield somehow let the soul of Greene's unorthodox Catholicism shine forth, abetted by Brook's superb visual and aural effects through which the Priest's furtive Mass among the Mexican peasants of the 1930's achieved a measure of the power and reverence in simulation of an actual Mass. In this way Brook early in his career experimented with returning to the theater its original function of expressing God's presence.

No less a theatrical colleague than Laurence Olivier expressed delight in and wonder in the presence of Scofield's performance and Brook's production, as he returned for repeated viewings of *The Power and the Glory*. Unfortunately not all members of the cast were up to Scofield's high level of excellence. Notwithstanding the superlative ensemble performances which Brook would become renowned for later in his career, it was not unusual for critics to note his erratic casting and direction of acting at this time, as often perceived in interpretation of minor roles.[1] Early and even later in his career Brook tended to leave characterization and line interpretation to his actors, his own directorial emphasis being rather on the pacing of the lines and the choreography of the stage movement. Graham Greene's Priest, despite his alcoholism and sexual misconduct, still showed sufficient faith in the redemptive powers of God to go about his Father's business in an oppressed world, and Scofield with Brook's direction found the means to realize the compassion of that triumph before a theater audience, fit though few.

Generally conceded to be the best-realized of the Brook/Scofield collaboration was the third production of the series, T. S. Eliot's verse play of an English rendering of the Orestes legend, *The Family Reunion*. Brook directed this play as the embodiment of stylish British drawing-room drama raised to a higher power by its intense analysis of responsibility, guilt, and atonement which deeply undercut the superficiality of drawing-room dialogue with choral chants, the appearance of the Furies, and other violations of theater realism. As on other occasions during his first decade in the theater, Brook presided over a superbly trained troupe of distinguished English performers: Sybil Thorndike as the fated matriarch who seeks to top time, Amy, Lady Monchensey; Gwen Ffrancgon-Davies as the oracular Aunt Agatha who helps her nephew to spiritual renewal and whose scenes with Sybil Thorndike and Scofield were particularly admired; Lewis Casson as the well-meaning family doctor; and Scofield himself as Harry, Lord Monchensey about whom Tynan wrote: "On Mr. Eliot's Orestean hero he bestows a sleepless mien, gently haggard, and an anxious warmth of utterance that very nearly cures the character of its priggishness. As he is softened by Mr. Scofield, we almost come to like Harry. Almost we believe that he might exist." (*Curtains*, p. 132)

Played within a simple but effective set also of Brook's design, *The Family Reunion* let Eliot's verse speak with eloquence and precision. The sobriety and discipline of Brook's production was not lifeless, though a trifle chilly and chilling as is Eliot's play. Brook stressed silences and quietness almost as much as the dialogue, anticipating later Pinteresque effects in the British theater. In this way Brook helped to underplay some of Eliot's theatricalism in *The Family Reunion* which sometimes proved distracting in the unfolding of the play's plot line. The guilt-ridden, deeply neurotic Harry, believing he has been responsible for his wife's death, returns to his family home, Wishwood, to celebrate his mother's birthday. He now learns of his father's earlier murderous thoughts against his own mother whose life was saved by Aunt Agatha, his mother's sister and his father's mistress, in order that young Harry could be born. Through this patrimony of sin Harry accepts identity with his father and transference of his mother's destructive love for him into enmity against his wife. He goes off to the desert to engage in some ritual of expiation, but Eliot implies that at a later time Harry will return to assume the improvement of the estate, the rightful and redeemed inheritor of it. Harry moves from reality toward a higher authority with theological implications, but, as with Hamlet, whom he greatly resembles, religious themes are more covert than overt in the character notwithstanding sensitivity to the divinity that shapes human destiny.

It may be recalled that in the same year as the Brook/Scofield collaboration John Osborne's *Look Back in Anger* also opened to revolutionize the British stage. Brook's work, in contrast, seems to be in a quite different key, "anglo-traditional" we might call it. With his Tennent management and essentially literary dramatic material, aesthetically, Brook accepted in these plays premises and practices of old-fashioned and upper-class English theater which Osborne set out to challenge, but shortly Brook, too, would turn to vehicles no longer British nor traditional.

II. American Drama: Arthur Miller and Tennessee Williams

Peter Brook has not shown much alacrity over the years to stage American dramas or plays roughly within the naturalistic tradition. It is indicative of his cosmopolitan nature that Brook's first venture into Arthur Miller, for example, was a French language production in Brussels presented at the Belgian National Theatre of *Death of a Salesman (La Mort d'un Commis Voyageur* – 1951) in a competent, if not especially noteworthy, production. Later in 1956, almost exactly a year after the American premiere of Miller's "A View from the Bridge," then a one-act play on a double-bill with "A Memory of Two Mondays," which had not been a large success in Martin Ritt's New York production, Brook staged a revised and expanded two-act version of *A View from the Bridge* to rave reviews and commercial success. The play was presented at the Comedy Theatre, London, under the auspicies of the New Watergate Theatre Club, formed to present sequentially three American plays "banned" for public viewing by the Lord Chamberlain for their suggestions of homosexuality: *A View from the Bridge*, Robert Anderson's *Tea and Sympathy*, and Tennessee Williams' *Cat on a Hot Tin Roof*, all now requiring "private" performance for "members" only. Brook's production of the Miller play starred Anthony Quayle as Eddie Carbone, Mary Ure as his niece, Catherine, to whom Eddie is attracted, Brian

Bedford as the illegal alien, Rodolpho, to whom more disturbingly Eddie is also attracted and at the same time repelled, Megs Jenkins as Eddie's wife, Beatrice, and Michael Gwynn as Alfieri, the "Chorus."

Brook acted as his own designer for *A View from the Bridge*. His imaginative, all-purpose set was strongly vertical comprised of a cage of girders which enclosed the trapped protagonist and implied a whole vertically-built neighborhood but which could also open to disclose a homely and realistic interior for family life. Off-stage Brook projected the clangor of a dock-yard wherein the hammer-blows of fate were being sounded for Eddie. Arthur Miller praised Peter Brook's conception of the play in the London production as according well with his own new perspective on *A View from the Bridge* which had led the playwright to revise the original text. In particular, Miller endorsed the central idea of Brook's set which was "to bring the people of the neighborhood into the foreground of the action. . . . The easier economics of the London theater made it possible to use many more neighbors than the three or four extras we could hire in New York. . . . The maturing of Eddie's need to destroy Rodolpho was consequently seen in the context which could make it of real moment, for the betrayal achieves its true proportions as it flies in the face of the mores administered by Eddie's conscience – which is also the conscience of his friends, co-workers, and neighbors and not just his own autonomous creation."[2]

Sheila Huftel, the author of one of the best critical works on Arthur Miller, assessed from first-hand experience the effect of Brook's production quite differently: "At the Comedy Theatre I felt I was watching a street accident, with the playwright as casualty. I could only wonder why Miller had (in my opinion) ruined his own work. . . . I am probably in a minority of one in damning the London version of this play."[3] Actually, Miss Huftel was not alone in finding the simpler, more taut and inexorable one-act version superior to the exciting melodramatic theater piece Brook staged. Margaret Webster, for example, wrote of the London production: "Gone is the sense -- so impressive to me in New York -- of a people of ancient lineage, reborn on the Brooklyn waterfront, yet still prey of those smoldering, buried passions which wrought the classic tragedies." ("A Look at the London Season," p. 29) As with Eliot's *The Family Reunion* earlier in the year, so Brook emphasized in his production of *A View from the Bridge* alternative conceptions to the naturalistic foundation and tradition of both plays. In the instance of Miller's drama Brook saw Miller conducting a kind of Brechtian experiment upon the limits of naturalism.

Brook ended his extremely active year of 1956 with another foreign-language production of an American play, Williams' *Cat on a Hot Tin Roof* in André Obey's French translation, *La Chatte sur un Toit Brûlant* (1956) at the Théâtre Antoine, Paris during December. The French press panned both the play and the production, but some American and British visitors in the audience still consider Jeanne Moreau's Maggie possibly the definitive interpretation of the role.

With considerably better fortune, Brook enjoyed his first large Parisian success two years later when he interrupted his British try-out tour of Dürrenmatt's *The Visit* to stage at the Théâtre Antoine Marcel Aymé's translation *Vu du Pont*, yet another even more radically altered version of Miller's *A View from the Bridge*. Originally Aymé wanted to leave Eddie alone and unkilled at the end of the play, but neither Raf Vallone who wanted to retain his big death scene as Eddie nor Peter Brook who felt he had to protect Arthur Miller's artistic design agreed. (Huftel, p. 161) Nevertheless, some significant changes had to be made because Brook was assured that French audiences would not accept the total lack of awareness exhibited by Eddie and Catherine about their desires and provocations. Thus in a highly Gallic alteration at the end of the play when Eddie asks for his "name," he, the betrayer, he is left alone to kill himself as he does rather like Racine's Phèdre with something approaching self-knowledge, no longer clinging tenaciously to his innocence and rejecting flaws in himself as he does in Miller's English-language versions. Brook's French production was enthusiastically received, as warm proportionately as the reception to *Cat on a Hot Tin Roof* had been cold, and *Vu du Pont* continued to run for three seasons in Paris.

In both the London and Paris productions of Miller's play, under Brook's direction, a somewhat more nearly "mythic" style and tragic

58

size were imparted to the characters than was apparent in the New York production. This result may be attributable to nothing more than the presence of classically-trained English actors in the London production and an even more pronounced classical tradition of French theater together with the added exoticism of *A View from the Bridge* presented in French. On the other hand, Brook may deserve more credit than the foregoing explanation for his capacity at once to affirm and transcend the play's naturalistic premises in a creative collaboration among playwright, director, and translator.

III. Dürrenmatt's *The Visit* (1958): The Commercialization of the Grotesque in a Modern Classic

Peter Brook's first major success in the American theater, his production of Friedrich Dürrenmatt's *Der Besuch der Alten Dame*, called finally in shortened form, *The Visit* in Maurice Valency's adaptation, after *Time and Again* was rejected as a suitable title in the midst of a tryout tour in provincial England, made its auspicious, if circuitous, Broadway debut, May 5, 1958. The plan originally called for the play to open in London after an extended tour under Tennent management of the British provinces, Scotland, and Ireland with the married luminaries of the American stage, Alfred Lunt and Lynn Fontanne in the leading roles of Anton Schill and Claire Zachanassian, but a suitable theater was unavailable. In addition, rumor had it that Dürrenmatt's tragicomic indictment of greed and grotesque study of revenge was too harrowing to risk a London production. Therefore, *The Visit* opened instead in New York at the recently renamed and refurbished Lunt-Fontanne Theater where it achieved immediate popular and commercial success, with a measure of glamour and hoopla which commented on even as it may have worked against the dramatic text.

Brook's brilliantly visual production, in retrospect, achieved the apotheosis of many earlier Lunt-Fontanne vehicles, now invested with new substance, perhaps almost profundity, beyond the customary theatrical style for which the Lunts were justifiably famous, but at some price to his dramatic source, first paid by Maurice Valency in adaptation rather than translation of Dürrenmatt. Actions and attitudes which are slowly built-up in the original text must be taken as a matter of faith in the quickly-moving, though more elliptical, Valency version. The original grotesqueries of the Old Lady are reduced, perhaps out of deference to Lynn Fontanne. For example, Claire Zachanassian no longer suffers from loss of limbs, as she does in Dürrenmatt's text. She persists in carrying a cane as an authority symbol and continues to smoke cigars, but as with other aspects of Brook's production the effect, to borrow Gordon Rogoff's apt phrase, was really "Grand Guinol with a velvet touch."[4] Lynn Fontanne, attired in clothes designed by Antonio Canovas del Castillo of the house of Lanvin-Castillo, Paris, appeared as a cool, impersonal beauty, not the hag-like fury of Dürrenmatt's imagination. Yet few who saw the production will ever forget Fontanne's first appearance in the play dressed in a single shade of red -- from cloche hat, to long red chiffon scarf, wool dress and cape, to matching shoes and umbrella. The monochromatic visual statement connoted, perhaps subliminally, the theme of blood vengeance which increasingly dominates the play.

The protagonist in Dürrenmatt's play is really the impoverished town of Guellen, in English "Dungtown," as Timo Tiusanen suggests.[5] Guellen contrives that Schill, a local shopkeeper, most popular man in town and mayor-elect, and significantly once Claire's lover, will be able to persuade his former mistress, now the world's richest woman, to save her hometown's economy. He is ironically successful in this aim but in an unexpected way. Claire Zachanassian's entourage is bizarre and sinister: her eighth husband, a butler, two brutes who carry her on a sedan-chair, two blind attendants, a pet black panther, and an empty coffin. The town learns that murder must be its price for economic recovery. The world's richest woman wants justice, since forty-five years ago in Guellen Schill won a paternity suit she had brought against him through bribes he made to two false witnesses whom she has subsequently blinded, castrated, and employed as her servants. The judge in the trial is currently her butler. Scorned by Guellen, the seventeen-year old girl, nee Clara Wascher, was forced to leave the town and became a prostitute after the birth of her child who lived only a year. Upon her return to

Guellen she has argued for reinstatement of capital punishment; now she demands the death of Schill. Civilized and humanistic Guellen at first forthrightly rejects such an outrageous proposal, but Claire is prepared to wait. In a drama of moral attrition, Dürrenmatt carefully traces the triumph of materialism over principles. Timo Tiusanen explains the process well: "Everybody is buying on credit: more expensive cigarettes, milk, chocolate, cognac. And pairs of yellow shoes: completing the above list of purchases these shoes of guilt turn bad omens into a certainty for Ill [called Shill in Valency's adaptation]. Guellen is speculating on his impending death." (*Dürrenmatt: A Study in Plays, Prose, Theory*, p. 230)

This sell-out of Schill was greatly reduced in Valency's adaptation over the Dürrenmatt's original treatment, and the hurried pace impaired credibility in Brook's production.

Claire Zachanassian, seated on her balcony, oversees the inevitable moral decline of the town which she has orchestrated. Lynn Fontanne in Brook's production played the Old Lady less as a Medea-figure, an implacable goddess of fate, than as a recognizable, plausible, and potentially sympathetic woman who has been wronged; in dress and style she might, as Rogoff observes, "have strayed in from the world of high comedy," ("Mr. Dürrenmatt Buys New Shoes," 33), consequently forcing the audience to accept her menace primarily by definition. Alfred Lunt's Schill was more appropriate to the playwright's conception. His meticulous performance carefully traced the growth of a small and insignificant shopkeeper into an unlikely character of strength and courage. In recognizing his guilt, Schill lives out justice to achieve greatness through death: he takes responsibility for making Claire what she is and for making himself what he is. His death, of course, makes the town fully corrupt as it is. With the community-executed death of Schill, Guellen stages a media-event, celebrating its own morality with great promise of future prosperity. Dürrenmatt's ironic chorus given to the townspeople at the end is omitted in the Valency adaptation, but it reads thus in the Patrick Bowles' translation:

> Protect all our sacred possessions,
> Protect our peace and our freedom,
> Ward off the night, nevermore

Let it darken our glorious town
Grown out of the ashes anew
Let us go and enjoy our good fortune.[6]

Brook's production tended to focus on Claire and Schill at the expense of attention to the inhabitants of the community, an emphasis consistent with Valency's version. At times, the director succeeded in individualizing the townspeople by giving them distinctive props, telling gestures, and revealing stage business while preserving the group character which assumes ineluctable force as it slowly closes in on Schill each time he seeks to escape. Brook still, though, concentrated on the stars, as in the memorable scene in the New York production when the crowd moves town Schill at the end of the second act. Their threatening presence was shown primarily through Lunt's appearing to retch and then vomit; the terror became psychologically horrifying less from the external threat of the crowd than from the involuntary physical reaction of Schill.

Brook's production of *The Visit* with the Lunts continued in performance with some suspensions for needed vacations for nearly two and a half years in the United States. At the end of the summer of 1959, the Lunts took the play on a cross-country tour, under the sponsorship of the American Theatre Society and the Council of the Living Theatre, which included seventeen cities in the United States and Canada where it frequently broke box-office records for a straight play. This tour ended back in New York for a two-week engagement at the City Center. Critics were even more enthusiastic about the play and the production during this second look than they had been first time round. On June 23, 1960, the Lunts finally opened *The Visit* in London, again inaugurating a new theater, The Royalty. Their limited engagement was scheduled for eight weeks, but it was extended on popular demand to twenty. Moreover in March 1960 Brook mounted a French production of *La Visite de la Vieille Dame* in Paris for the fourth season of the International Theatre Festival. This Gallic version seems a natural extension of the rather Frenchified Valency/Brook production of *The Visit*. Glamor proved a more commercial attribute than the grotesque, and Brook's production enjoyed international success.

IV. *The Physicists* (1963; 1964): Dürrenmatt Revisited

Having succeeded with *The Visit*, Peter Brook gamely turned to the other Dürrenmatt play of great popularity in European productions, *The Physicists* (1963), in an English adaptation by James Kirkup. It is a play of ideas as well as a thinking man's thriller. The setting is a strange Swiss insane asylum, Les Cerisiers [The Cherry Orchard!], presided over by Fräulein Doktor Mathilde von Zahnd, hump-backed, spinster owner and chief psychoanalyst who fends off the police with airtight please of insanity for her patients. The police come to investigate the murder of three nurses by three inmates, each of whom has credentials as a brilliant physicist, although they all exhibit singular delusions. One insists he is Sir Isaac Newton. Another has slipped into Albert Einstein's identity, complete with violin which the actual physicist played for relaxation. The third is called Möbius, and he possesses the secret of the ultimate nuclear weapon as well as the formula which will unlock all the secret of the universe and confer absolute power on those who control it [reminiscent of Einstein's theoretical unified field]. With a star-filled cast, including Irene Worth, who would resume the role of the Doctor eighteen years in the future as part of Stephen Porter's revival of the play, Cyril Cussack as Möbius, Alan Webb, Michael Hordern, and Diana Rigg, *The Physicists* entered the Aldwych repertory of the Royal Shakespeare Company where it rotated with other productions like Brook's *King Lear*.

An amusing and provocatively enigmatic first act is followed by a second act of revelations and debate -- the latter an almost Shavian examination -- on the responsibility of the scientist in extending his knowledge to a world morally incapable of handling it. East and West are seeking the Final Secret, the West in the name of scientific freedom, the East for service to the state. Their opposing contentions, represented by the scientist/agents Newton and Einstein, are reduced to a common denominator of cold-war absurdity and enmity that would turn the whole world into a madhouse. The playwright makes an ironic case that the duty of genius today is to remain unrecognized. Möbius has permitted himself to be incarcerated in the asylum for twenty years because he believes that thereby he has prevented society from appropriating his secrets for political ends. The genuinely mad person in the play is the doctor, a variation on the evil personified by the mutilated Old Lady of *The Visit*, who holds all the physicists in thrall. Dr. von Zahnd engineers them to commit the murders of their devoted nurses who alone could perhaps have saved them. Since the doctor long ago has stolen Möbius's secrets, she is about to establish an international cartel to control the universe. The once thought cannot be easily withdrawn, and other physicists outside the asylum pose on the threshold of repeating these discoveries at any time. *The Physicists* continues Dürrenmatt's theater of paradox, mixing comedy and tragedy through strange angles of perception and unexpected twists of thought.

Performed in John Burry's ingenious and menacing circular room set, complete with dome, which creates the effect visually of a pressure cooker or womb-like tomb, Brook's production of the play engendered rare showmanship, combining in performance style a broad spectrum of effects and readings from polished comedy of manners to zany, physical farce, in the main quite appropriate to Dürrenmatt's own method in the play of using, as Timo Tiusanen describes it, " a large orchestra of scenic means of expression: music, sound effects, action, scenes of pantomime, the setting, dialogue." (*Dürrenmatt*, p. 285) The London critics judged *The Physicists* the best foreign play of the season, and Brook appeared to be on his way to having another international hit like *The Visit*. This time the Dürrenmatt play was exported to the United States rather than vice versa.

Re-cast with nearly as distinguished a company in New York as in London, *The Physicists* opened in the United States during autumn of 1964 with Jessica Tandy and Robert Shaw in the chief roles, supported by Hume Cronyn, Martyn Green, and George Voskovec. Comparable American critical and popular enthusiasm for the play, duplicating its London success, was not to be Brook's destiny this time round. Some of the performances, especially on the part of the husband-wife team, Hume Cronyn and Jessica Tandy, were faulted; the Lunts had received much more critical praise in *The Visit*. Brook's attention-getting details seemed often extraneous to the play's content, self-consciously brilliant but superficial, even facetious. For example, the uncurtained stage, containing the corpse of a woman, one of the nurses as the play reveals within a few minutes of its action, which greeted the audience as it entered the theater and the presence of a second corpse during intermission on the same stage won less endorsement on this side of the Atlantic than it had abroad. To be sure, sometimes the subtlety of Brook's connections between external business and the play's theme was overlooked. At the beginning of the second act, three new male nurses, having replaced their deceased female predecessors, engaged in a remarkable acrobatic drill as they threw dishes and furniture across the stage in preparation for dinner – all without dropping anything. Potentially relevant, in addition to its pleasure as pure diversion, this feat of juggling skill perhaps commented obliquely upon Möbius the physicists whose formula had solved the problem of gravitation in the play. In this play, particularly, Dürrenmatt encouraged this kind of stagecraft. Brook obliged him with effects that on the surface resembled those of hackneyed thrillers like *The Cat and the Canary* – shutters opening and closing without apparent physical cause, flashing lightning and similar chestnuts – but which could be seen as conceits relevant to the play's darker intellectual and moral demonstration of the schism separating knowledge, morality, and political power. *The Physicists*, lacking the single-mindedness of Dürrenmatt's fable of greed, *The Visit*, attained only 55 performances during its New York run, but ultimately the play rather than Brook's imaginative production was thought to be responsible for the lack of success. The dramatist who provided the source of Brook's first American triumph proved less winning on this return visit.

V. Jean Genet's House of Illusion: *le Balcon* (1960)

In testimony of Brook's shifting interest from the nearly boulevard theater of the often-produced Jean Anouilh to the avant-garde during this period in his career, when the director took up a French dramatist he turned to Jean Genet and mounted the first Paris production in May, 1960 at the Théâtre de Gymnase of *le Balcon,* which as *The Balcony* had received its world premiere in English translation under the direction of Peter Zadek during 1957 at London's Art Theatre Club. The original producer who had optioned Genet's play for a French production had dropped his option for fear of police interference, and by the time Brook embarked on *le Balcon* the play had caused a furor in cities which had already seen productions of it such as London, New York, and Berlin. Brook appeared ripe, even eager, for controversy, as indicated by his change-over from Anouilh to Genet.

In *The Empty Space* Brook recalls the special challenge of Genet's play from a director's point of view and remarks on the workshop exercises he devised to generate an ensemble performance, a technique which would become quite standard in the increasingly experimental Brook productions of the years ahead:

> For a production I did of Genet's *The Balcony* in Paris it was necessary to mix actors of very different backgrounds – classically trained, film trained, ballet trained and simple amateur. Here, long evenings of every obscene brothel improvisations served only one purpose – they enabled this hybrid group of people to come together and begin to find a way of responding directly to one another. (*The Empty Space*, p. 103)

The play opens in a supposed sacristy where a Bishop, replete with appurtenances of his office, miter, surplice, brocades, and something extra, *cothurni*, the high-platform shoes traditionally associated with Greek tragedy, all designed to give this moral pygmy heightened authority and eminence. But this sacristy is actually only a stage-set in Mme. Irma's "house of illusion," the brothel called The Grand Balcony, and the Bishop is a gas man acting out his favorite fantasy with a female penitent who excites him with her tales of six sins. Brook created the sets for the Paris production, and they embodied to a higher degree than had been the case at the London premiere the opulence which Genet himself desired for this particular *mise en scène*. In a series of nine tableaux with a cast of twenty, *The Balcony* unfolds the fantasies of many visitors to this bordello whose private sensuality mirrors the public world of such primary institutions in the western world as the Church, the Magistrature, the Army, and the Police. Since French usage has described the brothel for years as a "house of illusion," Brook delighted in the metaphorical connection implicit in Genet's play between this brothel and the other great institution of illusion in cultural history -- namely, the theater. Genet's play pulls the weight of received culture into his brothel/ theater where it awaits interruption by the revolution raging outside its doors. The Chief of Police seeks to undermine the revolution by mobilizing the brothel's inhabitants as surrogates of the real power-holders in the state.

In a scene subsequently deleted early in its Paris run from Brook's production, the revolutionaries who pretend, in Puritan-fashion, to condemn role-playing and artifice, are shown possessed by their own sexual fantasies comparable to those of The Grand Balcony. The inclusion of this sequence slowed down the performance considerably, and Brook elected to eliminate Genet's own climax to act one in the interest of theatrical expediency. At the same time, that Brook recognized the importance of the scene where the revolution mirrors what it would like to overthrow and rehearsed it for performance bears witness to the director's usual predisposition to realize on stage as much of the totality of a dramatic text as is feasible.

In the ritualized enactment of roles both within and outside Mme. Irma's establishment, Genet's calculated arbitrariness of modern existence was given powerful embodiment, presented, insofar as Brook could, according to Genet's stipulation that the play should capture the solemnity of a Mass in a most beautiful cathedral, which, to be sure, makes a mockery of the sacred. The defeated revolutionary, Roger, comes to the brothel where he tries to impersonate the Chief of Police who, in turn, is happy finally to be the subject of impersonation, having feared he was deficient in the "sacred" and "mythical" by the nature of his social function. With new status the Chief of Police desires to have himself represented by a giant phallus, symbolic of his power and potency. Ironically, when in the guise of the Police Chief, Roger castrates himself – mutilation being perhaps the sincerest form of flattery for the man-god, mythically. The Chief himself retreats to his huge tomb to reign supreme for two thousand years.

The little prostitute, Chantal, who flees The Grand Balcony to join the revolutionaries is enlistened as the rebel's Joan of Arc, an action which later results in her separation from Roger whom she loves and eventually in her death. The roles keep shifting in Genet's play from appearance to being and back to appearance again, as they do when Brook leaves Genet's brothel for Peter Weiss' asylum in *Marat/Sade* a bit later in his career. Chantal temporarily may suggest reminiscences of Anouilh's *The Lark*, but Brook's career and his production of *The Balcony* take him away from early pieties and orthodoxies.

Genet's artifice in *The Balcony* has been ritualized into negation of sacred order which underlay the myths of the Greek theater. Brook, following Genet, makes the address to ritual without believing in it. His production of *The Balcony* may be seen as a critical address in lieu of what he cannot subscribe to, a negational analysis of the trappings of several millenia of culture through the de-idealization of the mythic. For Genet the formerly grotesque (and even perverse) become acceptable -- and not only in the brothel; he shifts the registrations literally and metaphorically downward, from the sacred to the derisive, from the mind to the genitals. Yet the interdicts remain and subsequently challenge Brook in his pursuit of theatrical ritual; for if everything may be presented directly, there is little need for the ritualistic, or for art itself. In his later renewal of ritual Brook finds the further renewal of repression necessary for art -- the distancing and concealment which affirms, despite the modernist calling into question what has characterized all past cultures, that there is some content so offensive that it cannot be expressed directly.

Philip Rieff has written on the subversive psychological implications of the artist's claim to express everything in the modern era which he sees as derived from the example of Oscar Wilde: "In such a mood," Rieff notes in language strangely appropriate to Genet, "all limits begin to feel like humiliations. Wilde did not know that he was prophesying a hideous new anger in modern men, one that will render peaceable existence even more Utopian than before."[7] Jean Genet, unlike his nineteenth-century precursor, Wilde, may be aware of and welcome his revolutionary animus in psychological terms rather than social ones. Mme. Irma in *The Balcony* celebrates with the new sacraments of sex and power in mockery of the old credal order. The extent of Peter Brook's assent to - or even recognition of -- such revolutionary elements in *The Balcony* cannot be established here; however, this Paris production of a seminal work of the modern theater heralded the opening of Brook's most creative and innovative decade in which he quickly moved beyond the commercial theater to become very nearly a charismatic institution in his own right. It is not coincidental that Genet and Artaud have often been linked in Brook's work as in commentaries on Genet; as Robert Brustein has written, "the opening scenes of the play [*The Balcony*] seem like an actualization of one of Artaud's scenarios, because -- in their unification of power, cruelty, and sex -- they owe a good deal to the writings of the Marquis de Sade."[8] *The Balcony* became a harbinger of things to come in Brook's activity of the sixties in a number of ways.

VI. The Theater of Cruelty Route to Genet's *The Screens*

Re-negotiating his continued association with the Royal Shakespeare Company in 1962, Peter Brook stipulated that he be permitted to work experimentally with a group of subsidized actors from the company -- but still independent of it -- without the necessity of staging a public or commercial production as a result of their activities. With this condition accepted, Brook seized the opportunity to go further toward experimental frontiers of the theater – director and actors welcoming some of the innovative freedom shown earlier by twentieth-century playwrights -- when he and Charles Marowitz, the American director, critic, and theorist who lived in Britain and who had assisted Brook in *King Lear* collaborated in November, 1963 on an experimental program under the aegis of the RSC. Their efforts in what was called, not without some misunderstanding, the theater of cruelty season led directly to Brook's far-reaching interest in establishment of his own permanent workshop and research ensemble. More immediately, subsequent Brook stage productions such as Jean Genet's *The Screens* and Peter Weiss' *Marat/Sade* were informed by the theater of cruelty workshop lessons and discoveries. Indeed, the Genet play, which both Brook and Marowitz desired to stage, required, in their opinion, a group of English actors trained in a new way for adequate performance, but the auditions for membership in the company were conducted, as Marowitz describes, without address to any particular play or reference to any definite theatrical end.[9]

The label of the theater of cruelty offered homage, of course, to Antonin Artaud. After the group of twelve actors nearly all of whom were in their twenties had been selected from more than fifty finalists in the auditions, Brook and Marowitz experienced some disagreement over the direction which the initial experiments should take. Marowitz, extensively schooled in the Stanislavski System, argued that some standard Method exercises would be in order before taking the plunge into the astringent sea of Artaudian thought. Brook prevailed with his insistence that the actors, coming from widely divergent theatrical backgrounds, were sufficiently experienced to embark immediately on Artaud-inspired improvisations. The most radical Artaudian feature of the workshop exercises challenged the actors to communicate feelings and ideas without recourse to words but with sound and their bodies: "Little, by little," Marowitz explains, "we insinuated the idea that the voice could produce sounds other than grammatic combinations of the alphabet, and that the body, set free, could begin to enunciate a language which went beyond text, beyond sub-text, beyond psychological implication and beyond monkey-see-monkey-do facsimiles of social behaviorism." ("Notes on the Theatre of Cruelty," 155) Artaudian, then, in their search for alternative means of presentation away from traditional naturalistic portrayals and the Aristotelian logic of plot unfolding, the directors, like their provocative antecedent stood at odds with the dominant contemporary theatrical culture characterized by Marowitz as "the well-upholstered, self-esteeming cul-de-sac in which contemporary theatre found itself." ("Notes on the Theatre of Cruelty," 172)

The group's experiments took place behind closed doors in a small church hall behind the Royal Court Theatre in Sloane Square, truly the crucible for experimentalism in the London theater of the times. Long daily sessions extended from 10:00 a.m. to 6:00 p.m. At the close of each day, Brook and Marowitz reviewed the work of that day and planned objectives for the next day, Marowitz was assigned the task of devising appropriate exercises for the following day's work; these were often embellished by Brook when the group put them into practice. The "cruelty" of the experience arose often enough from the discipline exacted on the part of directors and performers, reflective of a larger metaphysical cruelty which Artaud understood and Marowitz ably formulated:

> The cruelty that Artaud referred to (this is a truism worth repeating) did not refer exclusively to torture, blood, violence and plague, but to the cruellest of all practices: the exposure of mind, heart and nerve-ends to the grueling truths behind a social reality that deals in psychological crises when it wants to be *honest*, and political evils when it wants to be *responsible*, but rarely if ever confronts the existential horror behind all social and psychological facades." ("Notes on the Theatre of Cruelty," 172)

It is the cruel shock of this realization that Artaud-inspired exercises were meant to clarify for the actors. They, in turn, would embody this moral lesson of submission to necessity for audience recognition in the Artaudian theater.

The standard for evaluating a performer which evolved during the three months with the theater of cruelty workshop had as its hallmark the actor's capacity for rapid change and flexibility in characterization. Free association was encouraged as an alternative to the traditional approach to building characterization in logical dramatic situations. With the subordination of rational motivation in character development and abandonment of Aristotelian beginnings-middles-ends in dealing with incident, the theater of cruelty experiment contributed to a renewed English theater along modern rather than traditional lines.

Yielding to outside pressure against use of its own facilities, the RSC rented the intimate Lamda Theatre Club in London's densely-populated Earl's Court area for presentation of what became known as the "Theatre of Cruelty Season" of five weeks during in January 1964. Despite Brook's original hesitation about presenting work-in-progress as public performance and the tentative development work of the experiment which was meant to culminate in a possible production of Genet's *The Screens*, the directors and the young actors acceded to public presentation of some of their material as a way of testing their communicative skills. The theater of cruelty program consisted of a melange of scenes and improvisations, changing in content from performance to performance so that each audience discovered a program different from all preceding or succeeding ones. Sound exercises of an Artaudian variety were represented by two brief sketches by Paul Ableman. In homage to Artaud, the company re-enacted Artaud's own three-minute playlet, "Spurt of Blood," first without verbalization, only through sounds, and then with the original dialogue. Additional material from France was presented in a dramatization of a short story by Alain Robbe-Grillet which used only movement and gesture. A sketch, "The Guillotine," which was original with the company, and a mime sketch, described as anti-Marceauvian in Marowitz's chronicle, "The Analysis," were frequently staged. Each performance also included two "free" sections, the first of which always contained totally unrehearsed improvisations, often with challenges from the audience. The second "free" section usually was reserved for something special or extraordinary. One night, for example, Brook directed an impromptu section from *Richard III*, or discussions would take publicly between Brook and Marowitz. Once, when John Arden, whose short play, "Ars Longa, Vita Brevis" was included as part of the program, was present for the performance, he was asked to explain in public interview the justification for staging his play in the context of the theater of cruelty season.

The most controversial components of typical evenings at Lamda were the following: scenes from Genet's *The Screens* as prelude to the far-off theatrical event of the whole play which Brook and the RSC continued to imagine and desire; Marowitz's collage condensation of *Hamlet*, with key lines and scenes re-arranged and re-assigned in a twenty-minute version divested of the narrative features, appealing to everyone's collective unconscious "mythic memory" of the play; and, finally, the notorious Brook collage, "The Public Bath." In this latter ritualistic pantomime a girl in a raincoat, made-up to resemble Christine Keeler of the then memorable Profumo scandal which had rocked British politics, is arrested, for perhaps no other reason that she was a call-girl whose services took her to cabinet ministers and parliamentarians. She is stripped of her clothes preceding enactment of a required prison bath. The bath tub, suddenly raised and carried like a coffin, reveals a transformed girl, the ritual purification has produced Jacqueline Kennedy out of Christine Keeler, the former pristine in her recent bereavement and public show of valor. Martin Esslin, writing enthusiastically about this episode, relates "The Public Bath" to Artaudian principles:

> That the ritual also had the attributes of a strip-tease –
> one of the most daring events to be performed in a public –
> merely enhanced the effect. Here Artaud's demand that the
> audience must be physically affected, drawn into the action
> with an inescapable, inevitable excitement – that being the
> meaning of the word *cruelty* for Artaud – was here trium-
> phantly fulfilled.[10]

The actress subjected to nudity in "The Public Bath" was Glenda Jackson who would later participate clothed with a nude male actor in a similar sequence as part of *Marat/Sade*. "The Public Bath" received attention not for its ritualistic Artaudian transformation but as source of the epithet which gave the theater of cruelty season the reputation as "the dirtiest show in town." Both Peter Brook and Peter Hall, artistic directors of the RSC, rode out the storm of criticism which followed performances which included "The Public Bath." Hall reaffirmed the importance of experimentation in enlarging the form of theater which must be a part of the work of a group like the RSC and the necessity of subsidizing such activity, however great the economic loss. In the case of the theater of cruelty workshop and the Lamda performances, the cost figure Marowitz mentions is five thousand pounds. ("Notes of the Theatre of Cruelty," 166)

Financial support from the RSC continued after the close of the Lamda season when Brook and an expanded number of actors, now seventeen, augmented from the original apostolic number of the theater of cruelty workshop, began protracted rehearsals of another twelve weeks duration in preparation for staging twelve scenes, out of the total of seventeen with ninety-six characters, from Genet's *The Screens*, approximately half of the complete text. Because none of the original twelve actors could be promised assimilation into the RSC at a more generous salary, Marowitz sardonically remarks that

"An in-group definition of Theatre of Cruelty was twelve actors working for twelve pounds a week." ("Notes on the Theatre of Cruelty," 166) The serious side of this condition, apart from individual penury, was as an impediment to ensemble identity and security which adversely affected, in Marowitz's opinion, the quality of performance.

In light of the brouhaha over the theater of cruelty season, Brook decided to present his version in May, 1964 of *The Screens* before invited guests only for seven evenings in an improvised theater devised in the Donmar Rehearsal rooms near Covent Garden, thereby removing the necessity of the Lord Chamberlain's approval, during this last phase of official censorship in the British theater. Ostensibly about the struggle of Arabs against French colonialism in Algeria, *The Screens*, as Brook recognized, presents really a journey into the self seen as myth and apotheosis; the Arab, Said, and his would-be bride, are transformed through degradation -- Genet's favorite process -- and death with the ascetic figure, Said, becoming a legend. The principal scenery in the play are screens on which reality is painted during the performance and through which characters literally break out, indicative of movement from one world to another.

In manner and method, Genet's play seems almost an extension of Artaud's efforts to fuse life and death, the theater and its double, illusion and reality, consciousness and unconsciousness, the material and the spiritual -- all thinly separated by fragile screens. The company adhered closely to Genet's text during rehearsals, but they increasingly relied on stylized and symbolic effects to suggest naturalistic details. In Marowitz's judgment:

> *The Screens* was never an organic production, but a substructure and an overlay with a vital middle layer missing. The production made a kind of stark, physical sense in spite of, not because of, our work, and the intellectual uncertainty of cast and producers, the unresolved ambiguities in the text, left an inner fuzziness which a longer run would undoubtedly have revealed. ("Notes on the Theatre of Cruelty," 170)

On the other hand, Martin Esslin, using adjectives like "magnificent," testified that Brook's version of *The Screens* "contained some of the greatest moments I personally have ever witnessed in a theatre." ("The Theatre of Cruelty," p. 72) Esslin was particularly impressed by a scene in which the Arab rebels burn a European plantation which was represented by the actors painting the red flames of the supposed conflagration on the great white screen: "This was a marriage of theatre and action-painting. It generated an almost unbearable excitement as the stage blazed with tongues of flame that could actually be seen growing out of a paroxysm of rage and passion." ("The Theatre of Cruelty," p. 73) In this visual device Brook followed Genet's own suggestions but in a way which proclaimed the director's originality as much as it manifested Genet's. A great director does not so much discover a theatrical language as he releases the combinations, rhythms, and visual effects latent in the texts he stages. The surface brilliance of Brook's production of Genet's *The Screens* somewhat obscured the director's interest in the play's mythic quest, yet this concern would become more apparent in subsequent plays and films by Brook.

The intransigent material of Genet's most complex dramatic work let Brook and his well-trained company experiment with a multitude of approaches and theatrical traditions. It became the sponge which soaked up the new ideas and resources from the theater of cruelty workship. For the first time Brook presided over a company specially trained for the collective theatrical enterprise he ardently wished to pursue. In sharing of and education through communal discovery, the theater of cruelty experiment gave Peter Brook a new vision of what theater could be when directors, actors, playwrights, and audiences were equally attuned to possibilities of change. The momentum generated by these Artaudian experiments did not dissipate as Brook and some members of his workshop reintegrated with the RSC for *Marat/Sade*.

VII. Experimental Synthesis and Commercial Success: *Marat/Sade* (1964)

Brook found the perfect vehicle for his next step in theatrical experiment when he directed the RSC production of Peter Weiss' *The Persecution and Assassination of Jean-Paul Marat as Performed by the Inmates of the Asylum of Charenton under the Direction of the Marquis de Sade*, usually known simply as *Marat/Sade* (1964, London; 1965, New York). Weiss, an East German playwright living in Sweden, deliberately sought to bring together Brechtian elements of objectivity and Artaudian effects of sensibility and subjectivity in a highly eclectic script which proved quite complementary to Brook's current thinking about "total theater." Brook wrote an introduction to the published text of *Marat/Sade* which summarized his thoughts along these lines:

> Brecht's use of "distance" has long been considered in opposition to Artaud's conception of theatre as immediate and violent subjective experience. I have never believed this to be true. I believe that theatre, like life, is made up of the unbroken conflict between impressions and judgments – illusion and disillusion cohabit painfully and are inseparable. This is just what Weiss achieves. Starting with its title, everything about this play is designed to crack the spectator on the jaw, then douse him with ice-cold water, then give him a kick in the balls, then bring him back to his senses again. It's not exactly Brecht and it's not Shakespeare either, but it's very Elizabethan and very much of our time.[11]

Performed in Adrian Mitchell's verse adaptation of an English version of Weiss' play by Geoffrey Skelton, *Marat/Sade* brings together two significant figures of the French Revolutionary era fifteen years after the Revolution and establishes a fairly predictable dialectic between opposing views of history and human nature: Sade is the lyricist of individuality, keenly aware of the dark underside of nature on the basis of his own experience and imagination; Marat is the social activist and egalitarian theorist who embodies the will of the Revolution to transcend ideas and traditions of the past. Sade's writing, however horrific, was meant as a substitute for action, while Marat's writing prepared for subsequent action. In theatrical terms, a somewhat similar dialectic exists between Artaud and Brecht, as Brook seems to recognize even as he tries to ignore the contradiction. Such as it is, the debate between these two historical personages constitutes most of Weiss' intellectual substance.

Weiss proceeds from the historical fact that Sade was permitted to stage plays at Charenton during the confinement of his final years.

The play Sade is doing in 1808 concerns the stabbing fifteen years earlier of Marat, the Jacobin leader, by Charlotte Corday. The roles have been assigned, with the approval of the "enlightened" director, M. Coulmier, the spokesman for the new order, who adopts a Napoleonic pose. It is he who also promises that now everyone will be happy, a state of mind he believes will be achieved through his own therapeutic acts such as encouraging the inmates to perform plays.

Indeed, a similar purpose may underlie Brook's staging as he observes in a statement of his desired effect upon the audience which is nearly a paraphrase of Artaud with just a tincture of Brecht: "to put the audience in a state of self-conflict, to disturb, not for its own sake, for disturbance for its own sake is like sentimentality. But to scare, frighten and shake people so that, as a result they will reassess even one aspect of their thinking."[12] Brook's quest for "holy" theater frequently takes the form and vision of the therapeutic rather than the sacred, especially in *Marat/Sade* where the normative institutions of the culture seem to be the hospital and the theater combined into one. Richard Gilman expresses the dilemma of Brook's production astutely: "Flattering our sense of the fashionable, our desire to be at wicked, important happenings, but offering no light and no resurrection, *Marat/Sade* is to be seen but not believed."[13] Often within rave reviews of the stunning theater-piece Brook created from Weiss' play, other critics made similar demurs about the quality of the drama itself considered as the significant and even "holy" art which Brook seemingly hoped for. Brook's former collaborator, Charles Marowitz, ably deduced the difficulty for the director: "But just as the Group's work [the theater of cruelty alumni] itself had been diluted by being a demonstration of techniques, so the production of *The Marat/Sade* appeared the ultimate of a theory which had been hatched before the egg of the play ever arrived. It seemed to say: this kind of theatrical expression is soul-stirring and mind-widening -- if only there was a play to accommodate it." ("Notes on the Theatre of Cruelty," 183) Peter Brook, understandably, did not concur.

Not only in setting but also in content *Marat/Sade* presents consciousness hospitalized. Ian Richardson's Marat, suffering from an apparently incurable, if largely psychosomatic, skin disorder, passed the play in hydrotherapy [prefiguring, perhaps, the more recent therapeutic addiction in the United States to Marin-County-inspired hot tubs] -- his character inscribed upon his body, as in Kafka's "In the Penal Colony." Marat is played as an irritably itching revolutionary against the old order. Weiss' play allows Marat to express his revolutionary idealism; however, it also permits Sade to point out the mechanical bloodiness of postrevolutionary purges. While Marat speaks the most compelling lines in the play – and Peter Weiss has expressed his own sympathy for the Jacobin [and even more coincidentally Artaud himself played Marat in Abel Gance's film, *Napoleon* (1925) which has recently been revived] -- these lines are spoken supposedly in a play written by Sade. With such putative control over the machinery of the play within the play, Sade demonstrates a fairly thorough critique of Marat along the way. Consequently, Sade serves as the artistic-figure and even the chief theorist in the play, but he surely demonstrates no Ruskinian vision of the highest. As spectator and theorist, he is more voyeur, and he states that there is nothing else beyond the body. The intellectual put to his extremity becomes the sensualist in a negational manifestation of order.

The inmates of the asylum enact the French nation from lowest class to the highest and mime the executions of the Revolution, while at the same time projecting the intense theatricality of their supposed illnesses and rendering often unintelligible on stage the debate between Marat and Sade. Spastic, drooling, frequently distorted physically and mentally, Brook's inmates reflected their close attention to the iconology of madness as visualized by Breughel, Goya, and the graphics of Hogarth which their director had recommended to them. Brook himself, in preparation for both *Marat/Sade* and the play which preceded it, Dürrenmatt's *The Physicists*, also set, it will be remembered, in a mental institution, had paid visits to such therapeutic institutions and had discussed mental illness with his elder psychiatrist brother, but he discouraged his cast from pursuing the same field experience. Color was added to the antiseptic bathhouse interior of Sally Jacobs' design with its drably dressed nuns, male attendants, and nearly mummified inmates by a quartet of rouged and heavily made-up singers, dressed like clowns, who sang the Brechtian and Weill-like songs, compositions of Richard Peaslee. The evocative costumes were designed by the playwright's wife,

Gunilla Palmestierna-Weiss. Musicians, a kind of madhouse five, also participated zanily in the play's action from their box overlooking the stage and helped sustain the play's continuity with topical songs like: "Marat We're Poor"; "Song and Mime of Corday's Arrival in Paris"; "The Tumbrel Song"; "Copulation Round"; and "Fifteen Glorious Years."

Brook used every available space on stage for brilliant effect. The traps, suggesting the submerged tubs of the baths, became at one point the receptacle to catch the severed heads of the Revolution. A notable mime of the guillotine Brook devised with only the actor's heads displayed. Another memorable sequence revealed the symbolic blood of the Revolution flowing from buckets upon the stage in spectacular tricolor fashion: blue for the aristocrats; red for the people; and white for the pale Marat, after an initial "dry" run of potential black for which the white was substituted. Mme. Coulmier, the smirking wife of Charenton's director, was dressed à la the Empress Josephine, as her husband affected Napoleon, and her daughter, also too elegantly dressed, usually watched the audience more than they attended to the presentation of the hapless inmates, thus bring the contemporary twentieth-century audience watching *Marat/Sade* into this pastiche of French history. On this point Brook writes the following:

> The *Marat/Sade* could not have existed before Brecht: it is conceived by Peter Weiss on many alienating levels: the e- vents of the French Revolution cannot be accepted literally because they are being played by madmen, and their actions in turn are open to further question because their director is the Marquis de Sade – and moreover the events of 1780 are being seen with the eyes both of 1808 and of 1966 – for the people watching the play represent an early nineteenth-centu- ry audience and yet are also their twentieth-century selves. All these criss-crossing planes thicken the reference at each moment and compel an activity from each member of the public. (*The Empty Space*, pp. 67-68)

Brook further cites, with some obvious pride, the alienating ef- fect of the play's ending in which the inmates go beserk and begin their own revolution against their keepers. The stage image suddenly becomes threatening to the audience as well as the other performers trapped in seeming violence. At this moment, a stage manageress appears to blow a whistle which signifies the end of the performed madness, as Brook explains:

> A second ago, the situation had been hopeless: now it is all over, the actors are pulling off their wigs: of course, it's just a play. So we begin to applaud. But unexpectedly the actors applaud us back, ironically. We react to this by a momentary hostility against them as individuals, and we stop clapping. I quote this as a typical alienation series, of which each incident forces us to readjust our position. (*The Empty Space*, p. 68)

In the accomplishment of its theatrical effect, Brook's *Marat/Sade* may exemplify the supersession of the playwright by the director, although Brook would not agree with this claim. Through the splendid ensemble of RSC actors, with whom Brook carefully worked in numerous improvisations during rehearsals for *Marat/Sade*, it was easy to appreciate the pragmatic triumph of theater art; such technics rather than the rather specious debate between Sade as child of nature or Marat as creature of political reform were what endured after seeing a performance of Brook's production. Wilfrid Sheed refers to this circumstance of Brook's production in his acknowledgment that with the absence of traditional plot and conventional structure in the Weiss text and the presence of so many deliberate ironies, "the play gives itself to a director and says in effect, do everything you know, shoot the works – enlist every gesture and sound-effect you know; it won't be too much."[14]

When Barbara Walters asked Peter Brook in a *Today Show* interview shortly before *Marat/Sade* opened in New York if there was anything that he thought should not be shown in the theater, he replied: "Absolutely nothing whatsoever."[15] Though abandonment of interdicts invites disbelief in sacred order which alone can prevent the fall into pervasive nothingness, Brook presents the muddle of sensation which follows from such alteration with surpassing theatrical artistry. Transgressions represented or, indeed, enacted on stage become justified as therapeutic in the modern theater with its insistence, fully supported by Peter Brook, of the right to express everything that comes to mind, as *Marat/Sade* very nearly does. Yet those who would abolish the sense of guilt, as Philip Rieff observes, "suffer themselves to be heavily attended. . . . culture transformed into an out-patient clinic." (*Freud: The Mind of the Moralist*, p. 383) The "holy" institution of our time, then, is not the church but the clinic, and it is the latter institution which much twentieth-century theater emulates.

Not surprisingly, given the arduous condition of performance and the lacerating enactment of insanity daily on the stage, the actors of the RSC, on occasion, voiced the physical and mental strain incurred by their performance in *Marat/Sade*. Ian Richardson, Brook's Marat, for example, candidly acknowledged to Bernard Weinraub in a *New York Times* interview: "I hate doing this play, I loathe it, I hate every breathing minute of it. It's absolutely physically exhausting. I don't think any member of the cast enjoys it."[16] Other performers echoed Richardson's sentiments, including Brook's Charlotte Corday, Glenda Jackson, who admitted that "I've really hated this role":

> It's such a strain to do, to keep this curious thing alive. I am
> playing a character which nothing in the play supports. I am
> just a girl in a madhouse. I have nothing to go on except that
> she has sleeping sickness with melancholia. People seem to be
> stuck with the idea that I'm Charlotte Corday. Well, I'm not.
> I'm simply a girl in a madhouse. (*New York Times*, Feb. 13,
> 1966, II, 24X)

Apart from the teeth knocked out and the inevitable bruises of fight scenes and the like, the greater danger for the performers appears to have been mental and spiritual as Susan Williamson who played the cross-eyed Simonne Evrard, mistress and "nurse" to Marat, explained in the same *Times* piece: "Most of the actors have chosen a madness near their own idiosyncrasies. If it's played every day, and in London it wasn't, it becomes dangerous. After all, one is likely to have selected something without knowing it that reflects one's own fears and anxieties. It can be draining."

Increasingly in his theatrical experiments Brook reduced the distance between imitation of an action or a character and direct enactment in pursuit of expressive options, but the foregoing complaints from some of his actors suggest the consequences of Brook's method in their off-stage lives. Much of the appeal of Brook's *Marat/Sade* arose perhaps from the audience's awareness of the human toll being exacted before them, which was, to be sure, a distraction from the specific content of the Weiss text yet most compelling, as Walter Kerr correctly observed:

> The focus at all times was upon the mindless eyes, the
> spastic mouths, the cracked-egg skulls of the inmates of Charen-
> ton asylum, who had been assigned to perform the play-within-
> a-play that Sade had composed. We said to ourselves "How mar-
> velous the actors are! How can they possibly sustain these rigid
> attitudes for so long? Doesn't it hurt?" The manner of perform-
> ing was all we attended to or remembered; we sat through the
> evening, and then left the theater, feeling that the matter of
> the play needed scarcely to be investigated.[17]

At the opening night of *Marat/Sade* in New York, Brook and his actors encountered a particularly hostile audience, many of whom left before the end of the performance. The director argued, though, that the company turned in a superlative performance largely because of this negative reception. Mutual antagonism rather than love may be more conducive to excellence according to a theory that runs parallel to some of Artaud's notions. Thereafter New York audiences and critics lavished praise on and attention to the production. *Marat/Sade* won the New York Drama Critics' Circle Award for best play and numerous Tony Awards. The limited engagement of twelve weeks was extended to eighteen.

On October 19, 1965 Brook presented a public reading, prepared with the aid of David Jones, another dramatic text by Peter Weiss, *The Investigation* in a translation by Alexander Gross, performed by members of the Royal Shakespeare Company at the Aldwych Theatre, London. *The Investigation* documents the Auschwitz experience through court testimony against seventeen former guards of the concentration camp, based on an actual trial which began in Frankfurt during 1963 and extended into more than twenty months. The particular night members of the RSC was working through the Weiss text in London, thirteen theaters in Germany were presenting the play, and the Berliner Ensemble was also engaged in a public reading of it. In this instance, Brook eschewed the "art" which he brought to bear upon *Marat/Sade* and let the facts speak for themselves, largely the appalling details of life in the camp. J. C. Trewin movingly describes his experience of the event:

> With entire simplicity the Royal Shakespeare cast uttered
> a requiem for the Auschwitz dead. The mechanics of play-read-
> ing, the intermittent shuffling of positions, the rustle of scripts,
> ceased within a moment to obtrude; at once we identified the
> readers with the people of an investigation that in little over
> two hours held all conceivable horror. No sentences were pro-
> nounced. The narrative merely stopped; the readers dispersed.
> I had not known a quieter audience, either in the theatre or as
> it came into the hush of an early morning London. (*Peter Brook
> -- A Biography*, p. 150)

VIII. John Arden and Rolf Hochhuth en Francais: *La Danse de Sergent Musgrave* and *Le Vicaire* (1963)

Earlier than his involvement with Peter Weiss and later than it, Peter Brook staged challenging modern plays in French versions. In 1963 he staged productions of John Arden's controversial *Serjeant Musgrave's Dance* and Rolf Hochhuth's *The Deputy*, known in England originally as *The Representative* at the Théâtre de l'Athénée in Paris. Following the explicit instructions of the playwright, Brook presented a stylized production of Black Jack Musgrave's demonstration against violence through threat of violence. Without support from the Parisian press, which at the time manifested most power in its Right-Wing newspapers, the production seemed doomed to failure. After the major reviews were published, the performance following their release consisted of five people in the audience. Brook, then, advertised a series of three free performances which attracted a large number of people. It developed that virtually all such audiences could afford to pay for seats, but they had been discouraged by the poor press. J. C. Trewin reports about one evening, following a free performance, in which the Left Wing dramatist, Arthur Adamov, film directors, Alain Resnais and Jean-Luc Godard, joined Brook and his company on stage for a debate conducted in the presence of the audience who remained seated for two hours until after the departure of the last Métro [Truffaut, alas, was not apparently in attendance]. (*Peter Brook -- A Biography*, p. 137)

More successful with Hochhuth, whose *Le Vicaire* Brook directed with François Darbon, the directors found a waiting Paris audience who was eager to view the moral dilemma of Pope Pius XII in not officially condemning the Nazi slaughter of the Jews, notwithstanding almost nightly protests and demonstrations from various groups during the early run of the play. The references to Auschwitz in Hochhuth's play led inevitably to the RSC's public reading of *The Investigation*, where again there was some confusion about the work's claim to be taken as theater in its artistic sense rather than as document, which it most resembles.

IX. Between Mainstream Theatre and the Avant-Garde

The progression of Brook's work during this period of his career brought him to innovation and experiment predicated more than ever before on his own and his actors's intuitive and formal concerns rather than on the responses of the audience. Preoccupied with the need for a better understanding of the tools of the craft and the universal possibilities of the theatre, Brook, like a number of avant-garde directors at the end of the sixties, looked toward group creation and tighter links between the theatre and the plastic arts as the performing arts in general embraced a visual over a verbal emphasis. Unlike some of the more narrowly conceptual experimental directors, Brook continued his readiness to contradict or supersede himself with his next production.

In the company of his carefully chosen participants in his Paris-based research workshop and later theatre, Brook moved outside the mainstream to enlarge the connections between art and life in the next decade, as we shall see in a later chapter. If his work was no longer chiefly concerned with commercial or mainstream theatre, Brook's idea of theatre as a center around which diversities could be arranged as a means of discovering a fundamental unity -- the theatre as a powerful force to prevent further cultural fragmentation -- was sufficiently inclusive that it could not eliminate totally the best aspects of the commercial -- or more accurately the popular theatre. While Brook certainly borrowed from the avant-garde, he generated something different in kind from it as might be expected from his audacious eclecticism and capacity for ineluctable transformation of influences.

NOTES FOR CHAPTER THREE

1 Margaret Webster, for example, makes this judgment in "A Look at the London Season," *Theatre Arts*, May, 1957, p. 24.

2 Arthur Miller, "Introduction," *Collected Plays* (New York: The Viking Press, 1957), pp. 51-52.

3 Shelia Huftel, *Arthur Miller: The Burning Glass* (New York: The Citadel Press, 1965), pp. 158-159.

4 Gordon Rogoff, "Mr. Duerrenmatt Buys New Shoes," *Tulane Drama Review*, 3 (Oct. 1958), 27-34.

5 Timo Tiusanen, *Dürrenmatt: A Study in Plays, Prose, Theory* (Princeton: Princeton University Press, 1977), p. 223.

6 Friedrich Dürrenmatt, *The Visit*, trans. by Patrick Bowles (New York: Grove Press, 1962), p. 102.

7 Philip Rieff, "The Impossible Culture: Oscar Wilde and the Charisma of the Artist," *Encounter*, 35 (September, 1970), 33-44.

8 Robert Brustein, *The Theatre of Revolt: Studies in Ibsen, Strindberg, Chekhov, Shaw, Brecht, Pirandello, O'Neill and Genet* (Boston and Toronto: Atlantic-Little, Brown, 1964), p. 395.

9 See Charles Marowitz, "Notes on the Theatre of Cruelty," *Tulane Drama Review*, 11 (Winter, 1966). The aborted second half of the experimental season was to have followed Artaud's first Theatre of Cruelty Manifesto with Marlowe's *The Jew of Malta*, Büchner's *Wozzeck*, Alfred Jarry's *Ubu roi*, and Strindberg's *A Dream Play*, according to Christopher Innes, *Holy Theatre: Ritual and the Avant Garde* (Cambridge: Cambridge University Press, 1981), p. 131.

10 Martin Esslin, "The Theatre of Cruelty," *The New York Times Magazine*, March 6, 1966, p. 72.

11 Peter Brook's Introduction to Peter Weiss, *The Persecution and Assassination of Jean-Paul Marat as Performed by the Inmates of the Asylum of Charenton under the Direction of the Marquis de Sade*, English version by Geoffrey Skelton, Verse Adaptation by Adrian Mitchell (New York: Pocket Books, 1966), p. 6.

12 Brook's comments in Jules Arbore, "The Players Can Go Dotty," *New York Times*, July 17, 1966, D. 9.

13 Richard Gilman, "Assault on the Senses," *Common and Uncommon Masks: Writings on Theatre – 1961-1970* (New York: Random House, 1971), p. 169.

14 Wilfrid Sheed, "The Stage," *Commonweal*, January 21, 1966, pp. 476-477.

15 Barbara Walters, Interview with Peter Brook, *The Today Show*, NBC-TV, December 29, 1965.

16 See Bernard Weinraub, "Recording the 'Marat/Sade' Madness," *New York Times*, February 13, 1966, II, 24 X.

17 Walter Kerr, "The Case of the Vanishing Text," *Thirty Plays Hath November: Pain and Pleasure in the Contemporary Theater* (New York: Simon and Schuster, 1969), p. 61.

Chapter Four

BROOK AND SHAKESPEARE

Peter Brook won his greatest and earliest plaudits for bold innovation in staging Shakespeare, largely from three productions within
a ten-year frame, 1945-55, of less than major Shakespearean plays:
Love's Labour's Lost, Measure for Measure, and *Titus Andronicus.*
These productions were so very much revered that Brook had to persuade critics and audiences later in his career that he could stage with
equal success the Bard's major plays. With these three plays Brook
demonstrated his esemplastic power and integrated aesthetic sensibility necessary to mold the various materials of the theater into exciting unity. Further, in these plays Brook had at his disposal talent
like Paul Scofield's, John Gielgud's, and Laurence Olivier's respectively; and the director's vision was found thoroughly worthy of
these performers. Together director and actors salvaged lesser plays
from the Shakespeare canon and made them seem to be masterpieces.

Brook's method of directing also underwent significant changes
in the course of these ten years. Increasingly he came to rely on discoveries made in rehearsal, often encouraging the actors to take their
own risks in interpretation rather than representing theatrically the
director's reading of the text. The presentation of the play's energy
rather than representation of the text became Brook's desideratum,
the theater as exploration taking precedent over demonstrative theater. During this period and with these plays, Brook learned how to
work with actors individually to bring out the greatest strength each
one had for his role yet managing also to maintain ensemble balance
and a synthesis of theatrical means in the total performance. Although Brook is now known as a "conceptual" director of Shakespeare, he trusts Shakespeare's words and plots sufficiently to stage
the plays and not merely the director's concepts, however sophisticated. The rough and holy quality of Shakespeare Brook respects, as
he repeatedly manifests.

I. A Wunderkind's *Love's Labour's Lost* (1946)

At the age of twenty-one, upon invitation from Sir Barry Jackson who had recently been installed to produce the 1946 season at the Memorial Theatre in Stratford-upon-Avon, Peter Brook directed a triumphant production of *Love's Labour's Lost,* a most auspicious debut for the future great Shakespearean director. Brook, already declared the "boy-wonder" seemed ideally at home with this early Shakespeare comedy. Perhaps it is a truth universally acknowledged that the younger the writer [or director] the higher and fancier the style. The older Brook like the mature Shakespeare favors the plainer and more direct style. Nearer the present, in an interview with Ralph Berry, Brook observed that in staging *Love's Labour's Lost* he had a set of images in mind which he wanted to bring to life, a conception of the director as designer derived, in part, from his youthful enthusiasm to be a film director.[1] The images Brook advanced for this production evoked an eighteenth-century Watteau-like pleasure retreat, with the inclusion of melancholic suggestions reminiscent of the dark figure who is usually found somewhere in a Watteau canvas, the portrait of the artist himself as some would have it. J. L. Styan reports that the young Brook had seen a French production of Shakespeare's play the previous spring which had reminded him of Molière, Marivaux, and Musset, [2] and hence the pictorial means he used for his own staging were perhaps influenced by this prior Gallic context.

As a love comedy, *Love's Labour's Lost,* in Brook's presentation, is primarily intellectual, not physical, delicate in its juxtaposition of flippancy and sincerity. Though Shakespeare's play is highly satirical, the satire is never bitter, and the Watteau setting and costumes of Brook's production insured that everything is to be enjoyed in all the transience of youth and beauty. Brook captured this special essence superbly with the entrance of Marcade, dressed in black, amid the pastel colors of the five sets of summery couples to announce sadly the death of the Princess's father: "a fall of frost on the summer night," in J. C. Trewin's marvelous, eye-witness description of this theatrical moment. Trewin, moreover, remarks on the Brookian pause that this announcement inspired which possibly prefigures ever more extended ones in the director's career: "At Stratford (1946) the company remained stricken into absolute silence, a pause held for over half a minute."[3]

With one character in the play Brook violated Reginald Leefe's Watteau decor and costumes, as he dressed Constable Dull "as a Victorian policeman because his name at once conjured up the typical figure of a London bobby." (The Empty Space, p. 61) Presumably no one was bothered by this new anachronism in the production, and Brook's willingness not to maintain absolute consistency reflects his powers of imagination and invention revealed quite early in his career in this play about language, love, artifice, and reality.

In light of Brook's subsequent reluctance to assume always the primacy of words in the theater to the neglect of gesture, visual design, action, and non-verbal characterization, *Love's Labour's Lost* takes on a prophetic aspect in the director's career. Shakespeare, also early in his career, seems suspicious of some language at least and endows a character like Berowne with similar suspicion which subliminally might be extended to Peter Brook. The greatest rhetorical extremist in *Love's Labour's Lost* is Don Adriano de Armado whose virtuosity in Brook's production was assigned to the young, yet even then remarkable, Paul Scofield, with whom Brook would enjoy a number of later successes. Armado wills to simplify his life and language as a farmer, "to hold the plough," in order that love's labors need not be lost, even though for the moment they may appear to be. With a sense of balance restored, verbally and emotionally, the men of Shakespeare's comedy can still be worthy of the ladies they admire. Brook's visual style received warm and enthusiastic support in his first effort at Stratford.

II. A Controversial *Romeo and Juliet* (1947)

Less unanimously well-received than *Love's Labour's Lost* but in style an even more distinctive harbinger of later Shakespearean productions by Peter Brook was *Romeo and Juliet* (1947) at Stratford, which represented a radical departure from previous conceptions of this love tragedy of youth. Brook's was a thoroughly "de-Victorianized" *Romeo and Juliet*. Amid considerable controversy, Brook cast young people of the approximate age of Shakespeare's characters as the lovers. To his subsequent embarrassment and regret, Brook rejected the then fourteen year old Claire Bloom for Juliet; she would gain much notice in that role in 1952, though under Zeffirelli's rather than Brook's direction, albeit in a production indebted in some ways to Brook's earlier staging. A somewhat more mature actress, eighteen year old Daphne Slater played Juliet for Brook! Perhaps most fortuitously cast of all was Paul Scofield as Mercutio, fresh from his triumph in *Love's Labour's Lost*. Reminiscing about how to handle the Queen Mab speech, J. C. Trewin notes: "My happiest recollection is of Paul Scofield (Stratford, 1947) stretched upon the stage in the torchlight, his cape flung round him, his arm raised, and his eyes intent as he let the speech flower into the silence of the grotesquely-visaged masquers." (*Going to Shakespeare*, p. 95)

Zeffirelli in later productions of *Romeo and Juliet* on stage and especially on film would demonstrate to a larger public the truth which Brook had advanced in his earlier, precedent-making production; namely, that it is a play of youthful Southern European passion, its atmosphere described in a single line, "these hot days is the mad blood stirring," essentially virile and Elizabethan in spirit. Brook writes of *Romeo and Juliet*: "It is a play of youth, of freshness, of open air, in which the sky – the great tent of Mediterranean blue – hangs over every moment of it, from the first brawl in the dusty market to the calm and peaceful cadence in the grave. It is a play of wide spaces, in which all scenery and decoration easily become an irrelevance, in which one tree on a bare stage can suggest the loneliness of a place of exile, one wall, as in Giotto, an entire house."[4]

The sparseness of setting coupled with the intensity of violent action in Brook's production proved disquieting to audiences accustomed to traditional sentimental stagings of the play as almost a lyric love poem. Brook observed that his *Romeo and Juliet* seemed most alive and true to those theater-goers who were without an overclose acquaintance with the play. Many expository and recapitulatory portions of the text were cut from Brook's production. In time, Brook's audience would come to accept such surgery as necessary, but purists in 1947 still complained loudly about alterations and omissions in *Romeo and Juliet*.

90

Some years later, Clive Barnes looked back on Brook's production as a turning point in the history of British theater because "it tried to treat the text as if it were living theatre, and proved in the process that it was. . . . the fight scenes were magnificent and the actors did not speak Shakespeare as if they wanted to spit the plum-stones out."[5] The controversy surrounding his production of *Romeo and Juliet* catapulted Brook into the forefront of young, revolutionary British directors; however, he did not follow up on this reputation immediately with additional theater work. Instead Brook assumed Directorship of Opera Production at the Royal Opera House, Covent Garden, not without a flurry of public protest and criticism against the *enfant terrible* of the Stratford season whose liberated *Romeo and Juliet* augured for even greater liberties with rigidly traditional grand opera.

III. A Fully-Fathomed *Measure for Measure* (1950)

While surely not among the "unknown" Shakespeare, *Measure for Measure* (1950) never enjoyed a particularly steady success on the stage, even in the twentieth century, until Peter Brook's staging of it at Stratford. Eighteen years later Brook reflected upon this production and used *Measure for Measure* as exemplification of the mingling of what he terms the Rough and Holy Theatre:

> We have a base world, a very real world in which the action is
> firmly rooted. This is the disgusting, stinking world of medieval
> Vienna. The darkness of this world is absolutely necessary to
> the meaning of the play: Isabella's plea for grace has far more
> meaning in this Dostoevskian setting than it would in lyrical
> comedy's never-never land. When this play is prettily staged, it
> is meaningless – it demands an absolutely convincing roughness
> and dirt. Also, when so much of the play is religious in thought,
> the loud humour of the brothel is important as a device, because
> it is alienating and humanizing. From the fanatical chastity of
> Isabella and the mystery of the Duke we are plunged back to
> Pompey and Barnadine for douches of normality. . . . We need
> complete freedom, rich improvisation, no holding back, no false
> respect – and at the same time we must take great care, for all
> around the popular scenes are great areas of the play that clum-

siness could destroy. As we enter this holier land, we will find
that Shakespeare gives us a clear signal – the rough is in prose,
the rest in verse. (*The Empty Space*, p. 80)

The burden of holiness in Brook's production was carried by
Harry Andrews' Duke Vincentio, less in disguise than spiritually at
home in the role of Friar. In this regard, Brook applied to the stage
the consensus which had emerged from the most reputable criticism
and scholarship of *Measure for Measure* in the present century, which
interpreted the Duke as the play's moral touchstone and not merely
as a plot manipulator. Here is an admirable man no longer content to
hold the rottenness of his Vienna at arms length. As Herbert S. Weil,
Jr. has pointed out, Brook deleted a number of lines in *Measure for
Measure* which Shakespeare used "to laugh *at* the Duke and to find
meaningful flaws in his personal private character as well as in his
ability to rule."[6] A completely admirable Duke was no doubt a
distortion of the text in Brook's production.

As for the rough elements of corrupt Vienna, Brook established
the standard for their portrayal in most subsequent production of
Measure for Measure with three processions strategically placed in
the play of prostitutes, cripples, beggars, and degenerates. The most
audacious of these scenes evolved from the slightest of pretexts in
the play itself: Pompey's account in Act IV of the old customers
from the bawdy house he has met as new customers in prison.
Brook's repeated success with large ensembles representing the public
world was used to good effect in *Measure for Measure* to balance the
frequent private scenes with two or three characters.

It was Brook's good fortune to have John Gielgud as his Angelo
in this production, the first of many successful collaborations between Brook and this distinguished actor. Gielgud ably portrayed an
Angelo upset to discover that his total personality would not match
up to his ideals; nevertheless, despite his own personal failures, this
Angelo was too tenacious to permit his value system or that of the
state his public commitment requires him to uphold consequently to
crumble. Though he was no longer worthy, Gielgud's Angelo still saw
some honor and right reason in trying to maintain a public role, even
as he projected the psychological price an official pays for grave
imbalance between his private and public life.

Similarly Barbara Jefford's Isabella displayed a depth of characterization in the way she showed the process of change from a simple and Puritanical, if very intelligent, girl to a self-knowing woman. To crystallize Isabella's recognition that severe strictness will not do and her loss of former smugness about her own virtue, Brook devised an extended pause as Jefford knelt before the Duke to plead for the life of Angelo prior to her saying, "Look, if it please you, on this man condemn'd." Brook writes of this scene: "I asked Isabella. . . to pause each night until she felt the audience could take it no longer – and this used to lead to a two-minute stopping of the play [others have said the usual hiatus was more often around 35 second]. The device became a voodoo pole – a silence in which the abstract notion of mercy became concrete for that moment to those present." (*The Empty Space*, p. 81) Notable less for its duration than for its distillation through silence of the words and action which follows, this sequence articulated silently Brook's conception of the rough and holy meaning of Shakespeare's problematic comedy of forgiveness. Isabella's words, according to Richard David's account, finally "came quiet and level, and as their full impact of mercy reached Angelo, a sob broke from him. It was perfectly calculated and perfectly timed; and the whole perilous manoeuvre had been triumphantly brought off."[7] Earlier in the production Brook had captured the exterior roughness of Vienna's streets and prison; now his last memorable tableau of an unforgettable staging revealed how inner holiness made external can transform a rough world. No wonder such a man as Duke Vincentio desires to marry Isabella.

Brook's own design for the play's permanent set consisted of three prominent doors through which the action passed, stone pillars and arches which could be easily altered with a few details to represent palace, street, convent, or prison. The pace of the action was rapid in this all-purpose setting which let the rough and holy elements interpenetrate in approximation of the traditional playing areas on the Elizabethan stage. Instruments of torture gave sinister reality to Brook's stage with racks, whips, a block, and similar appurtenances scattered liberally; in complement the costumes of the production seemed reminiscent often of scenes from Hieronymous Bosch. Laurence Olivier was apparently not alone in judging Brook's produc-

93

tion the most enlightening interpretation of any play that he had seen, at least up to 1950. (Weil, 28) This production of *Measure for Measure*, after its season at Stratford, toured five cities in West Germany to great acclaim.

IV. A Triumphant *Winter's Tale* (1951)

Seeking to have lightning strike twice after the manner of the preceding year's *Measure for Measure*, Brook mounted another difficult and rarely produced Shakespearean play, *The Winter's Tale* (1951) which opened in June at the Phoenix Theatre, London as part of The Festival of Britain. As with its predecessor, Brook was again fortunate to have John Gielgud head his superb cast in the role of Leontes. On this occasion the innocent and long-suffering wife, Hermione, was performed with grace and beauty of speech and person by Diana Wynyard; a strong-willed, but sympathetic, Paulina was memorably portrayed by Flora Robson. Additional support was provided by performers of comparable excellence: Lewis Casson as Antigonus; George Rose as Autolycus, extending his Pompey of *Measure for Measure* somewhat further in *The Winter's Tale*, and the blossoming Virginia McKenna as Perdita. The production interrupted its successful London run for much-praised performances at the Edinburgh Festival in 1951.

From his first quiet utterance, Gielgud conveyed jealousy on the part of Leontes; here is a man caught in sick betrayal of himself and all he holds. Alice Venezky took note of Leontes' moments with his son, Mamillius, as Gielgud's "only touch of warmth and humanity," which the actor "shows by a subtle tenderness in voice and gentleness of motion, even when he is forcing himself to be harsh with the boy."[8] Later, by sixteen years, a repentant Leontes can accord Florizel the understanding denied him by his own father, and the play persuasively comes full circle in the wide gap of time, as the lost are found, and the supposed dead resurrected. Venezky writes of Gielgud's handling of the play's ending: "When Hermione's 'statue' comes to life, he falls to his knees with humility and joy in a final scene which is not only credible but moving." (Venezky, 339)

94

Graciously, Gielgud paid tribute to Peter Brook's direction for the success of the production: "He's wonderful. Me – a king in Shakespeare -- enter. No banners. No trumpets. Nothing. Incredible! Unprecedented! A Wonderful boy!"[9]

Brook used a setting by Sophie Fedorovitch which observed the basic structure of the Elizabethan playhouse with a central alcove at the back, and two smaller ones along each side, ending in two scene buildings, each with an acting space above reminiscent of the upper stage in what's imagined to be Shakespeare's Globe. Along with other critics, George Rylands praised Brook's grouping of the actors in relation to this set: "The sudden rejection of Hermione from a 'window-stage' as she played with her son in the courtyard below was remarkably effective."[10] Also highly commended was Brook's ingenious approach to the awkward appearance of Father Time in the play. The tempest which destroys the vessel of Antigonus turns into a whirl of snow – "as if one of those endearing glass toys had been shaken," as J. C. Trewin described it (*Going to Shakespeare*, p. 264) -- and out of the flakes materializes Time. He, in turn, melts away, skies clearing on an open stage where the rustics have their springtime in Bohemia.

Brook invested this portion of the play with earthy realism and plausible English shepherds in a raucous holiday mood. Venezky felt that Brook's results failed to achieve his aim. Her complaint is interesting as a minority report in its contrast with the usual praise Brook received during this period of his career for his handling of large ensemble scenes: "There is confusion in the handling of the crowd of shepherds who sit or cavort at the back of the stage while a weakly-realized Florizel [Richard Gale] and an inaudible Perdita exchange love speeches on the forestage." In addition, she faults Brook's production for "the lack of any over-all style or unifying spirit." (Venezky, 337) But the continous stage action of Brook's *Winter's Tale* achieved emblematic unity out of seeming disunity through time and seasons in the manner of Shakespeare's text itself. It must be conceded that the young lovers (and the youthful performers) were eclipsed in the production somewhat by the autumnal quality of the interpretation and those performers whom George Rylands, quoting Moth, named "their tough seniors!" (Rylands, 143) The generation which has sinned and suffered, repented and granted forgiveness, remains as the mythic center of the production.

V. The Reclamation of *Titus Andronicus* (1955)

Peter Brook's most spectacular excavation of a "lesser" Shakespearean play unquestionably was the widely-acclaimed Stratford production of *Titus Andronicus* (1955), historically the least performed of all Shakespeare's plays since the closing of the theaters in 1642. Indeed much scholarly debate had persisted well into the twentieth century concerning the authenticity of *Titus Andronicus* as the work of Shakespeare. In answer, the Polish critic, Jan Kott, who saw Brook's Stratford production in 1957 during its extensive and successful Eastern European tour, agrees with Brook that this early play contains, though still in rough shape, the seed of later great Shakespearean tragedies: "But it [*Titus Andronicus*] had pleased the Elizabethan audience and was one of the most frequently performed plays. Mr. Brook did not discover *Titus*. He discovered Shakespeare in *Titus*. Or rather – in this play he discovered Shakespearean theatre. The theatre that had moved and thrilled audiences, terrified and dazzled them."[11]

Using a judiciously cut text and a rapid, fluid mode of presentation which Kott identifies plausibly as cinematic, Brook's production sought to create an almost ritualistic ceremony of bloodshed. The carnage embodied in *Titus Andronicus* is justifiably famous even among those who are not very familiar with the play. "Everything in *Titus*," Brook writes, "is linked to a dark flowing current out of which surge the horrors, rhythmically and logically related – if one searches in this way one can find the expression of a powerful and eventually barbaric ritual." (*The Empty Space*, p. 86) Accordingly, Brook transcended the play's melodrama by illuminating the elements of genuine tragedy, some of which prefigure the greatest of Shakespeare's dramas, *King Lear*. As Kenneth Tynan observed: "The parallel with Lear is sibling close, and Peter Brook cleverly strengthens it by having the fly-killing scene performed by a wanton boy." (*Curtains*, p. 103)

In plot outline *Titus Andronicus* is nearly a parody of the revenge play. It may be recalled that the Roman general, Titus, returns to Rome, following a victorious campaign, with Queen Tamora and her three sons as captives. The eldest of Tamora's three sons is sacrificed by the four surviving sons of Titus in tribute to their twenty-one brothers killed in the wars. Although acclaimed emperor, Titus relinquishes the title to Saturninus, eldest son of the deceased emperor, who has promised to marry Lavinia, the daughter of Titus. Bassianus, the brother of Saturninus kidnaps Lavinia with the aid of her brothers and marries her. In his effort to regain his daughter for the intended Saturninus, Titus kills his own youngest son, Mutius. Meanwhile Saturninus weds Tamora. The latter schemes to avenge the death of her eldest son at the hands of the family of Titus. Tamora enlists the help of her lover, Aaron the Moor. Her sons kill Bassianus and throw his body into a pit. Lavinia is raped and her hands and tongue are removed. Aaron plants gold near the pit where Bassianus is buried, and his plan is for two sons of Titus to fall into the pit and then be accused of killing Bassianus for the motive of gold. Aaron then tells Titus that his sons will be pardoned by the emperor if either the third son or Titus's brother sends a hand in ransom. Heroically Titus sends his own severed appendage only to receive it back with the severed heads of his sons.

Kenneth Tynan wryly comments on this plot: "With acknowledgements to Lady Bracknell, to lose one son may be accounted a misfortune; to lose twenty-four, as Titus does, looks like carelessness. Here, indeed, is 'snip, and nip, and cut, and slish, and slash,' a series of operations which only a surgeon could describe as a memorable evening in the theatre." (*Curtains*, p. 104) The mutilated and ravished Lavinia writes the names of her attackers in sand with a staff, guiding it with her mouth and arms, and the surviving members of Titus's family determine complete revenge. At a banquet in the palace of Titus, a meat pie is served to Tamora, containing the remains of her sons. In a grand murderous finale, Lavinia, Tamora, Titus, and Saturninus are slain – in Brook's production like a strike at a bowling alley. Lucius, the sole surviving son of Titus, emerges as the new emperor and sentences Aaron to death by starvation.

Out of such uncompromising material, Brook fashioned a production of great dramatic beauty and strong visual images, often through stylized distancing effects which let the audience accept the horror of the play without experiencing total revulsion. For example, when Titus's daughter, Lavinia, entered following her mutilation and rape, she appeared with wrists swathed in gauze and streamers of red ribbon issuing from her mouth and arms. Likewise the heads of Titus's sons are brought forward concealed with black cloth and encased in steel baskets. And perhaps the most horrific sequence of all, where Lavinia holds a basin to catch the blood of Tamora's two sons before they become the ingredients of the "pasty," was removed to an off-stage kitchen. Such formal stylizations preserve the play's sacred order against lowering caused by the transgressions enacted in and through it. The beauty beneath the barbarism of *Titus Andronicus* requires the repressive mode for presentation. At this point in his career, Peter Brook seems quite sensitive to the distancing devices and balances created and recreated to do symbolically what otherwise is not done. If nothing is offensive, then nothing can be truly sacred or, the word Brook would probably prefer, holy. Later, Brook will call into question the existence of any content so offensive that it cannot be expressed directly, but his production of *Titus Andronicus* transformed the play's horror into the highly acceptable form of art even if "this obscure work of Shakespeare touched audiences directly," as Brook explains, "because we had tapped in it a ritual of bloodshed which was recognized as true." (The Empty Space, p. 43)

When Leslie Hurry, Brook's original choice for scene designer, became unavailable because of other commitments, the director again executed his own designs for both set and costumes. Richard David describes the versatility of Brook's use of three massive fluted columns with folding sides which could be arranged to achieve a number of effects in the ritual of blood:

> Festooned with leaves it [the set] became the murder pit and
> the forest floor above it; stained a yellowish natural wood color
> it provided a background of Roman frugality to the bereaved
> and brooding Titus at his family table; blood-red, it made a
> macabre eyrie of the upper chamber from which the Revenger
> [Titus] peers out upon his victims,. . . . In the court scenes the

closed pillars, supported by heavy side grating of the same
color and hangings of purple and green, richly suggested the
civilized barbarity of late imperial Rome.[12]

Likewise, Jan Kott rhapsodically admired Brook's colorful costumes
operating against the simple, bronze-gray set: "Like a true artist, he
[Brook] does not copy or impose artificial unity. He has freely taken
a full range of yellows from Titian, dressed his priests in the irritating
greens of Veronese. The Moor, in his black-blue-and-gold costume, is
derived from Rubens." (*Shakespeare Our Contemporary*, p. 348)

Moreover, the throbbing *musique concrète* of the production represented yet another contribution of the versatile director. Brook
took conventional fanfares of trumpets and played them at faster
tempo through an echo chamber to produce a tape recording of in-
human and unearthly quality. The baleful dirge played for the slain
Andronici stayed in the minds of the audience as a haunting and in-
cessant variation on "Three Blind Mice." At one point the slow
plucking of harp strings evoked the drops of Lavinia's blood. Penelope Gilliatt, for one, was less than enchanted by Brook's music for
Titus Andronicus, though her graphic description suggests that Brook
was effective in producing a score to conjure up the sensation of
cruelty: "a barbaric collage of noises that sounded rather as if it were
scored for Malayan nose flute, deep-sea tuba, and Gorgon's eye-
ball."[13] At least in all his many guises, as director, costumer, set
designer, and composer, Peter Brook showed himself at the end of
his first decade in the professional theater as a consummate artist.
Eye-witness J. C. Trewin remembers the opening-night at the Memorial Theatre in Stratford and the electric excitement which
greeted Peter Brook and his star, Laurence Olivier:

> *Titus Andronicus* came in the night of August 16 to the
> most sustained roar of applause I remember in the Stratford
> Theatre. . . . The curtain rose, fell, and rose again, while the
> house clapped until hands tingled and many people were
> shouting at the pitch of their voices. . . It was for Peter Brook,
> the director who showed again that he had one of the most
> imaginative minds in the English theatre, and for Sir Laurence
> Olivier, who turned upon the despised part of Titus the full
> beam of his genius.[14]

Praise for the performances resounded from all critical quarters, each reviewer trying to surpass the other in superlatives. Anthony Quayle, as Aaron the Moor, received laurels for his corrupt flamboyance, as did Maxine Audley for Tamora, the villainess audiences love to hate, and Vivien Leigh as the wretchedly sinned against Lavinia. But the loudest paeans went unreservedly to Olivier who captured from a number of critical sources the label of the greatest actor in the world on the strength of his performance in this production. Kenneth Tynan expressed it best:

> This is a performance which ushers us into the presence of one who is, pound for pound, the greatest actor alive. As usual, he raises one's hair with the risks he takes. Titus enters not as a beaming hero but as a battered veteran, stubborn and shambling, long past caring about the people's cheers. A hundred campaigns have tanned his heart to leather, and from the crackling of that heart there issues a terrible music, not untinged by madness. One hears great cries, which, like all of this actor's best effects, seem to have been dredged up from an ocean-bed of fatigue. One recognized, though one had never heard it before, the noise made in its last extremity by the cornered human soul. We knew from his Hotspur and his Richard III that Sir Laurence could explode. Now we know that he can suffer as well. (*Curtains*, pp. 104-5)

Peter Brook and his distinguished company of players re-discovered an early Shakespearean tragedy and found in it ritualized violence, hatred, cruelty, and pain. Shakespeare's Senecan stoicism led Brook to inventive stylization which permitted the horror of the ancient world to speak to contemporary conditions without imitating them. Hailed as a milestone in the English theater, Brook's production of *Titus Andronicus* was transferred to London late in 1956 and continued to play to packed houses well into the next year before it closed at home to resume performances in Paris, Venice, Vienna, Warsaw, Belgrade, and Zagreb.

VI. A Tentative *Hamlet* (1955)

As part of a series of three plays which Brook staged at the Phoenix Theatre in 1955-56 with Paul Scofield in leading roles, *Hamlet* was included. It was not Scofield's first *Hamlet*, but it was Brook's. The defects of the production would help sustain for some years the widely-held critical opinion that as a Shakespearean director Peter Brook's special forte was rediscovery and re-interpretation of other than the major plays. Brook's production was praised for its speed and for the vitality of the large crowd scenes, particularly in the play-within-the-play and the closing duel. Yet for all the movement, the production did not develop linearly toward any notable focus or destination.

Peter Brook admitted subsequently that he erred in this Phoenix production by treating the ghost realistically:

> When I produced the play [*Hamlet*] I. . . fell head first into this trap of making the ghost into a human figure, played naturalistically. . . making him talk like a father would to his son – but (through no fault of the actor), it was no good – it was the extreme opposite of the solution because it was against the whole conception of ghostness, and the scene just seemed drab and underplayed.[15]

Similarly, Paul Scofield's Hamlet achieved its own drabness; Kenneth Tynan comments on Scofield's interpretation: "Vocally and physically he is one long tremendous sulk." (*Curtains*, p. 110) This critic expresses greatest enthusiasm for Alec Clunes' Claudius, a portrayal Tynan considers definitive. Brook might have played Hamlet's sulking inaction off against this conscience-scarred, but still majestic, stepfather's actions for good effect. At times this tentative and unsure production revealed potential for a fresh approach to *Hamlet* through the nursery and the so-called family romance, raising what Freud termed the parent question of humanity and authority – "Am I thy master or art thou mine?" Instead the parent question became simply a question of parents, King Claudius vs. King Hamlet. That the court musicians at Elsinore in Brook's production were given toy instruments to play suggested possibilities of an audacious interpretation somewhat along these lines, but purpose and clarification do not emerge.

101

Brook's production had an unusual tryout tour before taking up residence in London. *Hamlet* was first performed in Moscow where it was the first British production to be staged in the Russian capital since the Revolution of 1917 and was accordingly warmly greeted by audiences and critics. Actually, during its London run, Brook's *Hamlet* chalked up 124 performances, according to J. C. Trewin, the third longest unbroken run of the play in English stage history. (*Peter Brook: A Biography*, p. 94) Audiences seemed to take to the production better than the critics did. Caryl Brahms cited as a frequent failing on the director's part Brook's tendency to work out brilliant moves, actions, and stage business for a character without sufficient concern for the character's inner motives.[16] This supposed defect Brook progressively turns to asset in later Shakespearean productions by his concentration on Shakespeare's narrative art, which begins and ends in motion and emphasis on what happens, without any irritable reaching after internal reasons and purpose.

Brook's production of *The Tempest* (1957) in Stratford will be deferred until a later section where his several approaches to Shakespeare's last great romance will be taken up together.

VII. *King Lear* (1962): Brook Soars with a Major Play

Peter Brook's first Shakespearean production as one of the triumvirs of the newly reorganized and renamed Royal Shakespeare Company, formerly the rather funereal-sounding Shakespeare Memorial Company of the Stratford Memorial Theatre, sharing directorship with Peter Hall and Michel Saint-Denis, was the controversial, but internationally acclaimed, *King Lear*, which opened at the Royal Shakespeare Theatre, Stratford-on-Avon, on November 6, 1962 and moved to the Company's new London playhouse, the Aldwych Theatre, on December 12, 1962. Following its very successful London run, Brook took *King Lear* to Paris where it was presented at the Théâtre des Nations and received the Challenge du Théâtre des Nations award and the Prix de la Jeune Critique awards for excellence; West Berlin; cities in Eastern Europe, and finally the Soviet Union. In 1964 the production came to the United states for an extended tour and generous run in New York.

102

Inspired philosophically by the absurdist world-view of Samuel Beckett as elaborated in the essay by Polish critic, Jan Kott, "*King Lear* or *Endgame*," reprinted, after Brook's production, as part of Kott's much-esteemed study, *Shakespeare Our Contemporary*, and theatrically by the ideas of Brecht, Brook's *King Lear*, perhaps not surprisingly, enjoyed its greatest audience response on the European Continent and its least critical and popular favor in the United States. Brook himself felt that the company's best performances "lay between Budapest and Moscow. . . . These audiences brought with them three things: a love for the play itself, real hunger for a contact with foreigners and, above all an experience of life in Europe in the last years that enabled them to come directly to the play's painful themes." (*The Empty Space*, p. 20) In contrast, despite the company's great expectations for bringing all the nuances they had cultivated during their foreign travels back to the English-speaking theater in their American tour, Brook experienced a quite different, even shocking, result:

> I was forced to go back to England and only caught up
> with the company a few weeks later in Philadelphia. To my
> surprise and dismay, much of the quality had gone from their
> acting. I wanted to blame the actors, but it was clear that they
> were trying as hard as they could. It was the relation with the
> audience that had changed. In Philadelphia, the audience under-
> stood English all right, but this audience was composed largely
> of people who were not interested in the play; people who
> came for all the conventional reasons – because it was a social
> event, because their wives insisted. . . . Undoubtedly, a way
> existed to involve this particular audience in *King Lear*, but
> it was not our way. The austerity of this production which
> had seemed so right in Europe no longer made sense. . . . I
> knew that were I doing a production of *King Lear* for the
> people of Philadelphia I would without condescension stress
> everything differently – and, in immediate terms, I would get
> it to work better. But with an established production on tour
> I could do nothing. (*The Empty Space*, P. 21)

Brook's *King Lear* was deliberately unsympathetic and cruel, played usually in bright, almost painful, light. Shakespeare's "unaccommodated man," with motives of conduct cut back to their roots, dominated this "naked" production, timeless and monolithic in the harshness of Brook's own designed wood and rusty metal sets and props together with unpliant, rough-hewn leather costumes. Norman Bel Geddes' Stonehenge-inspired set for *King Lear* in the nineteen-twenties was transferred figuratively now to the characters themselves in Brook's production; the human artifacts, though, unlike the stone monoliths, are worn away right before the audience's eyes. Brook especially emphasized the disintegration of all orders of established values, the decay and fall of the world, the defeat of all eschatologies. Jan Kott advances the notion of an absurd mechanism which has taken the place of God, Nature, and History. Brook translated this idea rather literally with openly displayed motorized rusty metal sheets which resonate to make the thunder of the play but in a larger sense produce the sound and fury signifying its prevailing nothingness and emptiness of "ruined nature." During rehearsals one of these sheets came loose from its moorings and fell to the stage perilously close to actors and director. Thereafter wily attention and projection of anxiety were always present when anyone approached these mechanisms.

That perverse Victorian, Algernon Swinburne, had argued long before Peter Brook, Jan Kott, and the absurdists of the post-Second World War years that the touchstone of *King Lear* was Gloucester's indictment of an indifferent universe: "As flies to wanton boys are we to the gods:/They kiss us for their sport –." But Brook gave uncompromising contemporary attention to the full implication of this Beckettian sentiment in a Shakespearean context.

Although presenting a nearly uncut text, Brook made some crucial deletion of lines in the play which militated against his overall bleakness of conception. For example, there was no appeal to "sweet sway," allowing obedience for Brook's Lear, and many of Kent's references to Lear's undeserved condition as well as Edgar's feeling asides were omitted. The dialogue between the Second and Third Servants, following the blinding of Gloucester in Act III, Sc. vii, which indicate their intention to offer succor to the old man was likewise deleted. Further, Brook eliminated entirely Act IV, Sc. iii, in which Kent receives the Gentleman's report on Cordelia's sorrow upon hearing about her father. Brook's Lear made no claim that "He

104

that parts us shall bring a brand from heaven,/And fire us hence like foxes." Not surprisingly, then, Brook's Edmund expressed no tardy, yet repentant, "some good I mean to do,/ Despite of mine own nature," in the same scene. Nor did Brook's Edgar try to re-acquaint Lear with Kent, "your friend," as earlier in the play Gloucester failed to acknowledge Lear's faithful servant as "that good Kent." In addition, Brook brought up final thunder, perhaps as harbinger of new storms, to drown out the last reconciliating speeches of the play and testimonies of abiding loyalty. It was as if Brook could not risk the least element of affirmation to creep into *King Lear*, notwithstanding Shakespeare's own practice, as those restless Philadelphians may have recognized with more attention to the text than Brook imagined.

Paul Scofield's Lear was powerful and different from any other of recent memory. Charles Marowitz who served as Brook's assistant director during rehearsals of *King Lear* incisively comments on Scofield's performance: "For me, Scofield has delivered only about fifty percent of Lear. Lear the ruler is there, as is Lear the madman; but Lear the father and Lear in those supreme final moments where the play transcends itself is only sketched out."[17] Whatever deficiency, in general correctly perceived by Marowitz, existed in Scofield's performance must be judged against the conception of Brook's production. The familial piety and interconnectedness which Lear impulsively abandons at the beginning of the play never occupied Brook's attention sufficiently for the audience to feel that an ideal had been lost. All the characters in this production were locked into their own existential isolation from the beginning, which, to be sure, affected the power and emotion of the drama's close. That existence is inseparable from relationships, both of blood and of service, was not the approach which Brook took to Shakespeare's study of vulnerable humanity; and without it vulnerability loses its tragic grandeur, which possibly Brook confused with emotionalism and sentimentality that he sought to avoid. However, Scofield's slow, almost incantatory delivery of lines matched with half-repressed gestures lay the rhetoric of the role aside for fresh precision of interpretation. This Lear virtually never shouted, but he was heard with a horrified acuity which surpassed the effects of declamation. Lear's "Howl! Howl!" had seldom been at once so muted and yet so commanding, as Scofield made his audience listen for his string of "never's" as if from the bottom of a limitless abyss.

Other notable portrayals in Brook's production included Alan Webb's compellingly ordinary Gloucester, Diana Rigg's somewhat too luscious, but stubbornly honest, Cordelia, Alec McCowen's extremely wise and knowing Fool, and Ian Richardson's Edmund [Richardson having replaced James Booth before the extended tour of Europe and the United States], treacherous, attractive, and eloquent. Brook took particular pains to differentiate Goneril, played with stunning sexual veracity by Irene Worth, and Regan, played by Patience Collier. The director cogently explained to an interviewer the basis of his conception of these two sisters: "The Goneril-Regan relationship is a completely Jean Genet one where Goneril wears the boots and Regan wears the skirts."[18]

Avoiding the traditional paradoxical exaltation of tragedy, Brook achieved a nearly Brechtian epic objectivity in his staging of *King Lear* through a variety of means, from decor to unheroic, understated acting. One of the simplest and most effective devices was the stark, bright stage lighting, which, on occasion, included the house lights as part of the presentation, as at the end of the blinding of Gloucester scene when the house lights came up but the action of the tortured man continued on stage in front of the audience eager to head to the bar for refreshment. Marowitz writes of this effect: "If this works, it should jar the audience into a new kind of adjustment to Gloucester and his tragedy. The house-lights remove all possibility of aesthetic shelter, and the act of blinding is seen in a colder light than would be possible otherwise." ("Lear Log," p. 142) Hereafter, in subsequent productions, Brook would often violate the conventional separation between stage and auditorium created by lighting. Because it is unorthodox and unfamiliar to most audiences, such effects can be truly enlightening, as they were in *King Lear* and later in Brook's theater.

Brook's *King Lear* became a tragedy without either "discovery" on the part of the protagonist or catharsis on the part of the audience. The play's ending in this production presented ambiguity and a moral stalemate, without the usual affirmation of the necessity of order or triumph of the spirit. Austere, cruel, atavistic yet contemporary, Brook's *King Lear* made an absurdist statement for the times. Harold Clurman summed up the relevance of the production expertly: "Peter Brook is to be congratulated on a *Lear* made to the measure of our day and the circumstances of the modern theatre." (*The Naked Image*, p. 181) Interestingly enough, in his essay on the Beckettian elements in *King Lear*, Jan Kott often compares Shakespeare's play and Durrenmatt's *The Visit*, The latter play, of course, Brook had staged first in 1958. Significantly, during its run at the Aldwych in London, *King Lear* alternated with another RSC production, also directed by Brook, Durrenmatt's *The Physicists*. Modern repertory programming has seldom made for stranger bedfellows, yet Peter Brook appeared happy with the juxtaposition, since both plays, in his productions, raised a shared question: Is it possible to achieve and maintain moral sanity in a "post-moral" world?

VIII. *The Tempest* (1957;1963;1968): Cooked and Raw Versions

Brook's association with *The Tempest* affords a gauge to his changing viewpoint on the nature of theater over the years. His initial production of the play was at Stratford in 1957 with John Gielgud cast as Prospero and the director responsible for the entire *mise en scène* -- sets, costumes, lighting, and music, everything grandiosely conceived and elaborated, though not necessarily with literalness. The opening scene, for example, was performed without much realistic detail. The ship itself was only suggested by a mast-head lantern dizzily swinging in an arc together with some flailing ropes and a burning fire-ball or two. J. C. Trewin comments on a distinctive Brook touch in the scene: "a moment few directors had vouchsafed, a spell-stopped, ominous quiet before the final split." (*Going to Shakespeare*, p. 268) Brook managed to impart an underwater effect by decorating the stage with streamers suggesting seaweed, as the company moved through the maze at least full fathom five. The wedding masque for Ferdinand and Miranda was celebrated by a frenzied masque, goddesses and dancers appearing to be silhouetted in fire floating in air. The stage decor was often changed quickly, before the eyes of the audience, as when the stage full of drooping vines was instantly transformed into an empty cavernous vault. While audiences generally appreciated Brook's effects, the critics were usually less enthusiastic about his production schemes. J. W. Lambert, standing for the nay-sayers, judged Brook's *Tempest* the "largest in scale of the recent Shakespeare productions, but the least effective."[19] In interpretation, Brook's 1957 *Tempest* was thoroughly traditional and dignified, embodied best in the performance of John Gielgud as the magus who loses his magic charms but gains human wisdom. After its presentation in Stratford, *The Tempest* moved to London for a succesful run at the Theatre Royal, Drury Lane.

In 1963 Brook again embarked on *The Tempest*, this time in collaboration with co-director, Clifford Williams, for the RSC at Stratford. The production was praised for its pictorial and decorative effects as well as for the musical score by Raymond Leppard. Some observers hinted that the music rather than the acting contributed most to the play's sense of enchantment. Perhaps the rehearsal process for the production had been difficult, with two directors sometimes giving conflicting instructions. The *New York Times* in a news-story on the opening in Stratford quoted Clive Barnes' review of the production from *The Daily Express*: " 'I hardly know whether to praise Mr. Williams for his imaginative direction and curse Mr. Brook for his wretched collaboration or vice versa.' "[20] No wonder that Peter Brook terms the play, "baffling and elusive," even as he finds it Shakespeare's "complete final statement" for its dealings with the "Whole condition of man" (*The Empty Space*, p. 86)

Discarding *The Tempest* as a pretext for costumes, stage effects, and music, Brook returned to the play in a strikingly radical context in 1968 when he accepted an invitation from Jean-Louis Barrault, director of the Theatre of Nations Festival in Paris to organize a theater laboratory that would make an investigation into audience-actor relationship in collaboration with directors and players from different countries. The international company Brook brought to Paris, which became the nucleus of his later International Centre for Theatre Research, included besides himself three directors: Geoffrey Reeves, a familiar Brook associate, the American experimentalist, Joe Chaikin, and a young Argentinian director, Victor Garcia. Actors were assembled from the Royal Shakespeare Company and The

Living Theatre who joined French and Canadian actors and Oido Katsuhiro, a Japanese actor trained both in Kabuki and Noh traditions. The "text" which Brook selected for workshop purposes was *The Tempest* but "translated" into a new hourlong "adaptation," in reality an original creation based loosely on some buried and not-so-buried themes in the play: magic, dreams, ambition, pride, violence, and hate. The director, no longer bound by his custormary interpretive function, goes beyond the text to something of his own authorship.

The French Minister of Culture made available to Brook the vast, empty space of a gallery at the Mobilier National, a warehouse for government furniture without any past theatrical connections. Unfortunately, volatile French politics intervened in summer of 1968, and Brook's company moved briefly to the Roundhouse in London, a building once used to reverse railroad and until recently likewise devoid of theatrical events, for four "open" performances of this new *Tempest* during July.

Brook was working on ways to encourage a more free exchange and intermingling of actors and audiences in pursuit of the transformation of traditional theater experience into something approaching modern ritual. He hoped that alteration of the performance space might significantly facilitate more expressive contributions between performers and audience. In the vast space of the Roundhouse, Brook hung a circus-like white canvas tent. Spectators and actors were seated on large movable pipe scaffoldings, equipped with wooden planks. As mobile units, these tower-like structures could be rolled into the midst of action. Spectators who wished to remain stationary could opt to sit in a "safe-area" on folding chairs, boxes, benches and stools rather than risk the high perches on the movable towers. Thus, Brook did not treat his audience as an indivisble whole, and part of the spectator's participation in the event came from the choice each audience member made as to his location relative to activity or passivity of involvement.

Before taking chosen seats, the audience was free to wander around the space of the Roundhouse, intermingling with the actors, the audience and actors being, for the most part, indistinguishable. The performers wore work clothes except for Ariel, portrayed by the

Japanese actor who wore a simple kimono, and Ian Hogg as Prospero who sported a white karate suit. The bright, white lighting of the Roundhouse was maintained during the performance. The actors slowly separated themselves from the audience by beginning to vocalize, dance, play ball, turn cartwheels, do handstands, and generally limber up. In the center of the open area a group of actors formed themselves into pairs and proceeded to perform "mirror" exercises, a device frequently used in American acting classes. In "mirroring," two actors imitate one another to the perfection of a mirror image; Brook added increasingly loud humming on the part of the actors to accompany their facial and gestural routines until the audience became quiet and attentive in their observation of the "performance." As appendage to the "mirror" exercises, the actors faced the audience and assumed "masks" made with their own facial muscles, accompanied by a variety of vocalizations, if not verbalizations. Presumably these "masks" were intended to represent the people aboard ship immediately prior to the "tempest."

Abruptly actors rushed to the platform, and this raw version of the play began with the chaotic shipwreck. While key words from Shakespeare's text were occasionally used, the non-verbal sounds of destruction really carried the meaning. Although Prospero and Miranda also often spoke lines from the play, they read them ametrically and without attention to ends of lines. Brook's mirror to *The Tempest* proved more a distorting lens, capturing hidden gesture and action, under, over, and against the Shakespearean text. As with the earlier RSC *King Lear*, Brook was profoundly influenced in his approach to *The Tempest* by Jan Kott's interpretation of the play, "Prospero Staff," also included in *Shakespeare Our Contemporary*. Kott explains the play as Brook embodied it: "Only the mirrors change. And every one of these mirrors is just another commentary on situations that remain the same. Prospero's island, like Denmark, is a prison. . . . Sebastian's gestures and motives are identical with Antonio's gestures and motives of twelve years ago, following the pattern of a real coup d'état. This is the essence of the Shakespearean analogy principle, and of the system of ever-changing mirrors." (*Shakespeare Our Contemporary*, pp. 256-57)

110

With gestures and actions inspired by scenes from Hieronymous Bosch, an analogue further suggested by Kott, Brook's 1968 *Tempest* gave tangible and concrete shape to the fears and evil implicit on Prospero's island and the larger anxities that haunt the mind of man. In this version, Sycorax, described by eye-witness Margaret Croyden, as a female King Kong in the portrayal by Ronnie Gilbert, was present to give birth on stage to Caliban who seemed to descend from her parted legs with a black sweater over his head – "Evil is Born," says Miss Croyden. ("The Achievement of Peter Brook" p. 248) Much additional grotesquerie was enacted during the production including simulated rape, heterosexual and homosexual, and a host of other sexual configurations. For example, no sooner do Ferdinand and Miranda meet, touching each other in the manner of the initial mirror exercise before the "play" began, than they make love [in direct antithesis to Shakespeare's virginal couple whose only dalliance is a game of chess], and their actions are then parodied in a homosexual encounter between Caliban and Ariel which stimulates the other men on the island to go and do likewise.

The anti-masque elements which Shakespeare has Ariel and Prospero turn loose on Stephano and Trinculo became in Brook's version dog-like men who fall upon Prospero himself in a scene of canabalism and violation reminiscent of nothing so much as Sebastian's fate described, but blessedly not portrayed, in Tennessee Williams' *Suddenly Last Summer*, all justified by Prospero's line describing Caliban as "This thing of darkness I do acknowledge mine." In Brook's version the line resounded amid the ensemble-monsters biting, sucking, and chewing upon Prospero. Then, out of sequence, the marriage ceremony takes place uniting Miranda and Ferdinand in a "mixed" affair which Miss Croyden calls "Hebrew-Hippie-Japanese rites." ("The Achievement of Peter Brook, p. 249) At this point Prospero announces, "I forgot the plot," echoing perhaps the director's own memory lapse with respect to the play. Out of the temporary silence, a member of the ensemble breaks into lines from the play's Epilogue, beginning with "And my ending is despair," a line which Kott considers pregnant and significant, though not necessarily indicative of Prospero's despair. The remaining lines of Prospero's epilogue are divided among the ensemble until an aural fade out of reiteration in which the only intelligible words are "ending. . . despair. . . relieved. . . by prayer."

Brook tried to present his *Tempest* as the ur-myth for Shakespeare's work in the theater, a Jungian myth in the sense of a turning point in consciousness, of Edens forsaken and Paradises lost. However, his repository of imagery and bright ideas seems something less than ancient and timeless – not derived so much from the collective unconscious as from a William Burroughs' novel. Like one of Ariel's troop, the play vanished into air and left not a wrack behind. Shakespeare's most archetypal play was treated locally and perversely: chaos against order and savagery against civilization. Brook's version of *The Tempest*, informed as it was by Bosch and the Polish Jan Kott, reversed the Italianate and Southern European premise of Shakespeare's romance that in spite of its evils the world ultimately is good, orderly, and beautiful for a more characteristically Northern European tone – that in spite of its joys and diversions the world is basically tragic, malevolent, and mysterious, familiar themes from the "theatre of cruelty" spectrum of Brook's work in the sixties.

This production was Brook's first full-scale venture into three radical directions for him in theater: his first wholly original theatrical creation without submission to interpretation of an existing text; his premiere experiment in environmental theater with encouragement of audience participation, particularly in the "mirror" exercise and "The Garden of Delights" segment; and, most far-reaching of all, this experiment with *Tempest* whetted his appetite for creation of his own permanent, experimental ensemble, with the purpose of exploring on a continuing basis fundamental questions about theater and its relation to life. The International Centre for Theatre Research was germinated in the Roundhouse with the risks, and even the failures, of Brook's version of Shakespeare's play. Another decade plus a year had passed between this *Tempest* and the elaborate 1957 staging of the play at Stratford. Never one to duplicate practices, Brook was ready as a theatrical artist to find new directions, but characteristically he preserved his nearness to Shakespeare even in striking out toward the unknown. Brook recognized that his chief value to the theater lay in living dangerously, as the gamut of *Tempest* productions witnessed.

IX. *A Midsummer Night's Dream* (1970): That Old White Magic

Marking his return to Stratford after an absence of eight years, Brook's production of *A Midsummer Night's Dream* in summer of 1970 was viewed as pure celebration, an imaginative dream of the theatre, and a much-appreciated antidote to the "theatre of cruelty" upon which Brook had been directing his attention. Shakespeare's great comedy on the transforming powers of love and imagination elicited Brook's own fullest creative resources for an unconventional staging of the play but one which Ariane Mnouchkine anticipated in her production of the play in 1968 within a circus setting, an antecedent which has been insufficiently noted. In the program notes for the RSC production, Brook alludes to Meyerhold's dictum that the fourth creator in a dramatic presentation besides author, director, and actor is the spectator whose imagination takes flame from the actor's creativity – a reciprocity dramatized brilliantly in the last act of Shakespeare's comedy. Donald Richie comments on the integral way the audience is repeatedly brought into Brook's production: "Over and over we discover that not only Puck (whose lines are occasionally written for our ears alone) but almost everyone else in the cast (including Bottom) are speaking over the footlights. These are not asides. They are halves of a conversation which the audience is offered and which, in the second half of the play it takes up."[21]

Sally Jacobs' design for the production places the action amid white walls rising to approximately eighteen feet to a gallery on the top where actors not on stage could survey the proceedings and participate, when necessary, in the mechanics of staging. A gymnasium atmosphere [or squash court] was suggested by the two upstage doors, reminiscent of doors in the Elizabethan theater, albeit of a smaller variety. These doors provided the only access at stage level. Trapezes and swings were hung from the flies. Ladders at the downstage end of both side walls permitted additional access to the playing area. Recently Brook's old friend and colleague, Sir Peter Hall, has spoken of the theater as "the gymnasium of the soul,"[22] a metaphor which may or may not be indebted to memory of Brook's *A Midsummer Night's Dream*. Sally Jacobs' "gymnasium" also assumes the aura of a clinic in its echo of the bathhouse in *Marat/Sade*, as Brook

113

probes [psycho]analytically "the fierce vexations" of this particular Shakespearean "dream." Trees, consisting of coiled wire mobiles, which extended from the gallery could substitute, on occasion, for wires whereby the characters as puppets might be manipulated in demonstration of the difficulty attendant upon Shakespeare's lovers pulling their own strings.

It was Brook's conviction that the play's outmoded fairy-land and magic, which doubtless spoke quite concretely to Renaissance audiences, could have slight visceral meaning to modern theatergoers. He endeavored to find substitute actions which would prove appealing in a breathtaking way, and his search took him to the arts of the circus, especially acrobatics and juggling, presented in *A Midsummer Night's Dream* as metonymy for the play's theatrical magic which would be free of Victorian conventions. Brook's only use of Mendelssohn's music in this production, for example, was in an unlikely context, indicative of his rejection of traditions associated with earlier stagings of the play. The "Wedding March" accompanied a scene of bestiality as Titania prepares to bed Bottom disguised as an ass, or in Brook's production, more as a clown with attached funny nose. In rather unworldly fashion, Titania's scarlet ostrich bed levitates; but the sexual and earthy denotations of Bottom are made very specific, as one of the fairies who is hoisting Bottom onto the shoulders of two other fairies produces by means of his upraised arms through Bottom's legs a grandiose phallaphoric effect, which is hilariously punctuated by strains of circus-band Mendelssohn. At the same time, Oberon sails across the stage on his trapeze accompanied by streamers, confetti, and paper plates. Whirling plates held aloft and exchanged between Oberon and his fairy crew, through dextrous manipulation of long sticks, stand for the magical skill invested in the hitherto fey denizens of *A Midsummer Night's Dream*. John Kane, Brook's Puck, proved the most accomplished of the production's acrobats, performing feats of derring-do on stilts, a skill he mastered in his youth, and ending the play by leaping into the audience to entreat surprised spectators to give him their hands, not in applause so much as in clasps. Often Kane would climb to the theater's balcony and then run around the rim of boxes and balcony, extending handshakes to patrons.

114

Throughout his production Brook intruded the "real" world into the "dream" world and vice versa to capitalize on the dualities which buttress the play. One way he managed this effect was to cast his actors in double roles. The actors who portrayed Theseus, Hippolyta, and Puck also played Oberon, Titania, and Philostrate, respectively, thereby unifying lovers and rulers in a single fabric of shared dream and reality. This device produced a more compact structure for the play than Shakespeare's division suggests. There was little difference in Brook's *Dream* between the rational decisions of Theseus and Hippolyta and the instinctive, subliminal manipulations of the King and Queen of the fairies. Brook exulted in the effect of such doubling upon Alan Howard's performance as Theseus and Oberon for its exercise of the actor's body and mind:

> Alan Howard played over two or three years with an ever-greater sense of secret meanings he found for himself. In the play on many levels, endlessly discovered and re-discovered, meanings came from him, that made vibrations passing through Theseus into Oberon and back again across the whole play. And the play was at its best when the whole cast was at a point of high attunement, so that within the performance those vibrations went across it. It's like those wire sculptures made out of tight wires making a complex pattern, where is the wires aren't tight you don't get the pattern. (Ralph Berry, *On Directing Shakespeare*, p. 128)

Brook used ritual in his production to prod his actors (and by extension, his audience) into knowing, a knowing that might require months, even years in light of the director's remarks about Alan Howard's evolving performance, to saturate, to seep down to the place where dreams are made. The psyche, whatever its own dreams are, wakes up for rituals. It hears the glad tidings of Brook's *A Midsummer Night's Dream* where the unconscious thematic quality of the play may be sexual but its external and conscious element – in this production self-consciously – is magic.

For this magic can exist only in the theater as Brook presented it – the play interpreted conceptually as the movement from circus to metatheater, all within a magic box, celebrating the play as performance, with consciousness turning back on itself and the nature of the theater. Hence Brook employed the Brechtian device of showing the elements of the drama as a performance by exposing the stage machinery as part of the theatrical experience. Conceptual issues of the nature of magic and performance were foregrounded as principal content in this *Dream*, from the child-like wonder of the circus world in the first part of the play to the jaded lovers' denial of their willing suspension of disbelief toward the well-intentioned performance by the rude mechanicals at the end. Brook invested the play of Pyramus and Thisbe with more poignance and credibility than is customary, in acknowledgment of the rough magic shared by all acting companies, whether under the direction of Peter Brook or Peter Quince, and the ritual acted out equally by all lovers whether they know it or not. The melancholy tone of Theseus in the last act, admonitory and even severe, carried a residual meaning of the first act's Oberon when in a mood to punish Titania, as now all the lovers "take time to pause" in order not to unleash new cruelty against one another. J. L. Styan noted that Brook's decision to cast his actors in double roles resolved much of the apparent contradiction of so much sobriety among so much revelry at the end of the play (*The Shakespearean Revolution*, p. 228) The originality of this device may well have had precedent in Elizabethan theater practice and represents a characteristic of Brook's production which Robert Speaight gracefully summarized and J. C. Trewin quotes: " 'Mr. Brook takes his cue from nothing but his own conscience, and from no one but Shakespeare himself.' " (*Going to Shakespeare*, p. 100)

The warmth of the costumes' colors and the fierce white lighting of Brook's production were not natural but, rather like the balancing of the plate in the air or of a juggler's wand at the tip of a magician's finger – an achieved state, in which an overconfident calculation, a graceless move, might prove as disastrous as a similar false step in love. Brook's production predicated a free exchange of imagination among all constituencies in the theater, embracing at least a total of Meyerhold's four creators in his combinatorial approach which during the length of performance made for a new community through the authenticating acts of theatre itself. There were, of course, dissenters to the proceedings like Kenneth Hurren who found Brook's production "a tiresomely self-indulgent display of directorial gimmickry."[23] Most members of the audience and critics in every

116

country where it was performed reacted enthusiastically, finding it a genuine revelatory experience. It has proved one of the most seminal and best-loved productions of the latter part of the twentieth century, the standard whereby other Shakespearean productions have been judged. It established new expectations for future performances within the so-called classical repertory – plays which definitively make their way through the director's daring out of the anthology books – truly a corrective to the Deadly Theatre.

X. *Timon of Athens* (1973): Supply-side Shakespeare

There was a certain propriety and inevitability in Peter Brook's staging of a French version of Shakespeare's sometimes assumed unfinished *Timon of Athens* in light of the director's earlier production of that other poor relation of major Shakespearean tragedy, *Titus Andronicus*. Assisting Brook was the talented Jean-Paul Wenzel who later would use his working-class background to revive realistic theatre with daily life dramas such as *Far from Harrisburg* in the neo-realistic stylizations. Wenzel's influence has not been much acknowledged – but probably should be – considering Brook's emphasis on an economic approach to *Timon* underscoring monetary concerns of waste, credit, consumption, price. and inflation in the life of a man living beyond his means. Timon tries to buy love and happiness for himself and his fairweather friends through vast expenditures of finite resources. Gold becomes the acid test of honor in Shakespeare's play and the motive for human behavior. The once philanthropic Timon discovers the uselessness of his former trust, and, jumping from one kind of failure of wisdom to another, he becomes a misanthrope. Like Lear's Fool, Apemantus speaks the truth to Timon when he utters the rebuke: "The middle of humanity thou never knewest, but the extremity of both ends."

Brook used as his text for *Timon of Athens* a new prose translation in French by Jean Claude Carrière to which the director himself made some contributions. Deliberately attempting to eschew the archaic language of the Shakespeare original which Brook thought often impeded understanding of *Timon* for English-speaking audi-

117

ences, Carrière's style was unashamedly modern. The production, presented in Brook's Paris theater, the Bouffes-du-Nord, used the total setting of the old gutted nineteenth-century theater, in the words of one highly enthusiastic spectator, Ralph Berry, as "a metaphor for Brook's harsh fable." Berry considers Brook's production, perhaps hyperbolically, the most important Shakespeare production seen in the West in recent years and elaborates upon what he calls "the verities of the setting": "The actors make their entrances and exits through what is left of the decayed machinery of the old stage. There is full light throughout (and no special lighting effects): nothing is done to soften the bleak realities of the house." (Appendix, *On Directing Shakespeare*, pp. 131-133) The "nakedness" of this setting offered a corollary to the naked essence of Timon as the unaccomodated man in the later part of the play. The image of the unclothed Timon has always been the special favorite of the indefatigable champion of this play, G. Wilson Knight: "His [Timon's] body," Knight writes, "confronts man with the human essence, which has been wronged by human iniquity. The actor in his nakedness, and through him Timon, radiates power. . . . The body should speak: this is the quintessence of acting. It is as a supreme exhibitionism, but it is more than that; it is prophetic."[24] With the antecedent examples of his *King Lear* and *A Midsummer Night's Dream*, Brook demonstrated a similar perspective on *Timon*, akin to Knight's, not only in his direction of the title character but in the decor itself.

Brook underscored certain peculiarly modern economic circumstances by presenting Timon's first feast as a somewhat Middle Eastern affair including Arab music and dancing. Moreover, the director grabbed for contemporary relevance by casting a black actor, dressed, according to Berry, as an Algerian laborer from perhaps the poorer quarters of Marseilles, thereby implying "a kind of Third World Critique of Timon's frivolity and extravagance," as Apemantus. Likewise Alcibiades' military coup against Athens was staged to bring out its terrible contemporaneity. In sum, to borrow J. C. Trewin's comment on this production: "Peter Brook contrived an inventive variety of mood for a play often slow and muscle-bound. In another poet's phrase, it was 'signed with conflagration.' " (Going to Shakespeare, p. 228) -- the darker reverse side of the Athenian coin proffered in *A Midsummer Night's Dream*.

118

In the person of François Marthouret, young and handsome, Brook found an actor to invest Shakespeare's abstract protagonist with some humanity – if more mythopoeic than dramatic. Brook's Timon was dressed in an elegantly tailored white suit suggestive of the best jet-setting embodiments of fashion; but despite this glamor, Timon's life has meant nothing, for in his death he has not redressed the wrongs that had been done him. On the other hand, Brook did not affirm any superiority besides strong-arm success for Alciabiades who could, and did, act against the similar affront that he had suffered.

Timon as odd man outside any community, indeed actively encouraging the capture of Athens, represents the antithesis of the renewed theatrical society so prominent in Brook's experiments during this periods – the republic of equals, for example, which had gone to Africa in pursuit of new exchanges across cultures through participation of everyone present for a theatrical event. Such destiny is not Timon's fate in the wilderness. There can be no retribalization for Timon with his misanthtropy, though he is courted by the community of Athens. Like a contemporary political exile, Timon seems a fugitive from all societies at the end of his life, defeated by the multiplicity of reality which he cannot apprehend. Brook hinted in his production of a possible connection between Timon's situation and the rebels, young and otherwise, of the late sixties and early seventies, who opted out of society because of its greed, lusts, and crime to take up life back in nature. Once again G. Wilson Knight and Brook may share a similarity of conception. Knight makes his own comparison between Timon and contemporary young people: "[Timon] turns to Oriental thought, longing for his 'Nirvana' in death, the perfect state of Buddhism, wherein 'nothing' is said to bring him 'all things'. He wishes to be buried by the sea. No cause of his dying is given us; we simply watch him dissolve into the ocean of being." (*Shakespeare's Dramatic Challenge*, p. 156) Brook at most inclined toward only some of the foregoing, since he did not endorse solely the heroic and self-sacrificing conception of Timon. Granted Brook's own penchant for the mystical and the arcane increased during the decade of the seventies, but in *Timon of Athens* Brook did not interpose all his mind wanderings beyond hints and suggestions. Talk persists of a potential English-language production of *Timon of Athens* to be staged sometime in the future, under Brook's direction. A new production, to be sure, would not duplicate this ever more distant Parisian *Timon*, yet the English-speaking theater should be most receptive to the continuing relevance Peter Brook finds in the often unreclaimed Shakespeare.

XI. *Antony and Cleopatra* (1978): A Tragedy of Intimate Behavior

Brook's long-anticipated and welcome return to Stratford's Royal Shakespeare Theatre following an eight-year stretch in other activities, frequently abroad, occured on October 4, 1978 with the opening of *Antony and Cleopatra*. Seven years before this production, Brook had asked Glenda Jackson to do the play with no one but him, pending his own readiness to stage this epic love story which surprisingly has remained one of Shakespeare's most rarely performed tragedies. Many theater-goers remembered quite fondly the notable production of the play staged in 1972 during the so-called Romans' season with Richard Johnson and Janet Suzman, marking the first time *Antony and Cleopatra* had been restored to the RSC repertory in twenty years. Brook's approach differed considerably from the earlier production in the seventies, but it was not flamboyantly "conceptual" as some had feared it might be.

Brook saw *Antony and Cleopatra* as a tragedy of intimate behavior rather than as a spectacular play; and, while conceding that the lovers are epic-sized people, he approached their characters to demonstrate private emotions and intimate human decisions, which incidentally affect the known-world. This deliberate scaling-down of the play's epic quality invited scattered negative critical responses about the prosaicness of Brook's conception, but, on balance, *Antony and Cleopatra* revealed Brook's skill at subordinating his own inventiveness and innovative tendencies to the service of a great text. Few productions have ever captured so fully Shakespeare's central paradox of the majestic poetry and the reality of two middle-aged lovers who frequently seem, at least on the surface, to have slight capacity for majesty at all. Brook's concentration on the small world of the lovers

120

was not really at the expense of the larger disruption in the macro-cosm which results from their affair. In Sally Jacobs' glass conserva-tory the lovers attempted to shut out inconveniences and instrusions of the Egyptian and Roman power struggle within their own intimate space, yet they appeared too conspicuously public in their glass pleasure dome ever to succeed simply as private citizens. Blood of the ignored political tragedy enacted outside occasionally splattered their glass barriers, and finally, as if to punish them for their self-absorption, the blood of their suicides had to be shed. Everything in Brook's production affecting Antony and Cleopatra must confront their private nexus. Appropriately, therefore, the floor cloth of their chamber at one point rose into the air to become a hugh sail, repre-senting the disastrous sea efforts of Antony as he clung precariously to the furls of the material, emblematic both of his ships' defeat at Actium and, by extension, of his amorous enslavement to Cleopatra. Additionally, the translucent screens of their glass pavillion turned a stony-green to insinuate symbolically the fate of Antony's forces at sea.

Glenda Jackson's Cleopatra, with close-cropped hair, moved with sinuousness in keeping with the attributes of the serpent of Old Nile. This Cleopatra expected mutual deceit and failure even as she was capable, rather as a surprise to herself and others, not only of love but also of forgiveness. Alan Howard's Antony was attractively virile, if paunchy, less in dotage than middle-aged physical decline. He re-mained enough of a Roman to be filled with self-disgust for his be-havior in Egypt even when he played the willing voluptuary and gave himself completely over to Cleopatra. Similarly, Patrick Stewart's Enobarbus in giving testimony to Cleopatra's attractiveness hinted at his own infection by things Egyptian at the expense of Roman virtue. His weariness offered good contrast to Antony's declining, but still manifest, vigor. An equally intelligent and sensitive perform-ance was achieved by Jonathan Pryce as Octavius, wholly Roman in his dedication to duty as well as his reluctance to enjoy release from responsibility. During the banquet scene Octavius very briefly let himself go with drinking and frivolity, and Pryce showed brilliantly the conscientiousness with which Caesar must make up for this lapse, epitomized almost shockingly by a pleased squeal which was quickly suppressed. There was a slight tendency in Brook's production for the RSC actors to demonstrate rather than embody the characters, as Roger Warren noted in particular of Alan Howard's portrayal of Antony.[25] If the production often was analytic of the characters with nearly Brechtian coolness, this approach seemed usually justified by permissible and consistent Shakespearean limits, since *Antony and Cleopatra* itself is strongly analytical. In this production Brook took an almost lapidary interest in the small but radiant insight but not at the expense of the play's comprehensive structure. Charmian's wry half-smile of incredulity as she listened to Antony and Cleopatra or the accompanying stare of tragic foreboding which Juliet Stevenson's Iras cast upon the oblivious lovers stay in the memory as examples of novel possibilities which Brook discovered within the larger, more familiar structures of the play.

Brook's staging treated the more than forty scenes of a nearly uncut *Antony and Cleopatra* with almost camera-like speed of fades and dissolves with one moment of action melting into another often quite opposite one, underscoring in the performance itself the play's reliance on the predicate *melt*, yet the verse speaking was never rushed. The considerable sensuality of the play was retained but presented with provocative understatement; again as with *A Midsummer Night's Dream* Brook turned to gestures, devices, and ideas of the Oriental theater to suggest rather than declaim emotions. Nor did Brook neglect the humor implicit and explicit in the play, as he once perhaps did in his production of *Hamlet*. Glenda Jackson delivered comic assault on Seleucas even in the last scene which complemented the antics of Richard Griffith's red-nosed clown with his two asps; Brook asserted earthiness before Cleopatra's ascent to the higher elements. In Act IV with the death of Antony, Brook employed a similar effect with the belts which Iras and Charmian shed in order to hoist the mortally wounded hero up into Cleopatra's tower. The action became at once comic and tragic, realistic in depiction of physical strain, and plausible in dramatic context. What first seemed to shatter the scene's atmosphere actually sustained and extended it in a durably direct and recognizably Shakespearean mixture of genres.

If the achievement of Brook's *Antony and Cleopatra* has not yet been adequately acknowledged, a number of critics praised the director's handling of the final scene in which Glenda Jackson underwent a stunning transformation, the fulfillment of much earlier promise in the play. Roger Warren's comments are pointed and representative of the critical consensus: "The last fifteen minutes or so existed on a higher, more moving, level than anything before them; what was unusual this time was Mr. Brook's deliberately cool handling of the first four acts so as to make the play's change of direction for Cleopatra's transformation absolutely clear." ("Shakespeare at Stratford and the National Theatre, 1979," 178)

XII. Affinity across Time: Brook's Shakespeare as Living Theatre

While numerous directors who like Brook came to prominence in the mid-twentieth century have staged more plays from the Shakespeare canon than has Peter Brook, the latter's productions have been among the most influential and memorable over the years. Generally freed from the necessity of having to stage many Shakespeare plays serially and systematically, Brook could pick and chose the particular play he wished to stage in order to seize the opportune moment for full theatrical realization. Brook continues to hold the conviction he expressed early in his career that "a production is only right at a given moment, and anything that it asserts dogmatically today may well be wrong fifty years from now. A production is only correct at the moment of its correctness, and only good at the moment of its success." ("Style in Shakespearean Production," p. 256) In light of that sentiment, Brook has found the means of making actual Shakespeare's ongoing theatrical potential in relevant and immediate productions which speak to and of our time without falsifying the plays' universality.

Attuned to the springtime of the dramatic imagination which was the Elizabethan age, Brook early in his life perceived related conditions of crisis and change which link the Renaissance and our own century. With a bridge, more spiritual than historical, Brook has captured the tradition of experiment in both eras by initiating bold risks on the intelligence, fortitude, and imagination of all constituents of the theater. In Brook's view, Shakespeare was "experimental, popular, revolutionary,"[26] and productions of his plays should accordingly seek out such qualities. While Brook oversees that the Shakespeare text, prose and verse will be well-spoken in his productions, he asserts at the same time, as J. L. Styan observes, "the primacy of the theatrical over the literary experience of drama." (*The Shakespeare Revolution*, p. 212) At their customary best, Brook's Shakespeare productions generated exciting Rough and Immediate Theater with aspirations toward (and even attainment of) what Brook understands as Holy Theater. At their very least, they avoided becoming Deadly Theater, the experience of which can still unfortunately be had in some luckless BBC adaptations of *The Shakespeare Plays* broadcast on American public television.

In production effects Brook moved toward what I would like to label a majestically plain style, but one possessed of the power to shape meaning with fully achieved artistic frugality of means – classicism in a contemporary context. His blend of tradition and modernism in conceiving Shakespeare for the twentieth-century theater represents a high achievement which has inspired others for forty or so years, but Brook may be subject to challenge now in the current neo-conservative challenge within nearly all the arts against the boldest, barest, and most uncompromising experiments of eclectic modernism. There is something ominous in Robert Brustein's report that "Lord Noel Annan was recently invited by the English departments of various Ivy League universities to excommunicate such heresiarchs as Peter Brook and Peter Hall (also Lord Olivier and Sir John Gielgud) for desecrating the holy relics of the bard with their irresponsible concepts and readings." Brustein's rejoinder is wholly appropriate that only in the study or classroom can the text be honored in the way Lord Annan demands, "because only there are we free from actors and directors with their insistent, fleshly intrusions. But these are hardly places designed to show the 'very age and body of the time his form and pressure.' "[27] It is one thing to revive the techniques and attitudes of the past; it is another and more difficult thing to make them work on the stage today. In the past Peter Brook has always returned to Shakespeare after an absence, however long, with vitality and vision; and audiences, eager to share his confidence, have been amply rewarded. We can only hope that the esthetic right will not deprive future theater-goers of the opportunity to enjoy the emotional, intellectual, and imaginative participation in subsequent productions of Shakespeare, conceived with more risk than reverence as Peter Brook so often manges to do.

NOTES FOR CHAPTER FOUR

1 Ralph Berry, Interview with Peter Brook, *On Directing Shakespeare: Interviews with Contemporary Directors* (London: Croom Helm/Barnes & Noble Books, New York, 1977), p. 117.

2 J. L. Styan, *The Shakespeare Revolution: Criticism and Performance in the Twentieth Century* (Cambridge: Cambridge University Press, 1977), p. 212.

3 J. C. Trewin, *Going to Shakespeare* (London: George Allen & Unwin, 1978), p. 69.

4 Peter Brook, "Style in Shakespearean Production," in *The Modern Theatre: Readings and Documents*, ed. Daniel Seltzer (Boston: Little, Brown and Co., 1967), p. 255.

5 Clive Barnes, "The Faces of Scofield," *Plays and Players*, January 1963, pp. 15-17.

6 Herbert S. Weil, Jr., "The Options of the Audience: Theory and Practice in Peter Brook's 'Measure for Measure'," *Shakespeare Survey*, 25 (1972), 27-35.

7 Richard David, "Shakespeare's Comedies and the Modern Stage," *Shakespeare Survey*, 4 (1951), 137.

8 Alice Venezky, "Current Shakespearean Productions in England and France," *Shakespeare Quarterly*, 2 (1951), 338.

9 "Theatre's Enfant Terrible," *Picture Post*, June 14, 1952, pp. 48-49

10 George Rylands, "Festival Shakespeare in the West End," *Shakespeare Survey*, 6 (1953), 145.

11 Jan Kott, *Shakespeare Our Contemporary* (Garden City: Anchor, 1966), p. 347.

12 Richard David, "Drams of Eale," *Shakespeare Survey*, 10 (1957), 170.

13 Penelope Gilliatt, "Peter Brook, a Natural Saboteur of Order," *Vogue*, January 1, 1966, p. 105.

14 J. C. Trewin, "All the Works," *The Illustrated London News*, August 27, 1955, p. 358.

15 Peter Brook, "Search for a Hunger," *Encore*, July/August, 1961, pp. 20-21.

16 Caryl Brahms, "Pace Without Poetry," *Plays and Players*, January, 1956, p. 23.

17 Charles Marowitz, "Lear Log," in *Theatre at Work: Playwrights and Productions in the Modern British Theatre, a Collection of interviews and essays*, ed. by Charles Marowitz and Simon Trussler (London: Methuen and Co., Ltd., 1967), pp. 133-147.

18 Peter Roberts, "Lear, Can It Be Staged?," *Plays and Players*, December, 1962, p. 21.

19 J. W. Lambert, "Plays in Performance," *Drama*, Spring, 1958, pp. 16-17.

20 "Shakespeare Fete in England Opens with The Tempest," *New York Times*, April 3, 1963, p. 43.

21 Donald Richie, "*A Midsummer Night's Dream*: The Royal Shakespeare Company," *The Drama Review*, 15 (Spring 1971), 330-334.

22 William B. Collins, "Broadway again looks to London for its hits," *The Philadelphia Inquirer*, July 26, 1981, F 1.

23 Kenneth Hurren, *The Spectator*, September 5, 1970, p. 248.

24 G. Wilson Knight, *Shakespeare's Dramatic Challenge: On the Rise of Shakespeare's Tragic Heroes* (London: Croom Helm, 1977), p. 135.

25 Roger Warren, "Shakespeare at Stratford and the National Theatre, 1979," *Shakespeare Survey*, 33 (1980), 177-178.

26 Address at the UNESCO Shakespeare Quatercentenary, Paris, 1964, from J. C. Trewin, *Peter Brook: A Biography*, p. 148.

27 Robert Brustein, "On Theater: Shakespeare Our Contemporary," *The New Republic*, August 22 & 29, 1981, pp. 23-25.

126

Chapter Five

PETER BROOK AND THE ART OF FILM

Brook's distinguished work in film has yet to be accorded the esteem which his theatrical achievement enjoys, but his cinematic panache apparent in the films he has directed is not appreciably less interesting and distinctive than his stage productions. Often Brook has brought his stage presentations to film, though in every instance he demonstrates impressive re-thinking of the stage material for cinematic rendering. Perhaps because his reputation was established in the theater prior to his first efforts on film, Brook remains neglected as a film director, despite his considerable originality and range demonstrated in this medium.

I. *The Beggar's Opera* (1953)

In 1952 the British film producer, Herbert Wilcox, persuaded Peter Brook to take a sabbatical from theater and try his hand at film. As pendant maybe to his recently concluded operatic activities at Covent Garden, not unmixed with a bit of satiric intent at the expense of traditional opera and the habitués of the Royal Opera House, Brook embarked on a long-desired project to film John Gay's eighteenth-century ballad-opera masterpiece, *The Beggar's Opera*. This Newgate Pastoral Brook conceived as a *gesamtkunstwerk* of theater, opera, ballet, and cinema, celebrating for the twenty-eight year old director, as Pauline Kael expressed it, "his tenth anniversary as the 'grand old enfant terrible' of the English theater."[1] Wilcox extended Brook a large budget and granted him absolute control in selecting cast and crew. Brook wisely chose for his set designer and costumer the highly respected George Wakhevitch who attired the company in gorgeous complementary colors and Guy Green as director of cinematography, a man who had won a number of awards for his camera work on David Lean's *Great Expectations* (1946). Brook's cast appeared to be an exercise in dream-fulfillment with Sir Laurence Olivier heading the ensemble as Macheath [notwithstanding the director's first choice of Richard Burton]; Dorothy Tutin as the ruthlessly winsome Polly Peachum; the distinguished actor/director, George Devine, as Peachum; Stanley Holloway as Lockit with Yvonne Furneaux, better known later for Fellini's *La Dolce Vita* (1959), as his daughter, Lucy; and Hugh Griffith as the Beggar. With equal taste and sagacity, Brook selected Denis Cannan and Christopher Fry to prepare a freely adapted screenplay from Gay's material, and renowned British composer, Arthur Bliss, provided the musical arrangement of the numerous songs. No wonder that Peter Brook had his own "great expectations" when he started filming *The Beggar's Opera* in Surrey during the late spring of 1952; here, he and his producers thought, Olivier being added on to Herbert Wilcox in that capacity, would be the film which would open up to this talented director another major career in cinema which, after all, had been his earliest aspiration.

The reversal of Brook's hopes and fortune relative to this film is well-known. *The Beggar's Opera*, distributed by Warner Brothers, was released in 1953 to sporadically favorable critical responses but to usually non-existent audiences. In the years since its first release, the film has won a considerable cult following, as a neglected masterpiece which is popular at revival houses and art theaters. Admirers of *The Beggar's Opera* are fiercely loyal, and even usual opponents like film critics Pauline Kael and John Simon have waxed enthusiastic about its abundant pleasures.[2] The film was ahead for its time, as Pauline Kael explains in her incisive summary:

> The only filmed opera that is light, playful, and sophisticated, it [*The Beggar's Opera*] may have suffered at box offices from the (deservedly) bad reputations of the many filmed operas that use the stage-set like an embalming table. It may have suffered even more from its greatest virtues: it is unrealistic in style, and the brilliant, unabashed theatricality, the choreographed chases and betrayals and captures, the elegant march to the gallows, the dazzling, macabre ballet under the titles at the end as the prisoners and jailers whirl amidst their stocks and irons, may have been too much of a jolt for movie audiences. Most movie directors attempt to conceal their artifice

128

in a realistic surface; here, artifice is used with the carefree delight and audacity of early Douglas Fairbanks films — delight in the film medium. (*I Lost It at the Movies*, p. 105)

Brook's use of the wide repertory of cinematic rhetoric such as narrow focuses, wipes, skillful dissolves as when the green drink Lucy prepares for Polly emerges as the green gaming table where Macheath gambles or the red roast beef shared by Lockit and Peachum after their collusion against Macheath dissolves to the red of the latter's coat, dizzying pans, and unexpected cutting rhythms anticipates the later success of Richard Lester and Tony Richardson with similar devices. The film opens with the quite realistic squalor of Newgate, colorless and drab, as Macheath is imprisoned. Then when the Beggar announces the creation of his opera, vivid color replaces the drabness; the dashing Macheath in his red coat rides forward singing lustily of his exploits, monetary and amatory — all irresistibly make-believe. The self-conscious artifice heightens the visual pleasure, but the effect is looser and more subtle than Tony Richardson's in *Tom Jones* (1963).

Olivier, emboldened by singing lessons, did his own songs, though most of the cast had their songs dubbed. His light baritone proved perfectly serviceable, if not exactly outstanding. Some commentators assumed that the undubbed (surely a paradox for the subsequently honored lord) Olivier contributed to the film's difficulties; possibly so, but now his vocal presence and still physically youthful appearance account for much of the film's enduring appeal. Dorothy Tutin does not herself sing in Brook's film, and the director cleverly calls attention to the fact of her being dubbed when he projects Adele Leigh's sweet sounds from the mouth of Tutin who rows a boat which in reality would render her incapable of such sounds. Pauline Kael remarks on this scene: [Tutin] smiles like a cat who has swallowed a canary, as indeed she has." (*I Lost It at the Movies*, p. 106)

While some of the satiric thrust of Gay's work may have been lessened by Brook's genial tone and quantity of production effects, *The Beggar's Opera* on film is true to Gay's assumption that the world is all alike whether the cast of characters includes prime ministers and noble ladies or highwaymen and prostitutes. In its Hogarthian evocations of London Brook's film re-creates the aura of the eighteenth century. However, in the pure delight of its joyous Eng-lishness and celebration of artifice, *The Beggar's Opera* transcends time, if not place, and merits comparison with Olivier's own *Henry V* (1944) in the annals of British cinema.

Vindicated as art by subsequent viewers, if not as a commercial success on the basis of original box-office receipts, Brook's *The Beggar's Opera* established a problematic precedent which has dogged the director in very nearly all of his later ventures into film. He did not return to films for a period of seven years. The exigencies of studio practices worked against Brook's usual freer theatrical meth-ods of trial and error, improvise, keep or discard through the rehears-al process. In an interview published a decade after the premier of *The Beggar's Opera*, Brook remembered some of the lessons he learned during his experience of shooting the Gay opera in the stu-dio; and, interestingly enough, despite a record of often incredible hardship attendant upon bringing his other later films to completion, he has not returned to the kinds of production circumstances which affected *The Beggar's Opera*:

> But when you are dealing with the full machinery of the conventional big film production, as I was with *The Beggar's Opera*, it's terrifying to find that all manner of things one has scribbled into the script as local color, notes one has made as a reader for oneself, possibilities to try out, have been taken deadly seriously and that months later someone will hold you to them. . . .
> All this means that you are put in the position of taking conscious, final and responsible decisions at a point where you really shouldn't and can't.[3]

Often controversial and usually tradition-breaking in technique, Brook's films represent the extension of his theater innovations into a complementary but often deeply resistant popular medium. Never really just right for the general movie public, Peter Brook keeps chal-lenging the medium of film and its audience, as he did with such op-timism in *The Beggar's Opera*. His usual result, though, might well permanently discourage a lesser director. As a film-maker, Brook em-bodies the tenacity and endurance of John Gay's Macheath who simply will not submit to hanging.

130

II. *Moderato Cantabile* (1960)

In early 1960 the independent French film producer, Raoul J. Levy asked Peter Brook to direct a film based on a *nouveau roman, Moderato Cantabile* by the critically-esteemed Marguerite Duras. This invitation, following the success of Alain Resnais's new wave film, *Hiroshima Mon Amour* (1959), also based on work by Duras, received an affirmative response from Brook who had been waiting to direct a film outside the studio setting which he felt had contributed to the problems of *The Beggar's Opera*. As he would subsequently do for *Lord of the Flies*, Brook worked largely from the novel itself, although script credit is also given to Duras and Gerard Jarlot. Brook went through the text, assigning close shot, mid shot, long shot and similar cinematic codes to details on the page.[4] Beyond these preparations, Brook did relatively little before moving his small French crew and cast to location shooting in the small provincial town of Blaye on the Gironde River near Bordeaux. Camera responsibility was entrusted to the talented Armand Thirard who shot the film in Cinemascope and subtly nuanced black and white which often a-chieves startling chiaroscuro effects.

The evocative, if perplexing, title derives from the tempo and style recommended for performance of Anton Diabelli's Sonata No. 4 in B flat, the piano composition which the young son of a bored and privileged mother, portrayed by Jeanne Moreau, plays throughout the film; the "gently and melodiously" admonishment to him from his piano teacher contrasts sharply with the inner turmoil of his maternal listener who accompanies him to his lesson. Brook skillfully scored his own music for the film, using the Diabelli theme with woodwind and some jazz variation/syncopation of it.

Anne Desbaredes, the character Moreau plays, is a latter-day Mme. Bovary without the capacity for action found in her nine-teenth-century antecedent but with all her languors and romantic longings. During her son's piano lesson, a scream is heard outside; and when the teacher, son, and mother rush to the window to see what has happened, they discover a crowd running toward a cafe. The teacher proclaims that her neighborhood is a rough one, and the mother hastily removes her protected son from this dangerous milieu.

131

However, before they go home to their bourgeois comfort, the mother sees enough to suggest that a crime of passion has occurred in the street: a man has killed his beloved. Obsessively pre-occupied with this supposed crime, Mme. Desbaredes repeatedly returns to the scene and strikes up an acquaintance with a workingman customer who often hangs around the cafe. This young man is named Chauvin and receives an admirable portrayal in Jean-Paul Belmondo's performance. Chauvin obliges her with presumed details of the troubled couples' relationship. In truth, these tales are imaginary accounts more appropriate to the psychological quirks of Mme. Desbaredes than to the former existence of the deceased girl. The young matron is attracted to a crime of passion for its embodiment of the romance and danger she feels is missing in her own life. At one point she acknowledges to Chauvin, "I want to know more, even if you have to invent it." He argues that the man killed the girl because she probably asked him to; thereby Chauvin voices the death-wish all too apparent in the Moreau role. But he cannot murder this strange woman who has accidentally entered his life.

Both people in this perverse relationship seem dead already, yet the energy and drama of either love or death elude such a somnolent pair. It is never clear that they have embarked on a romance; the only physical contact between them is hand-holding at a table. Otherwise, the camera tracks them on aimless walks and records their elliptical dialogues as they amble around the town. In the wake of a numbing dinner-party given by her industrialist husband at which she becomes quite drunk, Mme. Desbarades goes for a final visit to the cafe where she has always met Chauvin. He tells her he is leaving forever in order that she may resume her proper life characterized by her taking her son to his piano lesson. She screams, in manner reminiscent of the girl's cry during the murder early in the film, and falls to her knees by the bar as Chauvin leaves. Car headlights illuminate her. Her husband has come to retrieve her. She exits to the car, and the married couple drive off together to end the film.

As Brook's homage to and participation in the *novelle vague*, *Moderato Cantabile* was usually judged less than new but assuredly vague. Although the film never found much of an audience, it enjoyed some critical distinctions. Jeanne Moreau won the "Best

Actress" award at the Cannes Film Festival in 1960 for her role, and the film itself had there a number of admirers. David Stewart Hull, a critic for the British cinema periodical, *Film Quarterly* and the most ardent champion of *Moderato Cantabile* and admirer of what he termed Brook's "perfect exercise in technique," summed up the typical range of reactions to Brook's film: "One thought it either a small masterpiece or an irritating failure. . . . Brook has produced the most engrossing and personal cinematic document in many years. *Moderato Cantabile* is too personal a work to be accepted at once, but its spell is so powerful that it seems likely to gradually build an enormous following."[5] Alas, Hull's sanguine prophecy was never fulfilled for this film unlike the deferred success of *The Beggar's Opera*.

After poor audience reception in Europe, *Moderato Cantabile* was delayed release in the United States until January, 1964, when the French New Wave had declined in interest. *Newsweek* made a cruel, but in some ways apt, analogy when Brook's film opened stateside: "The delay in importing the film has been lethal, for the work, like a high-fashion gown has aged ridiculously." Brook gambled that his film would find an audience willing to work with and through the images presented to a drama which was more implied than enacted. The director wrote about his early fascination with the material filmed:

> What interested me in *Moderato Cantabile* [the Duras novel] was the story in which on the surface a woman meets a man, sees him a few time, and then parts with him. Looked at from the point of view of a small town, nothing could be less scandalous; she gets a tiny bit drunk and a bit distracted at a dinner party, and she is seen once by workmen in a crowded bar, and that's all. But if you follow the inner life of these people, this is the most gigantic, violent happening in their lives. . . total, vast, definitive, tragic, and violent." (quoted in Hull, 33)

The violence is so completely interiorized, of course, that its portrayal constitutes in its subtlety a subversion of the audience's usual expectation and often comprehension. *Moderato Cantabile* proved truly "anti-audience," in more ways than Brook first suspected in coining the phrase to indicate the necessity of reading between the lines in his film.

His intention, like that of other French New Wave directors, was to capture on film the "tempo of life itself," by recording significant moments during a period of seven days and seven nights in the experience of a young matron who registers, through characteristically New Wave long takes, internal emotions without much externalizing. The director found Jeanne Moreau a perfect choice for his purposes because, as Brook says, "she doesn't characterize." (Houston and Milne, p. 39) With her he could delineate a process of emotion seen almost as documentary, the director and his camera catching something as it happens. Brook makes *Moderato Cantabile* a sensitive and rich medium of personal expression often with nothing more direct than a slight movement of the cheek. The viewer must attend carefully to such slight registration, or else the drama, deprived of external theatrics, will be missed entirely.

Less daring and innovative than his acknowledged mentor, Jean-Luc Godard, Brook occasionally incorporates some Godardian disjunctive effects into the film. Brook credits Godard with successfully attacking the stability of the shot in his challenge to the classic theory of film editing and cutting, but his own practice in *Moderato Cantabile* exhibits only tentative exploration of this technique. He seems most like Godard in his apparent desire for the audience to remain restless and unsettled, caught like his protagonists between document and dream. Brook had his actors rehearse scenes which he had no intention of including in the film so that they would become comfortable portraying the narrative. In this way the actors took the director where they wanted to go, and the shaping of the material came later. In general, Brook permits the camera to record what is before it without comment or judgment; the atmosphere and relationships substitute for the plot.

The scenes between mother and son are among the most affecting in the film, if only because in them Mme. Desbaredes demonstrates more explicitly than elsewhere in other relationships her emotional resources. Nevertheless, the potential for Chauvin and Mme. Desbaredes to become sexually involved is cleverly and obliquely shown in the fleeting look of jealousy and resentment cast by the son on the man before the boy rushes off to play and leaves his mother and this stranger to share a park bench. In another memorable scene which takes place in the forest, the son rejects his mother's former explanation that the deer captured in nets are subsequently transported to other preserves. He insists that they are really killed, in an insight of sudden maturation beyond his previously sheltered youth. Following this pronouncement, he buries his mother with broken branches he has picked up. Less symbolic, but no less touching, are the almost wordless exchanges between mother and son as they ride a ferry, where her absorption in him temporarily releases her from the obsessions and longings which disturb her soul. Each time, in contrast, she seeks out Chauvin, her behavior takes on a disturbed quality, however well-concealed, adumbrated in the tones of the trees and landscape as well as on Moreau's physiognomy. As if to modify her death-wish, Brook counters with scenes of Mme. Desbaredes' richly sensuous appreciation of being in the world, especially with her son to share it.

In a thoughtful and important assessment of Peter Brook's work in film to 1967, John Russell Taylor argues that rather than breaking new ground Brook's films usually cast a backward look, a footnote gloss or farewell to a particular style or preoccupation derived from his theatrical work during the immediate past prior to beginning a film. In the case of *Moderato Cantabile*, Taylor places it on the hazy borderlines between half-hearted naturalism and half-hearted stylization, with its nearest antecedents being Brook's stage productions of Arthur Miller's *A View from the Bridge* and Tennessee Williams's *Cat on a Hot Tin Roof*, the latter in French with star, Jeanne Moreau.[6] With the decline of the brace of labels about artistic movements current at the time of its first releases, *Moderato Cantabile*, seen again more recently, takes on added freshness which has little, if anything, to do with the New Wave or the last gasp, prematurely noted, of stage naturalism. At his best in the film, Brook skillfully alternates between two kinds of dynamics, dramatic and pictorial; at his worst, the pictorial, however beautifully modulated, overwhelms the dramatic. Since all his characters carry an impartial emphasis on the condition of loneliness, Brook's images are plain and truth-telling. As a study of a woman in the midst of an emotional crisis of role and identity, *Moderato Cantabile* has aged gracefully on its own terms. His imagery locates the characters in persuasive, realistic settings

135

while simultaneously creating opportunities for spatial relationships which also illuminate emotional ones. Most impressively, Brook conveys a sense of intimacy preserved along with a sense of spaciousness in his deep focus photography. Domestic scenes appear curiously exalted by the luminous clarity of Brook's images, and the spare, eloquent movements of the camera support the understated narrative. The film grows organically from the opening scene of the piano lesson, but it does not grow to fulfillment, which may well be the point of *Moderato Cantabile*, a film of hyperbolic dramatic and emotional sparseness.

III. *Lord of the Flies* (1963)

Although Britain's Ealing Studios bought the rights to William Golding's *Lord of the Flies* (1954), the production of a film version was quickly abandoned as too risky. Then, producer Sam Spiegel enlisted Peter Brook as director at the beginning of the sixties when the book had gained enormous popularity both within and outside the school curriculum. Spiegel and Brook strongly disagreed over preparations for the film – the producer going so far as to suggest a new title and transformation of the English schoolboys into American boys and girls. When Spiegel subsequently dropped his option on the novel, Brook assumed the property and searched for a new producer whom he found in the person of Lewis Allen, a resourceful, young American theatrical producer who had previously produced a low-budget film version, financed by private investors, of Jack Gelber's successful off-Broadway play, *The Connection*. Together with his partner, Dana Hodgdon, the producers raised $ 250,000 from about two hundred Washington, D. C. investors. The eventual film cost more than half again that sum, but additional funds were raised through primarily small investors.

Golding's near-allegory of the primacy of evil symbolized in the foul-smelling pig's head, emblem of Beelzebub, literally lord of the flies, but actually embodied in the souls of depraved humanity manifested in the behavior of schoolboys who are lamentably father of the man parallels many of Brook's own preoccupations during this period of his career. With his genius for making virtue of necessity and for assuming auteurship of the film, *Lord of the Flies* (1963) in theme and method deserves recognition as a seminal work in Brook's canon.

In a famous interview given to *The Observer*, after release of the film, Brook explained his reason for translating Golding's novel into another medium, especially a primarily visual one. He argued that while a movie may lessen the magic and beauty of the novel, it introduces greater specific evidence, as only cinema can, thereby increasing the realistic novelist's certainties which Golding himself brought to Ballantyne's romantic *Coral Island* with his mid-twentieth-century pessimistic re-shaping of Victorian optimism. "The book," Brook observes, " is a beautiful fable – so beautiful that it can be refuted as being a trick of compelling poetic style. In the film no one can attribute the looks and gestures to tricks of direction. Of course I had to give the impulse to set a scene in motion, but what the camera records in the result of chords being struck on strings that are already there. The violent gestures, the look of greed and the faces of experience are all real."[7] Indeed, first-hand reports from the filming of *Lord of the Flies* frequently attested to the ease with which the non-professional actors, English children recruited ironically in the United States in order to save the cost of transportation from England to the small Caribbean island off the coast of Puerto Rico where the novel was filmed, began to take on rather frighteningly the darker elements of the roles they were playing.[8] William Golding was reputed to have remarked, upon hearing such tales of the filming, that he was surprised to learn the adults survived. Whether or not publicity hype inspired this kind of anecdote, it suggests the diminishing distance Brook sees in the interface between play-acting and reality, which he explores quite deliberately later in the sixties and early seventies in stage work.

Originally, Brook tried to develop a script for *Lord of the Flies* through traditional means. Spiegel had commissioned playwright Peter Shaffer to work on a script when Brook had been hired as director. After more than seven attempts, Shaffer's script consisted of an unwieldy six-hour epic which had badly attenuated the hard, almost marmoreal, narrative of Golding's novel. Moreover, Brook had

137

asked another author, Richard Holmes, to prepare an alternate screenplay which also was rejected. In the years ahead, it would not be uncommon for Brook to shelve texts prepared by distinguished literary collaborators -- usually without hard feelings. Out of this failure to find an acceptable screenplay, Brook took his thirty-four schoolboys and crew to the island and prepared to shoot the novel in three months with the boys simply enacting portions of the novel read to them before shooting began. Additional dialogue was improvised when necessary, largely under Brook's authorship and directtion. As had been seen in his stage-work and in *The Beggar's Opera*, Brook handled large ensembles and crowd scenes with skill and excitement. Understandably, the finished film evidences a spontaneous, improvisational quality which some viewers have called amateurish but which most critics and audiences have admired for its neo-realist, quasi-documentary effect so crucial to the film's seeming artlessness and unaffected sincerity. Enormous quantities of film stock were used in shooting [Brook estimated sixty hours of unbroken screening, about 415,000 feet of film], but the year-long editing, under Brook's supervision, resulted in a ninety minute movie remarkably faithful to the clean and concise silhouette of the novel itself.

Throughout the filming of *Lord of the Flies* Brook consistently used two cameramen, in a manner reminiscent of newsreel-documentary technique. His director of photography, Tom Hollyman, was highly regarded for his still photography and had not previously done a film or even handled a movie camera. The second cameraman usually shot simultaneously with the first, but he was free to locate the accidental and serendipitous elements which might have eluded the controlled shooting. Above all, this second camera had the opportunity to shoot expressive actions and reactions when the players were not aware of it, thus avoiding the self-conscious set-ups often imposed by the director. Brook conjectured that perhaps a third of the final picture came from this aleatory practice. In his later theatrical practice Brook would come to rely more and more on this kind of experiment.

Brook correctly mirrors and extends on film Golding's intense visual gifts, the precise nature of which V. S. Pritchett splendidly captures:

> He [Golding] is not cooking up freakish and exotic inci-
> dent; he is not making large proclamations about man and na-
> ture, God, destiny and so on; he is seriously and in precise,
> individual instances gripped -- as if against his will -- by the
> sight of the slow and agonizing accretion of a mind and a civi-
> lized will on one or two men, struggling against their tenden-
> cy to slip back, through passion or follow, and lose their skills
> in panic.[9]

This intense drama in Golding finds astonishing equivalence in
Brook's realization of *Lord of the Flies*. Indeed, the specificity of
film redeems Golding's material from the allegorical schematization
and broad generalization which some critics, possibly erroneously,
observed and objected to in the novel.

Brook's film opens with a montage of still photographs, review-
ing the boys' former life in civilized Britain at their elite public
school. These memories yield to shots of war planes bombing cities, a
shot of a rocket, a nuclear mushroom, and the crash of a plane, presumably the one from which the boys escaped to the island where
now we find them in motion but still recognizable at least in some instances from the earlier still photographs. We are introduced to
Ralph, Piggy, and the mystic Simon rapidly but appropriately, in
keeping with Golding's novel. Shortly thereafter, from a high-angle
shot, we see moving along the shoreline a group of black-robed choirboys, singing in march-time the *Kyrie eleison*, which will become a
recurrent motif in the film's unobtrusive, though haunting, musical
score composed by the contemporary conductor/composer, Raymond Leppard. The ineffable and sacred sounds accompany a menacing visual effect of a huge predatory creature with Jack at the head
of the parallel lines of boys. This disorienting image foreshadows the
subsequent change in the choirboys from songsters to hunters.

Brook succeeds in going beyond the surface strength of allegory
to the genuinely complex argument and reading of experience behind
it, as in the contest between what Frank Kermode calls "our physi-
cist-hunters and artist-shamans. . . . [which] Mr. Golding caught exactly in the Jack and Simon of *Lord of the Flies*."[10] The central conflict between Jack and Simon receive additional attention from Peter
Brook as he goes on to direct Dürrenmatt's *The Physicists* and becomes more deeply absorbed with the shamanistic possibilities of

ritualistic theater. The at once blessed and cursed Simon, like Cassandra gifted with prophecy yet doomed to be misunderstood or ignored, is played with golden beauty by Roger Elwin, a sweet-faced young actor. Curiously and regrettably, the crucial scene in the novel when Simon learns of mankind's own responsibility for the evil which dissolves the tenuously held-together community is not very intelligibly translated into visual terms in Brook's film. Nowhere else in the cinematic version of the novel is the absence of Golding's words felt so keenly. In the novel Simon hears the voice of the Lord of the Flies tell him:

> "Fancy thinking the Beast was something you could hunt
> and kill!" said the head. For a moment or two the forest and
> all the other dimly appreciated places echoed with the parody
> of laughter. "You knew, didn't you? I'm part of you? Close,
> close, close! I'm the reason why it's no go? Why things are
> what they are?"[11]

Later in the exchange the head warns Simon: "I'm going to get angry. D'you see? You're not wanted. Understand? We are going to have fun on this island! So don't try it on, my poor misguided boy, or else –" (*Lord of the Flies*, p. 133)

Whereupon, Simon, overwhelmed by such knowledge, swoons in another seizure, comprehending the identity of the beast but unable to do anything about it, as earlier he had found out the identity of the dead paratrooper, misconceived by others as a mysterious beast. While the camera "shows" the exchange between Simon and the Pig's head, no verbal revelation follows. The scene makes sense as does the later murder of Simon when he comes to report on his discovery of the paratrooper and his parachute only with reference to the novel itself, despite Brook's brilliant effect of the sound track switching from the murderous chant of the hunters' "Kill the beast! Cut his throat!" to the re-emergence of the *Kyrie Eleison* as Simon's body gently floats away, the little body which a moment earlier had been rocking back in the surf as if entranced.

From this point on the film devotes its attention to other hunts, culminating in the final pursuit of the rationalist/humanist Ralph. Brook's strongly-etched black and white photography limns in the physical menace of abundant tendrils on tropical plants and precipitous rocks as complement to the human menace of blood-instinct as the camera tracks Ralph across the island. With the voices of the hunters coming closer to the desperate Ralph, the film and soundtrack suddenly stop, suggestive somewhat of Robert Bresson's remark to the effect that the soundtrack invented silence. The camera discloses the shiny white stockings of the adult naval officer who has come, as *deux ex machina* or parody white knight, to rescue the band of pre-and post-pubescent British subjects. A slow low-angle shot encompasses the man who assumes gigantic proportions relative to the boys. With the appearance of this avatar of British authority and civilization, some of the savage hunters become once more contrite children, weeping and dependent. "And in the middle of them, with filthy body, matted hair, and unwiped nose, Ralph wept for the end of innocence, the darkness of man's heart, and the fall through the air of the true, wise friend called Piggy." (*Lord of the Flies*, pp. 186-187) James Aubrey's Ralph conveys by looks alone and through Brook's gift for direction the essence of that inner world and the certainty of its secrets which Golding describes so evocatively that astonishingly words become unnecessary. Under Brook's guidance and direction, the film of *Lord of the Flies* communicates immediately the non-verbal experience and realizes with great concreteness what is more distantly admirable and achieved in Golding's prose.

The reciprocal violence which locks Jack and Ralph into tragic rivalry and leads to the sacrifice of both Simon and Piggy is transformed into the ritual violence of culture and society represented by the appearance of the British naval officer, a survivor of the presumed nuclear war which had been responsible for the boys' presence on the island in the first place. Ralph's rescue, then, is really only a postponement of eventual later violence, Brook's film and Golding's novel intimate. The authoritarian structure which the adult officer brings with him has the force of violence behind it in contrast to Ralph's and Piggy's conch shell, formerly used as a symbol of authority. Moreover, life conceived as permanent warfare may prevail off the island as it did on it. *Lord of the Flies* as both novel and film brings readers and audiences to the brink of that awful abyss wherein differences disappear in unmitigated and undifferentiated violence.

What first attracted Peter Brook to Golding's novel may well have been the interstices in it, to appropriate Rene Girard's phrase from a completely different context, "through which violence and the sacred can pass."[12] The novel, rather in Artaudian fashion, illuminates whatever is latent and dormant in the psyche of civilization and releases it into consciousness. In Brook's film, this end is achieved in a further Artaudian way without recourse to verbalization, portending some later Brook theatrical experimentation.

Brook builds up his sequences, shot by shot, using motion to cut in and animate what began as still photographs in the film's opening moments and steadily becomes more syncopated and intense as the narrative unfolds but without wholly obliterating memory of the initial uncinematic effect – the plausibility of still photography, the documentary exhibit in the courtroom which underlies the film. Typically, Brook's patterns of shots opens with a close-up of one of the boys, with cut to jungle undergrowth or fast pan to other boys moving relentlessly over cliffs or through a tangle of trees. Daylight seems almost as terrifying as darkness on this island often for auditory reasons since Brook exploits sensitively the heightened sounds of insects, buzzing incessantly on the sound track, and the sudden crack of a branch. Yet the director never goes for the cheap tricks of horror films or tries to outstrip in visual effects the repugnant descriptions which Golding sometimes overdoes.

Lord of the Flies, though surely not a runaway hit, proved to be Brook's most successful film, critically and commercially, soothing somewhat his disappointment over the poor reception accorded *Moderato Cantabile*. In both these films, however, the director pursued the dissolution of duality between author and director which Artaud had argued for and which Peter Brook would implement still further in the future.

IV. Film Adaptations of Stage Works: *Marat/Sade* (1967); *Tell Me Lies* (1968); *King Lear* (1971)

Before members of the Royal Shakespeare Company performing *Marat/Sade* separated into other activities, it was decided to film the

142

Weiss play under Brook's direction. Young Lord Birkett, a governor of the Royal Shakespeare Theatre, became producer and acquired nearly $ 500,000 from United Artists for the project which consumed only seventeen days of actual shooting. Within six weeks Brook edited the twenty hours of footage to the film's two-hour running time. *Marat/Sade* as a play and stage performance seemes less the theater of ritual enactment addressing sacred order or achieving holiness in the manner of Artaud's theoretical theater of cruelty than an extension, albeit of a superior type, of the theater of mystification, sensuality, and perverse circus. Harold Clurman expressed the mode of the stage production cogently: *"Marat/Sade* converts our political and intellectual concerns into display, an artful fun house, a magnificent toy. It is distinguished decoration, first-class theatrical salesmanship."[13] In its failure to stipulate obedience to any authority beyond the existential subjectivity of Sade, Marat, Corday, Roux, and others who, performed by mad inmates, re-invent and re-imagine the past, the play reaches rarely beyond chaos. The cruelty and violence of history are witnessed, but they are not very adequately or meaningfully transformed or distanced by art; any address to sacred order appears to be negational, attentive primarily to two significant aspects of modernity – therapy and torture.

Ironically, on the basis of these deficiencies in the play and stage version, the film of *Marat/Sade* shows its own superiority. The praise, though, is ambiguous if one accepts, as I often do, Philip Rieff's judgment on the nature of the film medium: "Here, on film, we can see the first true anti-art, entirely incompetent to frame any vision of the repressive imperative. Film is the antitheoretical art of modernity. . . This gives us one reason why the theoretical culture of the book, lettered visions of the highest, cannot be put on film." (*Freud: The Mind of the Moralist*, p. 378) Rooted in lexicons of memory and the past, words celebrate the old and the unrepressed repressive; continually creating their own present reality, moving images perforce celebrate the new. Likewise, moving images enshrine the particular and individual, while words seek to attain the general, universal, and institutional. Consequently, words may secure authority outside the individual in contrast to the moving image's affirmation of the self-generated authority within the individual. As abstractions, words are monuments to the unseen, even agents of idealization and belief; images, on the other hand, as concrete and particular registrations, prize only the seen and serve as agents of action. Brook shares with Artaud a distrust of language, and *Marat/Sade* represents, in part, his challenge to the reifying abstractions of the word. Therefore, in a medium which deliberately works against a systematization of life in static, repeatable, and permanent forms, *Marat/Sade* on film has the courage of its negational convictions realized more completely and seamlessly than on stage.

The movie audience enters the "salon" of the asylum, as Mme. Coulmier calls it, for the inmates' performance along with the director and his family. Brook frames his movie as a play within a play within a film; an iron curtain of bars [restoring symbolically as a prison the theater's traditional fourth wall] separates the insane inmates of Charenton from the larger audience which watches them -- usually silhouetted but dressed in twentieth-century garb. These foregrounded spectators often rise to leave in the restless manner of contemporary movie spectators. The moviegoers who have come to see Brook's film of *Marat/Sade* are, of course, another audience behind this filmed one seen on the screen. The present tense of film may have inspired Brook in this successful device. David Watkins, Brook's cameraman, uses his hand-held camera advantageously to achieve mobility within claustrophobic madness (and when desirable to eliminate the separation imposed by the prison bars) and to penetrate seemingly even the minds of the inmates. The actual movie audience's point of view is sometimes inside the bathhouse looking out at the on-screen audience and sometimes behind this surrogate audience. We become something more than wanderers and voyeurs within the asylum; we are there. As with *Lord of the Flies*, Brook once more used at least two cameras for filming *Marat/Sade*: the fixed camera duplicating, more or less, the long and stationary view-point of the theater and the hand-held camera for action in the thick of things. Quick, almost subliminal, cuts from a principal to other inmates permit the audience to see reactions with the selectivity possible only in film. Interestingly, with the strategy of the close-up, the dialogue between Sade and Marat is often clearer on film than it was on stage without requiring suppression of the background insanity which the live performance often needed but failed to achieve sufficiently for full intelligibility of the text. At the same time, because the actual movie audience does not demand protection from excessive stage violence that might spill over into the auditorium, the filmed *Marat/Sade* could engage in more daring displays of violence and agitation than was hitherto possible during a live performance.

At the end of *Marat/Sade*, both on stage and on film, Sade watches the mad actors in their throes of ecstasy, almost indulgently with a faint smile. In the screen version, he breaks into a hearty laugh in the midst of the inmates' rioting. In the final tableau a chorus of inmates enact the loss of all resistances and assertions of self-command, as they shout:

> Charenton Charenton
> Napoleon Napoleon
> Revolution Revolution
> Copulation Copulation (*Marat/Sade*, p. 141)

This response answers Roux's final pleas to the performers: "When will you learn to see/When will you learn to take sides?" (*Marat/ Sade*, p. 142) The registration of the filmed action records the lowering of human behavior to chaos and mass psychosis. In Artaud's scheme, by giving vent to such extreme passions and cultural nightmares, the theater should be able to exorcise them. Artaud [and Brook] apply a homeopathic therapeutic to the troubled consciousness.

Almost all of Brook's images and effects serve the play's reliance on violence. Mme. Coulmier and even an attendant nun are knocked down in the film version. Just as the audience itself is about to be assaulted, literally as opposed to the relentless assault upon the senses throughout the stage and film version, the blown whistle secures remission. In the film version, the camera pulls back to show first the audience in the theater applauding the performance [recording the actual details of the stage performances of *Marat/ Sade*] and the cast applauding the audience. Some of the half-crazed inmates climb the bars of the grille, while others tear the cage, screaming for freedom at the few patrons in the filmed theater and at the larger implied audience watching the film wherever they may be. Brook has managed to suspend the usual easy identification and sympathy with characters so readily exploited through the camera in traditional movies. The result, though, takes on the quality sometimes of calculated arbitrariness of shamed characters caught in the act, the revelation of the otherwise properly concealed. *Marat/Sade*, in whatever medium Brook presents it, is a powerful negational artifact of modernity with new pieties addressed to what is lowering rather than exultant in the hierarchies of conduct and thought.

The film of *Marat/Sade* is often strikingly and perversely beautiful in its color, as was Brook's earlier stage picture. "Against the whites and grays of the asylum's bathhouse and the inmates' garb," writes John Simon, "the splashes of color from costumes, warders' uniforms, and props function in a similarly dual way as do focus and nonfocus: color solos performed dazzlingly to an accompaniment of amorphous drabness. The handheld camera, in harmony or discord, whirls around with or against the swirls of the spectacle. It is a split world, frightening yet not without its terrible beauty." (*Movies into Film*, p. 27)

Indeed the film's special vividness may reflect the condition of insanity wherein documented cases are often noted of heightened color and sound sensations. As in *The Beggar's Opera* Brook calls attention to his cinematic devices which parallel the often self-referential quality of some of his theatrical devices in the stage production of *Marat/Sade*. The hallucinatory world of the asylum at Charenton receives its due more adequately on film than on stage with over-exposed frames, "hot" shots of heavily made-up performers filmed against stark white tile, out of focus studies of characters, and related cinematic ploys. The film is cruelly fascinating to watch, at times actually painful visually. Brook's adaptation deserves to be called filmic and testifies to his continued fondness for the performance medium he espoused and aspired to work in as an Oxford undergraduate. His techniques demonstrate considerable subtlety as well as bold statement. Each principal is treated individually by the camera, relative to shots and angles, or edited differently with respect to rhythm. We see Sade frequently in profile at the extreme edge of the frame; Marat receives more frontal treatment. The Coulmier family is usually presented seated from low angle shots. Sade appears some-

146

times to have been shot with a longer lens than anyone else, thereby wiping out the background behind him in order to suggest his total self-involvement before the action of "his" play and the vagaries of the asylum once more intrude upon him. The memorable panning over the inmates gleefully guillotining one finger with another reinforces through parody the effect of the earlier enactment of the guillotine in which the inmates bowed their heads as special sound effects using materials in the bathhouse evoked the dropping of the blade and the fall of aristocratic heads.

Brook lets his virtuoso film-making get away from him in the sequence identified as "Marat's Nightmare," formerly "The Faces of Marat" in the play. The revolutionary looks back upon his history. What was a reasonably clear pageant on the stage becomes a surreal montage of dissolving shapes and left-over tableaux footage derived from the play, now scissored into fragments, visually provocative perhaps, yet otherwise unintelligible in contrast to Weiss's clear treatment of the material in the text. Although this device shortens the playing-time of the film, it eliminates much of the intellectual and emotional substance on which Weiss builds the character of Marat. On film the only meaning is the bafflement of the viewer. The address is to nothing but its own cinematic brilliance, and the weight of history and culture upon Marat is reduced to a blur.

Arguably, Brook's ideal and most appreciative viewer of the filmed *Marat/Sade* is Charles Eidsvik who praises the director for challenging "not only what a film should be 'about,' but also how it should work; ultimately he [Brook] has challenged traditional ideas of what a good film *is*."[14] Eidsvik especially admires what Brook achieves with respect to the viewer's affective response:

> The obvious artifices and ambiguities break down the barriers between the theater and the world outside. Further, the viewer's own complexity and inner contradictions (the deepest parts of his personality?) become part of his viewing role. He cannot leave that role on leaving the theater, the film-exercised part of his consciousness shoved to the side. There is more at stake than two hours of imaginative empathy in the dark. (*Cineliteracy*, p. 257)

If Eidsvik is at all correct in his evaluation – and I think he is – *Marat /Sade* both on stage and on film represents Brook's most successful experiment within broadly the commercial entertainment enterprise to affect the audience through the transformative powers of performance. To this end it stands as the culmination of his initial investigations in Brecht and Artaud.

V. *Tell Me Lies* (1967)

When *US* closed at the Aldwych, Brook and his company decided to produce a film based on the material of the play/happening. The new title for the film, *Tell Me Lies* is based on a frequently-heard refrain from one of the work's songs, "Tell me lies about Vietnam." Although many aspects of the stage production had seemed incipiently cinematic in technique, *Tell Me Lies* on film acquired a curious staginess. Because history and event can be re-created so much more persuasively on screen, the camera may have exposed the original material's lack of substance which had somehow been accepted as greater on stage during a performance that it looked now on screen. Actually very little of the stage script of *US* was retained in the film besides the songs, but *Tell Me Lies* was true to the spirit of the original Brook stage production if not its letter. As in *US* Brook tried to survey a wide range of attitudes in Britain and the United States about Vietnam through multiple means, including cinéma-vérité, documentary footage of interviews with right-wing spokesmen, student demonstrations, and actual fighting in Southeast Asia, comedy sketches, and conventional dramatic and narrative segments. Stylistically, Brook's greatest debt as film-maker seemed again to be to Jean-Luc Godard, extending even to sub-titles inserted to carry political comment at the bottom of the screen and excessive reliance on intercutting and jump-cuts. Likewise, in the Godard and Robert Altman manner, the soundtrack was often self-consciously at variance with the visual content of a sequence. While this technique was apparently intended to deliver an imaginative juxtaposition, it more typically produced confusion.

148

Once more Brook called upon resources of avant-garde cinema to mark a breakthrough in a highly personal film which was yet meant for a mass audience. The initial popular and critical reaction proved so extremely negative, however, that the film's distributor withdrew it from theater circulation. Those few who did have the opportunity to see *Tell Me Lies* frequently praised it and compared Brook's film favorably with the successful documentary on the Vietnam War, *Hearts and Minds*, most notably in the emotional effect of the photograph of a Vietnamese child who had been severely burned by Napalm which Brook used at the opening and close of his film. Brook's last line in *Tell Me Lies* asks: "How long can you look at this before you lose interest?" Then the camera pans away from the photograph of the burned child to a closed door in a freeze frame. The screen goes silently blank, the equivalent in movie effect to Brook's controversial ending to the stage production of *US* which was meant to stifle applause.

The play/happening and film on Vietnam prefigured new artistic and intellectual directions for Peter Brook and his subsequent collaborators. With its improvisatory and ritualistic provenance as well as in its substitution of ritual and genuine myth for the propaganda and debased "myth" of the war machine's newsmen and photographers, *US/Tell Me Lies* served as a harbinger for much in Brook's later career. Here he began a kind of cultural retrieval, looking increasingly at non-western sources for ideas, inspiration, and even language. His enlarged repository of options, while not completely successful in its application to Vietnam, points toward Brook's search for greater universality which will transcend theatrical cliché for archetypal form.

VI. *King Lear* (1971)

Brook's film of *King Lear* stands as an even more audacious endeavor than his acclaimed stage production which preceded it. The film was shot from January to April during 1969 in the frozen tundra of North Jutland, Denmark where the geographically and theatrically globe-trotting director found an unlocalized and empty acting space which exceeded the wildest imagination of anyone who was thinking of an Elizabethan playhouse. In this setting the film of *King Lear* could make use of infinite white and infinite black space as no giant white flats and black cyclorama on stage would match. Often, in exterior shots, the filmed *Lear* resolves background into pure white or pure black without break in the continuity as a stage blackout might.

The intervention of time and artistic activity on Brook's part which separates the film version of *Lear* from the Royal Shakespeare Company's stage presentation accounts for some of the changes made in the film. Although the stage production removed the positive and affirmative in *King Lear*, the text otherwise was reasonably complete. The film version's text amounts almost to what current critical parlance terms an act of "deconstruction." Originally, Brook called upon his frequent collaborator of the late sixties and early seventies, Ted Hughes, to write a "new" shooting script for the play. Despite admirable versions by the contemporary poet, Brook finally elected to go with the Shakespeare text, albeit often excised and revised form, derived, in part, from the director's own narrative treatment of the play without dialogue. The success of the Theater of Cruelty season, *Marat/Sade* on stage and film, and the Godardian experiments on film in *Moderato Cantabile* and *Tell Me Lies* further influenced the content and look of the filmed *Lear*. Even more so than on the stage, the film attempts to match its human cruelty to the cruelty of the universe, as indeed the actors and crew must have directly experienced it on location in Jutland during the winter months.

Given the weather conditions in Jutland and the possible inspiration of location shooting on an unused former mink farm, the costumes for the *Lear* film were significantly different from the stage version to afford some protection against the exterior cold. The fur-clad Goneril, Irene Worth retaining her original role, looks appropriately bestial; Paul Scofield, also re-creating his earlier stage Lear for Brook, swathed in furs to complement his glacial visage, resembles the embodiment of winter or the frost king out of some ethnographic study. This ritualized, frosty old man, a cold naked wretch beneath his arrogance of power, takes on more life, not less, on screen in Henning Kristiansen's stunning black and white photography reminiscent of Bergman's brooding studies of chilly medieval and contemporary Scandinavia and of the lighting in Carl Dreyer's films. The only other principal from the stage production retained in the film is Alan Webb as Gloucester. Nevertheless, Brook's replacements for the balance of the cast are firstrate, especially Patrick Magee's Cornwall, Ian Hogg's Edmund, Jack MacGowran's Fool, and the Danish actress, Annelise Gabold's Cordelia.

Perhaps fortunate in having so many alumni of Beckett plays in his film cast, Brook's repertory of Beckettian meanings (or un-meanings) continue unabated in transference from stage to screen. Interestingly, American critics, scholars, and audiences have generally been more enthusiastic about Brook's film of *Lear* than have their British counterparts – a somewhat ironic reversal of the reception accorded the stage version in the two countries.[15] Throughout the film Brook effectively plays off light against dark, literal and figurative conditions for sight and blindness, as well as sound against silence. The envelope for the film is silence, which begins and ends the action from the opening silent titles to the still fade-out to white at the close, indicative of the nothingness which Brook thereby makes palpable. The exchange between Gloucester and Kent which opens Shakespeare's *King Lear* by talking about an old man's issue and posterity has been omitted to begin with Lear's "Know" of his second speech – "Know we have divided/ In three our kingdom." This word -- *know* – isolated by strategic and dramatic pause, is easily mistaken for *no*, as Brook underscores by means of this ambiguous homonym the negational and existential epistemology of his Beckettian interpretation of the play. Likewise, our first introduction to Cordelia in the film is her verbalizing of "Nothing," Brook having eliminated the self-doubting asides of the youngest daughter before she makes her declaration in the love-test.

Paul Acker has perceptively noted that at this point with Cordelia's "So young my lord. . .," followed by a direct cut to Lear and her words, ". . . and true," Brook uses his first pure set of shot/reverse shots between father and daughter; but the communication is denied, since the context becomes that of Lear's curse. Instead of the expected exchange of glances, the shot/reverse shot must then be read as a

151

failure to see.[16] Thus the usual expectations of the shot/reverse convention are deliberately violated to underscore tensions and confrontations in the play. As Brook revivifies theatrical conventions on stage to transcend cliches, he subtly turns cinematic conventions upside down in the handy-dandy world of *King Lear* to make more impersonal the familial and service relationships in Shakespeare's tragedy. On several occasions in the film Brook uses fade-to-black effectively, perhaps most notably during the blinding of Gloucester when the audience hears the old man's screams but cannot see his suffering until the screen is lightened for us to see Cornwall pluck out the other eye.[17]

Frequently Brook moves the camera in the filmed *Lear* to duplicate experience from the characters' point of view or to reflect their state of mind. Other times, Brook denies such complete identification by using the camera as an alienating effect, in a manner more derivative of Godard than Brecht, by letting a character momentarily vanish from the frame or sway out of frame, or even photographing a Brechtian placard such as "Goneril's Castle." What has sometimes seemed to be inappropriate camera movement in Brook's film, upon reflection, usually may be seen to serve an aesthetic or intellectual purpose in his film conception of *King Lear*.

Brook uses particular cinematic wit in the Dover Cliff scene with Edgar and Gloucester. When Edgar comments on the difficulty of their progress, Brook captures a close-up of their feet followed by a tilted perspective and the camera zooming back suggestive of the supposed ascent. Jack J. Jorgens' appreciative description of the way Brook illuminates the human condition through cinematic artifice in this poignant sequence merits quotation:

> Set on 'the extremest verge,' Gloucester bids farewell to
> Poor Tom, and his final speech of despair is filmed in low-angle
> close-up — one of the most savagely beautiful shots of a human
> face ever put on film. As he falls forward, however, Brook jolts
> us with an illusion-shattering cut to an extreme overhead shot.
> From this godlike perspective, we watch a tiny old man take a
> silent pratfall on a barren stretch of sand. Edgar rushes to his
> side, and in one of those disjunctions so frequent in the struc-
> turally parallel storm scene, the screen is suddenly filled with
> what seems to be a vortex or a huge inscrutable eye. When the

camera zooms back, our disorientation, which parallels
Gloucester's, is resolved as we see that it is a knot in a piece
of driftwood (a microcosm, not a macrocosm) upon which
this piece of human flotsam rests his head. In a kaleidoscopic
series of voices, Edgar repeats the act of Cordelia and jars his
father back to life. Thus, in emotion, theme, and style, this
expressionist, absurd tumbling off the imagined edge of the
world is for Brook an epiphany of the *Lear* experience.[18]

Brook's turning of *Lear* into a landscape of a mind encountering
the cruelty of life and nothingness reaches its climax in the madness
scene of Lear on the heath. Here Brook captures the creative-destruc-
tive duality of Lear in possibly a symbolic, cinematic realization of
Artaud's notion of the theater and its double -- theater and "true
life" as well as the other metaphorical doubles -- the plague, cruelty,
and alchemy. A shot of Lear is offered looking frame right, followed
by a shot of him looking frame left. The conventions of realistic,
illusionist film are abrogated, but the expressive power which Brook
has gone for replaces our usual way of movie-viewing. We see Scofield's Lear in dialogue with himself, creating out of his own madness
and destruction renewed tragic selfhood and human significance in
the midst of cosmic cruelty.

At the end of the film the head of the deceased Lear slips out of
frame. The cold world in the frame always has difficulty containing
Shakespeare's narrative or holding his protagonist, Brook seems to
suggest. The reductionist nature of Brook's stage version persists
amid the truncations of the film [we still lament the absence of the
sublime "Pray you, unbotton. . ." at the close], yet this *King Lear*
compels in its single-mindedness of conception and mastery of film
techniques put in the service of the text as few film adaptations of a
Shakespeare play ever have. Indeed, Brook's fragmentariness of the
Gloucester sub-plot may strengthen the cruel, insistently absurdist
interpretation of the principal action. This filmed *King Lear* invigor-
ates without consoling in its radical and revolutionary Artaudian implications, which Charles Eidsvik fully recognizes:

> He [Brook] attacks every verity in our culture, from Shake-
> speare to reason itself. He attacks *us*. And the only way to re-
> spond is to strike back, to think, to act so that Brook's vision
> stand as a challenge rather than a condemnation. . . . Brook

makes his audience think. And people who think are dangerous. They are capable of anything, even of not lying to themselves. (*Cineliteracy*, p. 262)

Less disposed critics and viewers of the filmed *King Lear* found the
mannerist cutting Brook uses, the sudden shifts from one angle to
another, and the visual punishment of exploding flashes merely
alienating without theoretical recourse to Brecht or Artaud. But even
more than in the stage version, Brook's film of *King Lear* brings a
level of concentration and intensity to his Shakespeare material
which demands the same from the viewer. That these demands were
more stringent in the film than on the stage suggests Brook's further
daring in his attempt to enlarge the possibilities of film relative to a
mass audience. It is gratifying to have via the permanence of film
evidence of Brook's cool, methodical, formal intelligence, and of the
fervent attention with which he continually applied it. Not surprisingly, *King Lear* on film was a box-office failure.

VII. *Meetings with Remarkable Men* (1979)

Brook's fame [or notoriety] for filming unlikely and seemingly
unpromising subject-matter reached its zenith with the release in
1979, after a protracted seven-year endeavor, of *Meetings with
Remarkable Men*, a film based on portions of the autobiographical
work of the same title by George Ivanovich Gurdjieff (1877-1949),
philosopher, writer, musician, and searcher after mystical truth, who
was the founder of a movement which now appears to be the direct
antecedent of the numerous awareness and human potential/develop-
ment movements of the nineteen-seventies.

In his desire to convey nothing less than a numinous vision of
spiritual development on the part of Gurdjieff as a young man,
Brook faced a nearly insuperable task. He expressed his intent for the
film in a *Parabola* interview:

> I feel the film [*Meetings with Remarkable Men*] is a story
> -- a not totally truthful story, somewhat oriental, sometimes
> accurate, sometimes not, sometimes in and sometimes out of
> life, like a legend. It is told like a legend in the remote past,

for a purpose: which is to follow in a certain order the search
of the searcher who is the central character. The entire film
has been constructed around that one essential thread. . . . the
film is a direct expression, for the person watching it, of a
growing search; the sense of the growing search and the changing taste of it is what the film is there to show.[19]

Brook disavowed that his purpose in making the film was to recount
the biography of Gurdjieff. Thus Brook follows a protagonist whose
principal action occurs within the mind, and the director counts on
his viewers being affected by the spiritual process without their fully
knowing how and why it is happening. As Brook himself expressed
it: ". . . you have to let the film wash over you to follow the central
process. If you ask yourself about logical reasons for transitions, that
sets up a difficulty that I don't think is there otherwise." ("Leaning
on the Moment," 58) Brook's eagerness to win audience reflection
on the ineffable far surpassed his desire for box-office success in this
highly personal film. He chose as his Gurdjieff, Dragon Maksimovic, a
young, unknown Yugoslav actor who learned English for the role,
though usually without speaking he stares fixedly into space, representing Gurdjieff when in the throes of higher consciousness. Sequence after sequence ends in this manner as if Brook somehow
trusts the viewer will become caught up in the experience and thereby absorb something of Gurdjieff's spiritual essence. Unfortunately,
matched to the often arresting visages in the film is incredibly banal
dialogue about great, abstract verities. In making that judgment, I
doubtless ally myself with those people, according to Brook "whose
developed reflexes are so powerful that they are registering at every
second what they are *not* with, [italics are Brook's] and that prevents
them from entering into what is there." ("Leaning on the Moment,"
58)

Brook collaborated on the script with Mme. Jeanne de Salzmann,
one of the then few surviving members of Gurdjieff's earliest dis-
ciples who at a truly venerable age headed the world-wide movement
based on his work with headquarters in Paris. It was she who helped
Brook in the presentation of the sacred dances which Gurdjieff
learned in Central Asia and which subsequently constituted the
major physical regimen of his movement for human development.

This collaboration between Brook and Mme. de Salzmann was most fortuitous. Gurdjieff's numerous, and often celebrated, followers traditionally shun publicity in any form, preferring to pursue their inner work inspired by the master with the greatest possible measure of privacy. Inasmuch as Peter Brook counts himself among those followers, *Meetings with Remarkable Men* was a film which he greatly wanted to do.

Brook budgeted the film at $ 2.5 million, which for a movie of epic scope is assuredly minimal, but he could not find anyone willing to produce his approach to *Meetings with Remarkable Men* – as a study of the early process toward greatness rather than as a biography of greatness – in the worldwide film industry. Finally he resorted, as he had done eighteen years before with *Lord of the Flies*, to funding provided by a large number of generally small, private investors, three hundred of whom came up with $ 3 million on the basis of their faith in the project perhaps a testimony to the actual power of Gurdjieff, to say nothing of Peter Brook! Production took the company, which included the distinguished South African playwright, Antol Fugard, Terence Stamp, Colin Blakely, and Natasha Parry (Brook), into remote locations of exotic and often politically troubled countries with the bulk of the film being completed in Afghanistan only months before the Afghan king was supplanted by a pro-Soviet government. As with his African pilgrimage, Brook took particular pleasure in the reception accorded him and his company by the people in Afghanistan who permitted him to record what he considered to be the deep spirituality of their daily lives.

Nowhere is this special quality more clearly demonstrated than in the opening of *Meetings with Remarkable Men* where the long shots of the locale gives way to close-up studies of Afghans, Turomen, Kafirs, and Kurds, in appearance comparable to the wise men of the Russian-Turkish border where Gurdjieff grew up. The boy Gurdjieff used to accompany his father who was a famous rhapsode engaged professionally to chant the epic poetry of Asia Minor, sometimes as part of great tribal contests. The film opens with another kind of contest, a ritualistic ceremony wherein men playing various instruments meet in order to discover who will produce the sound which will cause the rocks themselves to echo in answer. The drama of

156

human physiognomy dominates this evocative sequence as each performer takes his turn and Gilbert Taylor's haunting photography slowly and lovingly pans from face to face in anticipation until the rocks do, finally, respond.

The winner receives a lamb as reward, recorded by Brook in a sequence which renders quite matter-of-fact the inexplicable, even ineffable event of wonder which has preceded except that the audience sees on the face of the young actor playing Gurdjieff more than a trace of discovery – hereafter he will seek additional remarkable men and their more remarkable truths. The early portions of the film with the young Gurdjieff and his boyhood discoveries, rivalries, and adventures are among the most satisfying moments in *Meetings with Remarkable Men*. They manifest a kind of hypnotic plausibility reminiscent of Brook's success with Golding's novel of boyhood so much earlier in the director's career. With the adult Gurdjieff, his meetings with the Gobi Desert landscape often assume as authoritative interest visually and dramatically as his sage and eclectic human encounters. Mystical truth as Brook explores it in this film is a form of benign terrorism. He plants little time bombs in Gurdjieff's head and those of the other searchers he meets without always showing the flash when they go off. We must take on faith that not all the bombs are duds.

One notable later sequence shows Gurdjieff at the foot of the Sphinx, surreptitiously studying a map of ancient Egypt which he had earlier stolen in a copy from an Armenian monk. He is surprised to find an older man standing above him, looking down with a shock of recognition indicative of prior acquaintance with the map. Thus Gurdjieff meets the wealthy and remarkable Russian, Prince Yuri Lubovedsky [Terence Stamp], who had tried unsuccessfully to obtain the map or a copy of it from the same Armenian monk. Separately, both this Prince and Gurdjieff eventually reach the Sarmoung Brotherhood, an order founded in 2500 B.C. which was thought to have disappeared after the sixth century. There the viewer discovers figures and symbols first found on the map of "pre-sand Egypt" seen earlier in the film. The Prince and elders to whom he introduces Gurdjieff insist that thinking and knowing are not synonymous. As the Prince explains at one point, "Learning happens only when not even a thought stands between you and your knowledge. Faith cannot be given – it comes from direct knowledge." For both men, the Prince and Gurdjieff, true wisdom is suffered information. Their relationship Brook presents as the apotheosis of the extensive criss-cross of relationships in Gurdjieff's biography which the film distills to relatively few.

His final ordeal before attaining entrance to the Sarmoung Brotherhood requires Gurdjieff to traverse a narrow swinging bridge over a mountain gorge. Filming Maksimovic from below the timbers of the bridge, the camera records Gurdjieff's careful, steady, and purposeful crossing toward the locus of his greatest discovery. Here Gurdjieff learns the sacred dancing central to his disciplined exercises. Brook appropriately ends *Meetings with Remarkable Men* with enactment of these dances which are designed to liberate the energies of the body. From these physical movements Gurdjieff evolved his language of the body as a means for advancing the harmonious development of the whole person. Members of the monastery community alone can read the alphabet of the body in these sacred dances, but the film viewer who may not be a true-believer in Gurdjieff can still find enormous appeal in this mystical choreography. And Brook's often static film does acquire some energy and even ecstasy through demonstration paradoxically of such perfect discipline as the dances themselves.

Brook presents in the film enactment of the famous "stop" exercise which Gurdjieff eventually taught at the Institute for the Harmonious Development of Man outside Fontainebleau. Upon command, participants in the "dance" would freeze for as long as the leader required. The bodily control of such exercises only hints at the corresponding mastery of the mind required by them. Brook said of these activities:

> It should be quite clear that what we are showing in the film is not a series of ceremonies and rituals. You arrive at a monastery and you expect to see the sort of ritual you might see with the dervishes at Konya. But the head of the monastery says: "Go to the courtyard and you will see people doing certain *exercises*." An exercise is very different from a ritual, because it means that as a beginner you do an exercise to learn. ("Leaning on the Moment," 59)

The attitude expressed in the foregoing quotation relates to Brook's own theatrical practices of recent years as much as it does to Gurdjieff's experience. Again the emphasis is placed upon the process rather than the product.

Meetings with Remarkable Men presents itself as a metaphysical travelogue, vague in content, yet reverential and portentous. Like the young Gurdjieff, Peter Brook may subscribe to the notion that certain kinds of occult wisdom and practices are preserved only in remote and faraway places, as the director's own pilgrimages continue and even multiply in both frequency and difficulty. Notwithstanding the similarity in the method of financing *Lord of the Flies* and *Meetings with Remarkable Men*, the two films afford a way to contrast art and value terms in Brook's career. The earlier film with its statement on human beings as a dangerous species, brutal and barbarous if left to their own instinctual devices, complements the many stage productions directed by Brook which dealt with cruelty in the decade of the sixties. However, *Meetings with Remarkable Men* implies a more sanguine assessment of human capability which is distinguished by the absence of violence in any form. If formerly Brook used cruelty as the chief means whereby people entered imaginatively into the loves of others, this study of Gurdjieff during his formative years offers a gratifying alternative to such pessimism about the human condition. Nevertheless, a price may yet have to be paid for new-found transcendence of previously conceived limitations on human freedom; namely, the tag of therapeutic control and anti-egalitarianism which subordinates independent existence to the dictates of the leader. Anyone who is good at setting people free, as Gurdjieff assumed he was in his role of professional liberator, is also potentially good at enslaving them. Both Gurdjieff and Brook, of course, repudiated such power; the former never claimed that he was able to give his students knowledge which they did not already possess – only that he could help arrange the existing knowledge in a new way. Brook's approach as theater director is quite similar. Further, Gurdjieff remained highly eclectic in his appropriations from world philosophy and wisdom literature. The discovery of precise origins in his work proves ultimately elusive and frustrating. Brook's own intellectual debts are similarly obscured by eclecticism and amalgamation.

159

Not many critics who saw *Meetings with Remarkable Men* took Brook's images, ideas, and practices dedicated to defining, liberating, or cultivating the self in quite the ingenuous way the director apparently hoped they would be taken. Derisively, Brook's sense of reverence for Gurdjieff's quest was compared with Cecil B. DeMille's suspect standard of reverence in his biblical epics. A typical description of Brook's film is Erika Munk's: "a humorless hill-and-desert guru-hunt."[20] Or more excoriating is Philip French's assessment:

> The acting varies between three modes – the questing-cataleptic, the eureka-agitated, and the transcendental-smug. The dialogue suggests an acquaintance with the Orient restricted to Maria Montez B-features of the 1940's. The shangri-la where Gurdjieff penetrates the arcana looks like the musical version of "Lost Horizon" or a yoga and eurythmics evening at a North London community centre.[21]

Once more Peter Brook failed to achieve in film comparable success to his innovative theatrical work. The representational directness of film's visual medium may have contributed to Brook's problem in suggesting Gurdjieff's spiritual ascent. On several occasions in the film we see the enneagram, Gurdjieff's mystical emblem of triangles enclosed within a circle, but no explanation is forthcoming of its exact significance. Maybe Brook meant it as a test of the initiated: the necessity of accepting on faith the mystery which the director has made the core of his film. The audacity of Brook's film lies in his address to his audience, initiated and uninitiated, as fellow remarkable persons meeting in the movie theater, not a monastery, for purposes of mystical discovery.

Admittedly, a vintage Gurdjieffian like Kathryn Hulme may be attuned to nuances in *Meetings with Remarkable Men* that the unacquainted will probably miss, as in her comments on the musical score for the film:

> As the Sacred Dances must be seen so must the musical accompaniment to the film be heard rather than described. Thomas de Hartmann, a well-known Russian composer, one of Gurdjieff's earliest disciples from 1917 and the days of the St. Petersburg group, wrote the extraordinary music for the dances which Gurdjieff memorized as he had heard it years earlier and had kept intact in his great trained memory. Ar-

ranged and added to by Laurence Rosenthal, the special music composed by de Hartmann under Gurdjieff's influence is the basis for the film score.[22]

While not exactly a cinematic triumph for its director, *Meetings with Remarkable Men* comes closer than any other Brook film to challenging the affective responses of the audience by releasing some process that goes on within the moviegoers but without their knowing that it is happening. As corollary to Brook's recent theatrical experiments, this study of Gurdjieff has considerable interpretive usefulness for showing how performance may be one way into myth as in the depiction of the sacred dances and the meeting point of the ordinary and the remarkable within the actor. Moreover, it is quite pleasurable to watch the development of a protagonist propelled by an inner energy. Brook's young Gurdjieff captures a renewed spirit of romance popular at the moment in the West, manifested in upward projection toward recovery of self through the creative power of mankind returning to original mythic awareness. *Meetings with Remarkable Men* fulfills in its structure the three states of the successful romantic quest: the perilous journey, the crucial struggle, and the exaltation of the hero. A new generation of mythically-inclined young people may yet salvage Brook's film at future box offices. True to the pattern of Brook's film career, this most recent film continues the honorable, if romantic, search for an elusive audience. Not unexpectedly, therefore, those Brook films which have endured and have gained quantitatively in admirers tend to have the reputation of cult films. Will this be the destiny of *Meetings with Remarkable Men?* Portents suggest it could be, if not in spades, at least in mandalas.

VIII. Toward an Evaluation of Brook and Film

Without a companion volume on his work in film like *The Empty Space* on his theater experience or the large body of work in the former medium comparable to his achievement in the latter, any evaluation of Brook's films proceeds tentatively and speculatively. The two performance media are linked principally by the director's attitude toward his audience and what he asks of it. Given the diversity of Brook's films, it would be absurd to over-emphasize the unity among them, especially with respect to the usual criteria of subject-matter or style. But there is remarkable uniformity in the way Brook invites his movie-audience to engage with him in ludic collaboration and/or cognitive, even mystical activity. This appeal has only recently gained wide currency in mainstream films, yet Brook was exercising it from the very beginning of his cinema career, despite the incapacity for large audience to accept the invitation.

That a number of Brook's films have attained a kind of cult-status testifies to the willingness of at least some members of his audience to let their movie-experience of *The Beggar's Opera, Lord of the Flies,* and *King Lear* become part of consciousness long after initial viewing. Perhaps as a result of his earlier and later theatrical experience, Brook deliberately extends to his films some of the visual freedom enjoyed by playgoers during a Brook stage production. Brook, rather like Jean Renoir, often avoids the imposition of meaning in portions of his films by permitting spectators to explore his images through long takes and with relaxed panning camera in order for us to reach inferences on our own quite apart perhaps from the director's conclusions. Such indeterminacy is radical in a popular medium like film. Much of the appreciation of a Brook film rests on what the audience brings to it as much as what it sees. When the collaboration works well, the film endures as a happy and active memory. Long ago, then, Brook gave up conceiving the film as object; instead it is an event, to adapt Stanley Fish's vocabulary from literary criticism, something that happens to, and with the participation of the audience.[23] Familiarity with Brook's stage work and the theory behind it reveals the application of these principles in his theater productions; the only surprise comes when they are applied to film which has been conventionally regarded as more of a mass medium than the theater.

Though Brook could surely be seen as an auteur on the basis of his control over the various phases of his films -- usually from script to final editing -- and in the signature of his visual style through his flair for camera angles and composition, his touch and rhythm in the editing room, his most consistent and distinctive contribution to the

162

art of film has been, in the opinion of this study, enlarging the interpretive dynamics of the interaction between film and viewer. In this regard, Brook was very much ahead of his time. We are only now catching up to him. In a contest between theatre and film, Brook would probably choose the former for its art which is fluid, spontaneous, alive as opposed to cinematic art frozen in time. In film the audience changes, but the art remains the same; Brook's theatre art in its relationship to the audience offers greater reciprocity.

NOTES FOR CHAPTER FIVE

1 Pauline Kael, "The Beggar's Opera," *I Lost It at the Movies* (New York: Bantam Books, 1966), p. 107.

2 See review of "Marat/Sade," by John Simon, *Movies into Film: Film Criticism, 1967-70* (New York: Delta, 1971), p. 28.

3 Penelope Houston and Tom Milne, "Interview with Peter Brook," *Sight and Sound*, Summer, 1963, pp. 40-41.

4 Ibid., pp. 31-41.

5 David Stewart Hull, "London," *Film Quarterly*, 14 (Winter, 1960), 33.

6 John Russell Taylor, "Peter Brook or the Limitations of Intelligence," *Sight and Sound*, Spring, 1967, pp. 80-84.

7 Interview with Peter Brook, "Filming a Masterpiece," *The* [London] *Observer*, July 26, 1964, p. 21.

8 See Robert Wallace, "A Gamble on Novices Works Almost Too Well," *Life*, October 25, 1963, p. 104.

9 V. S. Pritchett, "Pain and William Golding," *The Living Novel and Later Appreciations* (New York: Random House, 1966), p. 311.

10 Frank Kermode, "Hunter and Shaman," *Puzzles and Epiphanies: Essays and Reviews 1958-1961* (New York: Chilmark Press, 1962), p. 44.

11 William Golding, *Lord of the Flies* (New York: Capricorn Books, 1959), pp. 132-133.

12 See especially, "The Unity of All Rites," Rene Girard, *Violence and the Sacred*, trans. by Patrick Gregory, (Baltimore and London: The Johns Hopkins University Press, 1979), pp. 274-308.

13 Harold Clurman, "The Theater," *The Nation*, January 17, 1966, pp. 82-84.

14 Charles Eidsvik, *Cineliteracy: Film Among the Arts* (New York: Random House, 1978), p. 250.

15 See comment about the poor British reception in Frank Kermode, "Shakespeare in the Movies," *New York Review of Books*, May 4, 1972, pp. 18-21.

16 Paul Acker, "Conventions for Dialogue in Brooks's *Lear*," *Literature/Film Quarterly*, 8 (1980), 219-224.

17 A particularly fine essay on the Brook film to which I am indebted with perceptive commentary on this point is Lillian Wilds, "One *King Lear* for Our Time: A Bleak Film Vision by Peter Brook," *Literature/Film Quarterly*, 4 (Spring, 1976), 159-164.

18 Jack. J. Jorgens, "*King Lear*: Peter Brook and Grigori Kozintsev," *Shakespeare on Film* (Bloomington and London: Indiana University Press, 1977), p. 240.

19 "Leaning on the Moment: A Conversation with Peter Brook," *Parabola: Myth and the Quest for Meaning*, 4 (May, 1979), 56-57.

20 Erika Munk, "Peter Brook: The Way's the Thing," *The Village Voice*, May 12, 1980, pp. 36-38.

21 Philip French, "Cinema," *The* [London] *Observer,* September 16, 1979, p. 14.

22 Kathryn Hulme, "*Meetings with Remarkable Men*: My Impressions of the Film," (New York: Remar Productions, Inc., 1979), n. p.

23 See, for example, the well-known essay by Stanley E. Fish, "Literature in the Reader: Affective Stylistics," *New Literary History*, 2 (Autumn, 1970), 123-162. I am indebted also to Carole Berger, "Viewing as Action: Film and Reader Response Criticism," *Literature/Film Quarterly*, 6 (Spring, 1978), 144-151.

Chapter Six

NEW DIRECTIONS; NEW INSTITUTIONS:
BROOK TO THE PRESENT

Before Brook became established in Paris with his own research workshop and its multifaceted pursuits, his career had already branched out beyond his usual loyalties. For the first time Brook considered staging a classical tragedy from the Greek theater. His choice was the Aeschylean tragedy, *Prometheus Bound* which he planned to direct for the Royal Shakespeare Company with his friend and frequent collaborator, Paul Scofield, in the lead. Owing to other commitments, the actor was forced to forsake the proposed production, and *Prometheus Bound* was withdrawn from the RSC. Meanwhile, Kenneth Tynan and Sir Laurence Olivier of the newly-established National Theatre of Great Britain invited Brook to stage *Oedipus* by the Roman Stoic and dramatist, Seneca. Tynan, then the National Theatre's Literary Manager, had recently discovered a new translation of Seneca's version of the Oedipus story by David Anthony Turner, which, in turn, had been freely adapted by Ted Hughes, with whom Brook would frequently work in far-flung projects during the seventies. As he wrote in the program for his production of *Oedipus*, Brook was searching during this period for dramas to express the invisible currents of our lives in ceremonious ritual whose form dictates the architecture of the occasion. The working-out of this search in *Oedipus* was startling to behold and augured for new directions in Brook's career.

I. Seneca's *Oedipus* (1968)

Seneca's *Oedipus*, despite or maybe because of its lack of a performance tradition and history in English, proved a most congenial vehicle for Brook in 1968. This same year saw the publication of *The Empty Space* in which the director had celebrated the rough and ready Renaissance theater and had urged movement away from sophisticated theater to a harsher, more primitive form. Inasmuch as the Senecan influence had been pervasive in the Elizabethan period and Brook had staged quite successfully a strongly Senecan play by Shakespeare with *Titus Andronicus* a decade or so earlier, *Oedipus* stood as a work to be theatrically reclaimed. Likewise, Seneca remained a particular favorite of Artaud whom Brook continued to admire, and indeed the French director/theoretician had staged Seneca's *Thyestes* as the second offering in his Theater of Cruelty. The fact that Seneca usually reduced the profound and dignified moral questioning of Greek tragedy to melodramatic bombast handicapped Brook not at all. Many of Seneca's wise-sayings (sententiae) succumbed in Brook's production to non-verbal sounds on the part of the approximately thirty performers comprising the cast. Wails, chants, cries, shrieks, groans, and pants punctuate [and eventuate] in the tragedy of Oedipus as Brook staged it.

Since there is little which could be called regal about Seneca's protagonist, the *Rex* of the original Sophoclean tragedy may be appropriately deleted from the Latin title. Suffering no loss of pride or significant alteration of soul through self-discovery, Seneca's Oedipus is simply forced to accept as fact what he already knew as obsessive fantasy. Seneca characterizes Oedipus almost exclusively in relation to his mother unlike the Sophoclean actions which display the king in other roles as monarch, father, and husband. It may be relevant to recall that early in his career Brook staged Jean Cocteau's *The Infernal Machine* which in regard to its portrayal of Oedipus seems more indebted to Seneca than to Sophocles. Brook's Oedipus in the person of Sir John Gielgud salvaged surprising dignity.

Similarly Seneca's Jocasta assumes principally the role of mother to Oedipus at the sacrifice of other functions. Again Brook's production benefited from the services of the distinguished actress, Irene Worth, in the role of Jocasta which Ted Hughes expanded somewhat from the Senecan version. One notable addition explains that she did not regret the murder of Laius because he "owed her a life," i.e., the life of her infant son, Oedipus, whom she presumed died on Mount Cithaeron. In Seneca's version, instead of hanging herself as Jocasta does in Sophocles' tragedy, she commits suicide by impaling herself through her womb, "which (horrible!) both son and husband bore."

166

Brook staged this act realistically, but Irene Worth's face took on a mask-like quality with stylized open mouth as in classical statuary representing the tragic performer. Throughout the play Worth's Jocasta walked with legs stifly spread, knees bent but rigid.

Because Seneca unlike Sophocles has Oedipus blind himself before Jocasta's suicide, it is the latter action which commands the greater theatrical effect. Brook treated the blinding of Oedipus with inspired understatement. The blind Tiresias, wearing black patches on his eyes, merely walks over to Oedipus who has been seated at the edge of the stage listening with head averted to the messenger's recital of his own blinding and transfers the patches to Gielgud's immobile, mask-like face. The horror of the messenger's language is complemented but not upstaged by the simplicity of the stage business.

In the aftermath of his blinding, Gielgud's Oedipus stood motionless as Irene Worth moved toward impalement on the golden spike, a symbolic phallus which embodies for Jocasta her past pleasure and pain. Seneca's Oedipus takes responsibility for killing his mother, claiming that in this death he has outdone the impious fates who constrained him only in parricide. With rueful humor, Oedipus cautions the audience to watch its step, lest one stumble over his own mother. Seneca's tragedy ends with Oedipus calling for disease, emaciation, black plague, and rabid anguish to accompany him into exile.

Peter Brook, however, ended his production of *Oedipus* quite differently and very sensationally. In the final moments of Senecan anguish, members of the chorus wheeled out on stage a huge object covered with a red silk cloth. At the exit of the last principal, the covering was removed to reveal an enormous seven-foot phallus. This sight was accompanied by increasingly intense drum beats until the house lights came up, signifying that the play was over. While Brook may have been after strange gods in this ending, the content and purpose were not clear to the audience. Therefore, Brook altered his effect with a substitute ending in which the stage suddenly fills with revelers immediately upon removal of the silk covering from the immense object on stage. This Bacchanalian celebration spilled over into the auditorium, as a six-piece Dixieland band played the unaccountable, if plausibly Freudian, "Yes We Have No Bananas."

In a well-known interview conducted by Margaret Croyden with Colin Blakely who had played Creon in Brook's production, the actor explained what he understood as Brook's intent to provide release through lustful pleasure from the tragic tension which had preceded in *Oedipus*. Then Blakely went on to articulate what the ending said to him:

1. You've just seen a load of cock.
2. In olden days the Romans used to do this after the play.
3. You see what can happen when you fuck about?
4. Don't go to bed with your mother.
5. Don't take it too seriously, now you've been through hell, forget it, you can deal with it.

Number five is valid. The rest is unfortunately belittling.[1]

Brook's ebullient ending undercuts the boding sense of worse to come which Seneca's Oedipus enunciates at the play's close. Images in Seneca often seem deficient in dramatic and moral significance, and Brook's phallic idol offers the last heightened ornament of *Oedipus* as symbolic of the dramatist's incestuously generative obsession throughout the play. The effect may be truer than the attitudinizing which is more characteristic of Senecan dramaturgy.

The National Theatre Company was treated to Brook's increasing reliance on improvisational rehearsals partly inspired by the work of experimental directors like Joseph Chaikin, Grotowski, Julian Beck, and his own experiments earlier in the decade. The production of *Oedipus* received a full ten weeks of rehearsals and would serve as a harbinger of Brook's later extended rehearsals for his work in Paris. The classically-trained performers like Blakely and his eminent colleagues gave high praise for what Brook was able to achieve without words but with sounds and gestures. By the same token, London critics who had responded favorably to earlier Brook experiments rejoiced over new indications of his continued brilliance, risk, and inventiveness. Martin Esslin, for example, praised the director for being among the first Englishmen to employ Artaud's "storehouse of primitive emotion successfully in the theatre."[2]

Oedipus was staged without intermission in order to sustain uninterruptedly two hours of ritual enactment on the stage of the Old Vic. In content, Seneca's drama is punishing: death, disaster, plague, and horror are the main ingredients. The sun itself shines painfully to illuminate the action of the drama. Brook made use of a large golden cube in the middle of the stage which sometimes was opened to serve as the boundaries of a room but which often was closed to revolve, as the sun might appear to do, catching stage lights and reflecting them harshly into the eyes of actors and audience alike, a technique anticipatory of avant-garde director Richard Foreman at a later date. At such times, Brook's art truly became ordeal, as Artaud would have it – the mind's conception transformed into material event. In contrast to this production of *A Midsummer Night's Dream*, presented two years later, Brook's *Oedipus* in its sensory objectification of Seneca was Artaudian rather than pleasant and charming as it was for Shakespeare. Without mitigation, Brook presented Seneca's tragic vision of life in which passion is fate, choice illusion, and both innocence and guilt have little meaning or moral relation to suffering.

II. Director as Founding-Father, Mentor, Playwright: International Centre of Theatre Research [the performing wing "for Theatre Creations"] or, in French, Le Centre International de Recherche Theatrale (C.I.R.T.) [performing wing "de Créations Théâtrales,"]; for our purposes here, the blanket English version and abbreviation will be used, ICTR. (1970)

Following the triumph of *A Midsummer Night's Dream*, Brook began fulfillment of one of his own dreams with the establishment in Paris on November 1, 1970 of the International Centre of Theatre Research. The Ministry of French Cultural Affairs made available, a bit later than November, the Mobilier National as headquarters for the Centre, and Brook, as producer/director, secured funding for the first eighteen months of work for what Brook projected as a three-year operation. In truth, the Centre in Paris continues at present and gives every sign of great longevity. It took the director about two years to acquire adequate funding for the Centre, the search for which he began back in 1968 when Jean-Louis Barrault invited Brook to form an experimental theater group. France, of course, suffered its own mini-revolution, politically with the student population, the same year. When Brook took up residence with his collaborators in 1970, little was left of that earlier revolution except the graffiti on the buildings around the Musée des Gobelins on the rue Berbier de Metz, the 150 feet square room which Brook was given to share on rare occasions with the Mobilier National -- the French government's collection of furniture.

The principal sponsor during its first year of operations was the Iranian government in the name of the Festival of Arts at Shiraz-Persepolis. An important component of the research effort envisaged by Peter Brook was foreign travel, discovery, and performance. The Shiraz-Persepolis Festival, in addition to providing needed funds, also offered an artistic destination where the product of group theatrical process could be presented and tested by an audience. From the beginning of the Paris-operations, Brook desired to free the Centre from the obligation of regular, scheduled performances in order for the group to have adequate time and scope to explore and develop material. On the other hand, he recognized equally the value of performance as the completion of the theatrical process which absolutely requires an audience and its response. Consequently, in means and end, the Iranian sponsorship insured the fledgling Centre a beneficient beginning. Additional funding came from the Ford Foundation with a $ 200,000 to support "international training. . . of actors, writers, directors, musicians and designers from all over the world."[3] Other sustaining contributions were made by the Anderson Foundation, sponsored by the Atlantic-Richfield Corporation, the Portuguese Gulbenkian Foundation, the John D. Rockefeller 3rd Fund, the David Merrick Arts Foundation [Merrick having produced a number of Brook's successful presentations in the United States such as *Irma la Douce* and tours of *Marat/Sade* and *A Midsummer Night's Dream*], and lastly UNESCO of the United Nations which provided fellowships for special collaborators like Irene Worth who joined the ICTR for the Iranian pilgrimage. Subsequently, the French government has preserved Brook's experimental workshop far beyond the originally projected three years of its work to the present time.

The director along with a carefully selected group of multinational, polyglot performers began a shared search -- or perhaps more

accurately, a shared research – for the roots of drama, anthropologically, mythically, philosophically, for the possibilities of a "new"
dramatic language of universal communicability, and for a theatrical
simplicity achieved by an ensemble beyond the limitations of individual actors. This enterprise has been genuinely collaborative, a community of questers, in which whatever theatrical truth emerges from
exercises and research is created by the group rather than in imitation or representation of a truth lodged elsewhere, through carefully
developed expressive means. As desiderata for theatrical art, Brook's
goals were not especially novel; they share much in common with
Meyerhold's theatre, for example, and more recently, nearly every
avant-garde experimenter in the theatre of the 1960's from the
Becks, Joseph Chaikin, to the Polish guru, Jerzy Grotowski, and
the Argentinian director, Victor Garcia, to name only those innova-
tors with whom Brook and his company interacted at various times
during the decade of the seventies.

The essential function of Brook's theatre in this initial Paris
phase was to elicit connectedness among all the constituencies of
performance, including the audience. Since so many international
movements in the arts of the late nineteenth century and the twentieth century have first blossomed in Paris, and the very term for experimentation in the arts takes the form of a French phrase -- avant-
garde -- Brook's locus for a global theatre appropriately sports a Paris
address as poste restante no matter the exotic perimeters of his far-
flung travels. Paris and the French government remain surprisingly
hospitable and generous to foreign theatrical directors who elect to
work in France.

The gathering of an international company never engendered for
Brook the creation of a homogeneous or synthesized performance
theory or style. Truly the son of chemist-parents, Brook looked forward to holding in suspension the multiple cultural traditions represented within the ICTR and using the "chemistry" sparked by inter-
action for enrichment but not merger. He voiced his enthusiasm for
what separate cultural traditions could bring to communal work in
remarks about the Japanese actor, Yoshi Oida, who as " 'a fully
trained Noh actor. . . can co-ordinate his movements with an awareness and a sense of space and rhythm that you couldn't learn in any

171

dramatic school in the West.' "[4] Usually about fifteen or so different nationalities and/or cultural traditions have comprised the participants in the Paris workshop at any one time. A sometimes smaller number may participate in the field experiences to foreign countries, but then Brook enlarges his human resources by including indigenous talent from his host countries.

With such a linguistically varied group of participants, verbal sharing presented a considerable challenge that Brook welcomed for its opportunity to restrict the language of the theatre exercises to a small, fixed vocabulary of invented syllables, an extension somewhat of the linguistic experiment used in the radically shortened version of *The Tempest* directed by Brook in 1968 with little actual use of Shakespeare's text. In the early experiments of the ICTR, each actor contributed one syllable, and the order into which they were organized, despite the theoretical possibility of any order, began *bash/ ta/hon/do*, by which the language was later known. This language was used for improvisations as well as for other exercises; subsequently, it became a pattern for the inspiration of a new theatre language. Brook's linguistic experiments during this early period with the ICTR relate him most consistently with the avant-garde experiments current with other contemporary theorists and theatre experimenters in the decade of the seventies.

The language of Bashtohondo was employed in the first public performance the Centre staged in a unique Christmas offering to the children of the workers in the Mobilier National, a dramatization of the American short story, "The Bee Man of Orm," written by Frank Stockton. Though the "production" was given only once, it proved a deeply satisfying experience for all concerned, with the audience joining in improvisations with the actors long after the performance itself had ended.

Apart from attempts to forge a new theatre language, about which more will be said shortly, Brook pursued further linguistic experimentation by having his company work with a number of international texts in their original languages. The director endorsed this somewhat bizarre practice in a notable interview given during the maiden year of the ICTR in Paris:

It is possible for actors, whatever their origin, to play in-
tuitively a work in its original language. This simple principle
is the most unusual thing that exists in the theatre. We've been
rehearsing Japanese, ancient Greek, Spanish, and we're about
to add Arabic and Persian texts. Our actors play in the language whose sound texture has meaning.[5]

With his developing interest in linguistics and anthropology, Peter
Brook inevitably invited comparison with French structuralists
whose achievements were being celebrated during this time. The director never identified himself as a disciple of structuralism. Yet as
he engaged his actors in the interconnected process of theatrical experiment wherein separate roles were subordinated to emphasize the
relationships between them in such a way as to point up the essential
dramatic structure and language of theatre, Brook shared the desire
of the structuralists for a system that transcends race, individualism,
and localized culture. However, Brook's approach is based less in a
belief in the structuralist order of things than in an almost mystical
conviction that the sounds and movements of the human body are
capable of striking an identical chord in any observer, despite his or
her own cultural or racial conditioning.

III. Now Voyager: Orghast in Iran (1971)

The culmination of the ICTR's experiments during its initial
months of operation was the pilgrimage to Iran for the fifth annual
Shiraz-Persepolis Festival of the Arts, the year of the 2500 centenary
celebration of the establishment of the Iranian monarch, an event
which the Pahlavi dynasty as successor to an ancient heritage was
eager to commemorate. Thus in 1971 Brook and a company of 25
actors, representing ten nationalities, together with four directors of
similarly diversified background, including Andrei Serban, Rumanian-
born but increasingly American-based, the British director, Geoffrey
Reeves, and the Iranian director of Armenian descent, Arby Ovenes-
sian, besides Brook himself, arrived in Iran with indeed a new theatrical language especially created for the scheduled presentation by
the distinguished British poet, Ted Hughes, who termed his tongue,
"Orghast."

173

Because everyone in the Centre was equally unfamiliar with the language Hughes had created, the group's linguistic education was truly democratic, as Brook would like most discoveries to be. Many of the roots of Hughes' Orghastic words suggested onomatopoeic versions of assumed universal physiological states or conditions meant to mirror the mythic basis of the content to be presented, some of which described in the following way in the program for the performance:

> Orghast [the "play" and its language shared the same label]
> stems from certain basic myths – the gift of fire, the massacre
> of the innocents, the imprisonment of the son by the father,
> the search for liberation through revenge, the tyrant's destruc-
> tion of his children, and the search for liberation through knowl-
> edge -- as reflected in the hymns of Zoraster the stories of Pro-
> metheus and Hercules, Calderon's *Life's a Dream*, Persian leg-
> ends, and other parallel sources.

Other material such as excerpts from the Aeschylean tragedy, *The Persians*, which reported the defeat of the Festival's host country by the ancient Greeks was daringly included but in the original Greek which escaped the notice of Iran's censors. Christopher Innes in a recent book identifies a structuralist view in this material and in Hughes' method similar to that advanced by Claude Levi-Strauss to the effect that myths operate in people's minds independent of their consciousness of that fact. "This organic unity," writes Innes, "also brings the linguistic exploration into the frame of an all-encompassing myth, with connection (again following Levi-Strauss) between the gifts of fire and language, the use of both being what distinguishes man from nature, the cooked from the raw."[6] Throughout the decade of the seventies Brook pursues strong links which unite the cultures of the world at the mythic level, sometimes with gratifying accessibility and universality, occasionally with quite esoteric results.

The plan for the presentation of *Orghast* called for the first part to be performed at the tomb of Artaxerxes II twice a night on successive nights, beginning at sunset for a duration of about one hour, and the second part to be presented at Naqsh-e-Rustum, the burial ground of other Persian kings, including the great Darius, once or twice at dawn a few days later. After rejection of an elaborate stage design by the Swiss designer, Jean Monod, it was decided that no set would be constructed: the sites for performance were viewed as sufficiently dramatic spaces in themselves, acoustically and visually. Little artificial lighting was used in order to concentrate on the natural Promethean element of fire which was integral to the thematic content of the production.

Notwithstanding the efforts at universalizing through the actors' preparations and the nearly Jungian repository of ancient images and ideas of *Orghast*, the audience often found the presentation curiously one-sided in its address, as Christopher Innes explains: "This appeal to the primitive night side of nature seem only to have worked with the over-educated, intellectually sophisticated spectators at the Persepolis festival – perhaps because of the highly literary sources for that collage of creative myths." (*Holy Theatre*, p. 142) Most observers apparently found the unity of history, nature, and myth more or less successful and intelligible within the spectacular space of Iranian ruins, but Brook found the effect not readily transferable to other theatrical spaces, as he discovered when he tried to revive moments of *Orghast* back in Paris and on his subsequent African tour.

Margaret Croyden, the indefatigable and enthusiastic unofficial American publicist of Peter Brook, witnessed the Iranian production and remarked on it: "Hughes has, in his way, attempted a passion play. Brook directed it as if it were sacred art, and part of the audience received it as if it were an epiphany."[7] There were, to be sure, critical dissenters whose reactions to *Orghast* were something less than glowing, perhaps the most outspoken being the German critic, Ernst Wendt who wrote:

> The attempt to combine stage, performance and spectator in a *unio mystica* was a highly artificial, over-perfected experiment which will serve to confuse the course of theatre. In seeking to awaken mythical powers below the detritus of civilization, the production has gone so far beyond physical reality that it has reached the radically abstract point of pure theatre-craft, formalistic acting. . .[8]

In contrast, Andrew Porter, the famed music critic and opera translator who had been instrumental originally in enlisting Brook's participation in the Persepolis Festival, wrote on the basis of his eyewitness attendance at the ICTR performances in Iran: "The Playgoer who has entered deeply into *Orghast* has passed through fire, and can never be the same again."⁹ *Orghast* had the advantage [or perhaps weakness] of being tantalizingly vague and grandiose that nearly any interpretive hypothesis could be applied to it and any emotional response seemed permissible from total belief to complete disbelief. The predilection for magic and mystery that has taken hold in the decade of the eighties Brook anticipated a decade earlier heralded by his *Orghast*.

Brook's visit to Iran revealed his instinctive rapport with alien customs and mentalities. Unlike foreign policy experts of the period, Brook did not view Iran as a characterless cipher, an oil exporter, arms market, or strategic ally, but as a nation whose history, religion, and social mores made it unique and dramatic. Brook exulted in seeing a performance of the Persian *Ta'zieh*, enacted by the Shi'ites who alone had broken with the Islamic proscription against representation of sacred matters. Brook considered the performance the living form of an extant mystery play because during the theatrical event, as the director expressed it, "an event that was told as a remembered happening in history, six hundred years ago, actually became a reality at the moment."¹⁰ Wherever Brook travels he actively seeks out the native theatre of the region.

During his stay in Iran, Brook tried to avoid what he considered a colonialist attitude which a western visitor might easily fall into as a result of staging an elaborate dramatic production without the support facilities and techniques ordinarily taken for granted in Europe and the United States. " 'The only way,' " Brook submits, " 'to get close to any people different from your own is to enter into their rhythm, and to do that you must be on a non-result-producing stint.' " (*Orghast at Persepolis*, p. 243) Accordingly, Brook and his company would be less concerned about production-oriented activities on their African journey a year later. The Iranian pilgrimage consolidated the collaborative approach of the ICTR at the end of its first crucial year of existence. The legacy of the trip would be considerable. One of the small ways its influence continued in Brook's staging may be seen in his devotion to Persian carpets as a principal element of stage decor for the next decade and beyond. In Iran, a country half-way between East and West at that time, if not tragically at the moment, Brook found a rich field-trip experience for collaborative effort with a truly international company.

Upon his return to Paris, Brook takes up a dramatic text once more from the current modern repertory but one with enormous linguistic interest. In 1972 the ICTR begins work on Peter Handke's *Kaspar*, a contemporary masterpiece which had been introduced into the workshop by the German director, Frowin Haas, during a brief residency with the company before the Iranian trip. Handke's character, Kaspar, can almost be taken as emblematic of Peter Brook himself who worries more than the other theatrical directors of his generation, nationality, and first name – Hall, Wood, Glenville – about what words in theatre and in life can and cannot do, what limits of thought and action they can impose. Handke's play of "speech torture" affords a theatre degree zero, a *tabula rasa*, in which the protagonist is taught and then imprisoned by language, as Brook often implies the theatre's empty space may likewise be.

As early as World Theatre Day on March 5, 1969, Brook articulated his distress about the institutions of the theatre which is somewhat analogous to Kaspar's sense of entrapment expressed by his one and only sentence:

> In the theatre we are all prisoners of the forms through which we live and to which we owe our everyday existence, and these forms perhaps more than any other forms in our society are marked by periods that are not our own, marked by these periods for sentimental and economic reasons. We work in buildings that distort the nature of our activities because these buildings were built a long time ago and it is neither expedient nor economic to change them. We work for audiences which rarely change because the structures that draw those audiences toward us are complete in themselves and make change very difficult. . . . We are forced always to the same point, our immediate role is to re-examine, re-examine deeply, fundamentally, destructively, and we hope creatively all the forms by which we live. . . . Perhaps our starting point must be in taking in the teeth the challenge that comes from facing a very unpalatable fact, that we have so little world theatre in which to rejoice.[11]

177

Brook and his company set out to rectify that situation, to find something worthy of celebration in theatre, both "rough" and "holy," to borrow the descriptions which Brook finds operating in the best of Elizabethan theatre. The director has never been able to find the combination of excellence in a twentieth-century playwright which he finds in Shakespeare who remains always his touchstone. It is true that association between Peter Brook and a particular living dramatist with whom triumph after triumph can be achieved has always eluded the director of the ICTR, whether by choice or by accident. More typical of his practice is occasional work on something like Handke's *Kaspar* but rarely follow-through to a definitive production.

IV. Africa: Process and Deferred Product (1972-73)

It was an exotic text Brook and the ICTR travelers took to Africa for their trip in 1972-73. Ted Hughes, again, was developing a dramatization of what has been called the Catch 22 of Islam, a work of twelfth century Islamic or Sufistic mysticism, *The Conference of the Bird*. The work deals with a symbolic pilgrimage which proves that Mecca is wherever you are, but without the actual attempted journey you would never understand that you need not have it in the first place -- a premise, it may be recalled from a parallel source, shared with the Good Witch Glinda in *The Wizard of Oz*. Hughes' version of this story constituted the work-in-progress which Brook and the ICTR company hoped to refine in the course of presentations in Africa. No final version, however, emerged as part of this African expedition. Most of the public presentations there took the form of largely improvisatory performances, implicitly questioning traditional categories, identities, and boundaries of theatrical experience. With titles like "The Box Show," "The Ogre Show," "The Noise Show," "The Bread Show," "The Shoe Show," and "The Man and Woman Show," performed often in make-shift theatre space, open and empty as Peter Brook could wish until his actors filled it, in the middle of an African village. Brook's company investigated the connection between life and art, seeking to reveal some of the deepest and most universal aspects of human experience in a manner which would be immediately recognizable and meaningful to any observer. This trip to Africa contributed significantly to Brook's continuing quest for the zero-base of theatrical experience wherein the body of the actor becomes the chief working source and reference through which the audience discovers an action becoming a drama.

In an interview Brook explained the special appeal Africa held for him:

> The African who has been brought up in the traditions of the African way of life has a very highly developed understanding of the double nature of reality. The visible and the invisible, and the free passage between the two, are for him, in a very concrete way, the two modes of the same thing. Something which is the basis of the theatre experience -- what we call make-believe – is a passing from the visible to the invisible and back again. In Africa, this is understood not as fantasy but as two aspects of the same reality.
>
> For that reason, we went to Africa to have the possibility of experimenting with our own work in relation to what one could consider an ideal audience.[12]

The company set out from Algiers, proceeded straight through the Sahara Desert – a rather ultimate empty space for the director to confront – into northern Niger and Agades. From southern Niger the company entered Nigeria and then crossed into Dahomey, returning eventually to play in the capital of Niger, Niamey, before turning north and cutting across a bit of Mali and Gao. After a return trip across the Sahara, the company arrived again in Algiers. Part of Brook's motivation for the pilgrimage was to give his actors respite from what he calls "Western conditioning" in the theatre which he considers strongly result-oriented. As the earlier extended quotation indicates, Brook sought audiences in-experienced with Western forms in order that his company could concentrate on the creative process itself independent of "product." Wary of the so-called Western dualisms, especially the division between emotion and intellect, Brook almost required a trip to Africa to test his new-found instincts about a mythic and ritualistic theatre.

In Oshogbo, Brook and his company visited a sacred forest where they were privileged to see a ritual staged by the White Priestess of the Sacred Forest. Somehow, in experiencing as a group the sacred quality of this ancient ritual, the players in the work-in-progress version of *The Conference of the Birds* found themselves inculcated with a sense of wholeness hitherto missing in their work which they carried over into their presentation to the delight of the African audiences.

Their capstone experience, demonstrating the reciprocity between members of the Paris-based ICTR and their African hosts, occurred Daru Lapidu's open-air theatre in Oshogbo. The preceding night, Brook's company had watched the celebrated Lapidu troupe brilliantly perform a Yoruba legend. At the end of this performance, the great African director/actor invited his audience to come the next evening to see a presentation by his good friend, Peter Brook. Consequently, in such a supportive and even transformative context, the performers in the incomplete *Conference of the Birds* rose to the occasion, as reported by eye-witness John Heilpern in his delightful book-length study of Brook's African pilgrimage:

> Incredibly it was as if the shape and form of Brook's longed-for theatre of the future were at last bursting open. And something wonderful, something more that Brook had waited years to see. For there was the unique and individual colour of a real group, sensing each other out, playing with danger and care, care for each other, but performing as one, absolutely as one true group of people who have come together to share what they have to offer. . . .
>
> For the first time in the long journey, a true sense of this mysterious search of the birds was captured in the twilight. But just as quickly as it had been caught, it was gone again. [13]

The evanescence of the precious moment of connection Brook freely acknowledges; his re-sacralization of the theatre cannot become institutalization of the "holy," nor can it be made to order. It is for this reason probably that Brook demurred in claiming any new or theoretical principles about theatre from his African expedition. Always more the explorer than the discoverer, Brook in Africa did not conclude a search the way a finder might. At most, he was a seer, less in the prophetic sense than in the literal perhaps. Brook and his company came to Africa, as earlier they had gone to Iran, not like theatrical imperialists bent on taking something away but rather in the spirit of exploration to establish a working relationship with an artistically rich continent in human terms for performance ends. The Persian rug which customarily was unrolled by the ICTR members in typical African villages to designate the playing area functioned symbolically like a magic carpet – even a flying one – as it made possible new unity of races and cultures wherever the company traveled.

In the years following the African trip Brook worked ever more seriously on cultivating with his company a sense of global awareness. He challenged thereby a number of assumptions too often associated with Western culture from white supremacy to excessive faith in the merits of modernization and high technology. For example, Brook increasingly eschewed in his imaginatively minimalist and simple production values reliance on the complexity of sophisticated electricity. As the decade of the seventies proceeded the ICTR gave demonstrations and workshops around the globe, held invitational performances of works-in-progress, and sought out mutual exchanges with diverse performing groups as varied as the American-based National Theatre of the Deaf, the Chicano theatre company under the direction of Luis Valdez, El Teatro Campesino, and Grotowski's famed Polish Laboratoy Theatre.

Possibly as a result of his work on *The Ik* which will be discussed shortly, Brook became fascinated with the land rights debate in Australia where the government had sought to take over the aboriginal lands for their rich mineral deposits to the sacrifice of territory sacred to the aboriginal gods, lands which belonged to the aborigines for forty thousand years. Consequently Brook journeyed to Australia and became acquainted with elements of aboriginal culture which paralleled other explorations he made elsewhere. Before the aborigines Brook presented *The Ik*. Summary comments about this experience Brook published in the London *Sunday Times*, and these may be taken as representative of his thinking, anthropologically and theatrically, during the seventies:

> Aborigine stories come from an indefinite prehistory, when
> legendary figures moved through unformed space. Each of their
> adventures became fossilised into boulders, rocks valleys, so that
> the landscape was created like a series of words in Braille. At first,
> a child learns just his and his family's tales, then through initia-

tion he learns other fragments, until one day he is ready to take part in a ceremony with other tribes which fills in the gaps. By the time he is old, the many scattered pages bind together in a complete and coherent book and he becomes the possessor of the totality of tribal understanding.[14]

In particular, Brook responded favorably to the aboriginal notion that for a people on the move life itself is a walk toward wisdom, a conception not unlike Brook's own experimental inquiry during this phase of his career into the theatricalization of everyday life and thought through global and intercultural connections, the triumph of performance without the intervention necessarily of a theatrical text – theater without the authority of literary drama as in the Western cultural tradition. If this manifestation on Brook's part is seen as avant-garde, it is an avant-garde which transcends any particular style and theory pioneered by an avant-garde theorist. Brook's eclecticism militates against any such focus, which is the reason this study terms him the explorer rather than the discoverer, the latter more often associated with the avant-garde artist in whatever medium. Some of these generalizations can be tested by considering Brook's retrospective performances with the ICTR at La Mama in New York during 1980 where much of the experimental work of the company during the seventies attained the look of completeness and culmination.

V. Retrospective at La Mama (1980)

While Brook and the ICTR had paid visits to the United States to present workshops and work-in-progress occasionally during the seventies, most notably in 1973 at the Brooklyn Academy of Music, the retrospective of three evenings of performance at Ellen Stewart's bastion of experimentalism in New York, La Mama E.T.C., from April 30 to June 15, 1980 constituted a kind of temporary summing-up for Brook before new embarkations. This visit was eagerly anticipated by theatre-goers and critics. The four plays presented, though widely divergent in source, content, and performance style, achieved in presentation often unexpected, but brilliantly realized, thematic unity – a microcosm binding together the physical, social, and spiritual dimensions of existence which moved progressively from stomach to soul.

The evening of comedy consisted of a double bill: "L'Os," (The Bone), based on a story by Birago Diop from African folklore and dramatized by Malick Bowen and Jean-Claude Carrière of the Paris Centre; and Alfred Jarry's *Ubu Roi*, which included excerpts from the complementary *Ubu enchaîné* in a combination of French, English, and Franglais. A contemporary tragedy, *The Ik*, an adaptation by Denis Cannan, Colin Higgins, and Colin Turnbull from the latter's anthropological study, *The Mountain People* (1973), composed the second program. Finally, the mystical romance, *The Conference of the Birds,* the same work which Ted Hughes had attempted to adapt from the twelfth-century Persian poem by Farid Uddin Attar in the early years of the seventies, was presented in a new adaptation by Jean-Claude Carrière and Peter Brook. *The Conference of the Birds* restored theatrical artifice and high style to the minimalist legacy of the other two evenings of repertory without violating the performance premises of simplicity and audience discovery of the invisible in the visible – the principle which undergirded all the performances at La Mama with the goal of enriching the lives of those who participated in the activity, whether director, actors, or audience.

The African "L'Os," used as the curtain-raiser to *Ubu*, introduced in bold and comic terms major thematic concerns that figured in all the subsequent repertory by the ICTR at La Mama. It is a farcical cautionary tale about human greed with Malick Bowens, one of the collaborators of the adaptation, portraying a man of such fundamental pride and possessiveness that he gives up his humanity and then his life rather than share a bone with his neighbor and friend. The bone is all that remains of a cow he once owned. In this almost Beckettian play, Mor Lam, the protagonist of "L'Os," feigning death in order to keep his precious bone all to himself, finds that he has been buried alive in the company of his bone. Appetites, often those actually of the stomach, unify and intensify other themes of universal experience that touch humanity most profoundly presented in the repertory at La Mama. "L'Os" takes the audience directly – even literally – to the first rung of that ladder where, as W. B. Yeats says, all ladders start "in the foul rag-and-bone shop of the heart."

Alfred Jarry's once sensationally avant-garde play, *Ubu Roi*, with some additions from elsewhere in the Ubu canon, that scandal which once provoked riots in the Paris of 1896, received a curiously apolitical interpretation in Brook's staging. Again the emphasis is placed on appetite and greed with corresponding diminution of the play's political theme on the nature of power. The corpulent and gluttonous Père Ubu does, indeed, embody the bourgeois who has dined well, but mysteriously Ubu's large belly is used only in the middle portion of the play. Gratuitously Brook adds hints of castration for Ubu which the text does not support at the beginning of the play; then, in contradictory fashion, the director has Ubu fall upon his wife in sexual congress at the end, once more without textual evidence. The set for the production consisted of large and small cable spools used imaginatively as throne and much else in a way reminiscent of the Théâtre Vincinal's inspired foolery in "Real to Reel." Ubu's holding court with a toilet brush proved emblematic of Brook's ridicule of Ubu's world which took precedence over exploration of the horror and savagery of Jarry's burlesque version of *Macbeth*. Perhaps Brook used *Ubu* as a comic catharsis of his own gory and often brilliantly cruel stagings of Shakespeare's tragedies like *Titus Andronicus* and *King Lear*. That the comic mode prevailed in Brook's staging separates his *Ubu* from the special cruelty which Artaud perceived in *Ubu Roi* and which he sought to implement in his theoretical theatre as indication of humanity's thralldom to cosmic malignity. Brook's former Artaudian phase seemed to have metamorphosed, if not actually passed, as witnessed in the productions at La Mama to include a number of other theatrical viewpoints. "L'Os" and *Ubu Roi* taken together formed a comic whole predicated, as the program for the La Mama performances expressed it, on "Mr. Ubu's infinite stupidity, his crazy greed, his extraordinary hunger -- they thrive in his fatness, but they bite us close to the bone." Brook pulled down even the ruins, as Jarry insisted the play must do, with bricks strewn over the stage; Ubu recited his paternoster from atop a fallen brick rather than perched on a high rock as the text would have it. Brook's treatment of a classic avant-garde text from the later nineteenth century was simple, rough, and funny, possibly the only declension for an avant-garde piece eighty years later.

Besides the brief "L'Os,: Brook's ICTR presented a major statement about Africa in a piece which had evolved over the years, *The
Ik*, based on anthropologist Colin Turnbull's best-selling field study,
The Mountain People, a genuine tragedy recording the fate of a tribe
in Northern Uganda. The Ik were banished from their traditional
territory in 1946 in order for the government to create a national
park of their former lands. Originally nomadic hunters, the Ik were
supposed suddenly to become farmers. Therefore, they were required
to alter their whole way of life immediately and without instruction.
Partly as a result of severe drought, the intended transformation of
the Ik failed. When Turnbull investigated the consequences of the
government edict upon the tribe eighteen years later, he discovered
that the Ik, once a flourishing society capable of mutual support, had
ceased to function as a civilized society. What Turnbull found was a
case study of mass malnutrition, apathy, notable sexual lassitude,
greed, and despair. All remaining energy left to the Ik was centered
on finding enough food to insure individual survival. The Ik wouldn't
store food supplies. Their philosophy insisted that what is not carried
in the stomach cannot be stolen. The Ik's price for random survival
was loss of compassion, love, affection, concern and care even for
offspring and aged parents in need. Beyond these large personal
losses stood the utter collapse of the even larger cultural institutions
such as history, religion, morality, and art. In Brook's presentation,
based on Turnbull's findings, the drama suggests that in the dilemma
of the Ik may reside a foreshadowing of possible worldwide decline
of the so-called advanced contemporary civilizations as they, too,
succumb to selfishness and narcissistic detachment. The dramatic version of *The Ik* becomes then symbolic rather than documentary, set
in the universal community of neglect and pain.

In its deliberate avoidance of sentimentality, which appeared to
extend even to legitimate sentiment at times, Brook's company
achieved a measure of distanciation perhaps more appropriate to
ethnography than to the theatre, since audience identification with
the suffering Ik in emotional terms often was thwarted. In Brook's
version, Turnbull as a character, played by Andreas Katsulas, did not
change from empathetic concern to heartlessness as he does in *The
Mountain People*. A moving exception to this cultivated detachment

was Yoshi Oida's portrayal of Turnbull's guide; his compelling performance of an African by a Japanese actor validated Brook's international casting.

The evocation of Africa through sweeping the dirt covering the floor of the playing area into paths, the building of a hut on stage, and the starting of numerous campfires captured brilliantly the anthropological constituents of the Ik's elemental culture. The success here may be partly attributable to the performers' direct exposure to Africa itself some years earlier which they were able to call upon in their re-creation of certain episodes in Turnbull's book. The actors achieved something on the order of what Victor Turner, in another context, terms performative and reflexive anthropology wherein "there would be a constant back-and-forth movement from anthropological analysis of the ethnography, which provides the details for enactment, to the synthesizing and integrating activity of dramatic composition, which would include sequencing scenes, relating words and actions of the characters to previous and future events, and rendering actions in appropriate stage settings."[15]

Turnbull shares the physical experience of the Ik, but identifies with them at a level beyond the physical. Because of the nature of the theatrical experience, Brook's production forced recognition largely through the physical – especially the shockingly physical exemplified by snot blown on stage and putative vomiting, the latter quite a bit more vivid than Alfred Lunt's simulated action years earlier in Brook's production of *The Visit*, as the Ik gorge themselves on grain at one point. On the other hand, Brook's use of the objects the Ik so desperately needed for survival attained a special kind of poetry, particularly when accompanied by comments in the Ik language. The words were made meaningful because the things represented by them were tangible on the stage. The registering of moments of physical sensations in *The Ik* sometimes reminded one of Richard Foreman's experimental work except that Brook seemed much more concerned with unity of effect than Foreman does. As with a pair of peasant shoes in a Van Gogh painting where we are able to see the essential nature of the reliability which characterizes the being of all equipment and the sum of its involvement in human life, Brook projected beyond the usefulness of simple materials to the roots of art in the world of everyday work and everyday things. The ensemble's encounters with the simple materials of Ik life – a teapot, a container of water, a sack of grain, some firewood – derived some of their excitement from the theatrical techniques developed improvisationally for the basic vignettes which the ICTR members performed during the African expedition. Moreover, the making of theatrical event out of quotidian objects anticipated the recent avant-garde return to [neo]-realism on the part of certain directors and playwrights in the contemporary French and German theatres. Immediate reality acquires the transformative power of elementary hierophany with the manifestation of the sacred in some ordinary object. Brook's Ik revealed reverence for the purpose of things, and their collaboration with these things occupied much of the action.

The story of the Ik is tragic in its inexorableness. As Brook's production unsparingly dramatized, the Ik's decline and eventual fall would not yield in any permanent way to remedial attempts. At best, custodial care might preserve life for a short period, but no permanent transformation of the Ik would be possible. Brook captured the horror, qualified somewhat by macabre humor, of this inevitability with an excellent scene where Christian missionaries arrive to impose memorization of "Rock of Ages" upon the Ik as a pre-condition for obtaining food. The Ik dutifully learn the hymn, after a fashion; however, when they, in turn, receive the food, instead of storing some of it for a later time, they eat all of it until they become ill. In light of the fact that Americans consume from thirty to fifty times as many goods of all descriptions than most residents of the Third World, the gorging of food by the Ik has considerable relevance to our own pursuits.

One of the most disturbing characteristics of the demoralized Ik, according to Turnbull, was their alacrity for laughing at the suffering of others and often at their own suffering as well. Brook's production displayed this laughter as a species of degradation, to borrow the apt description of laughter by Henri Bergson. With excellent dramatic effect, Brook sometimes implicated the audience in inappropriate comic responses only to draw everyone suddenly up short. In those intense moments of *The Ik* when Brook's company brought to

187

consciousness the concrete, existential relationship between wealth and poverty, the years of work on this material seemed well worth the effort. Despite the audience's satisfied stomachs, like Père Ubu's, we left the theatre feeling a little less smug.

The most beautiful and moving of the ICTR presentations at La Mama was the latest version of the long-standing work-in-progress, *The Conference of the Birds*, now co-authored by Peter Brook himself and his frequent collaborator in Paris, Jean-Claude Carrière. It may be recalled that Ted Hughes, no slouch as a poetic aviarist, judging from his extensive body of bird-inspired and bird-titled verse – though his birds have been known to wag wings as heavy as oxen, was unable to complete a satisfactory version years earlier. What Brook and Carrière produced is a rather Gurdjieefian journey, almost a "Meeting with Remarkable Birds," as the birds, led by the Hoopoe, search across desert and seven valleys for their true king, called the Simorgh. Notwithstanding its inspiration in ancient Sufism, *The Conference of the Birds* as presented by Brook appeared closer to contemporary notions of self-fulfillment through the triumph of the therapeutic than to twelfth-century Islamic mysticism. The secret revealed finally to the pilgrims who attain audience with the king is that the Simorgh is themselves and the journey itself is Truth. If there is little distance between archetype and cliché in the content of *The Conference of the Birds*, the written text providing not much more than the impetus for improvisation and performance realization, what is seen on stage deserves the accolades bestowed upon the production.

The hitherto bare stage of the other presentations at La Mama was transfigured for this production by the simple opulence and color of Persian carpets on the floor and back wall. The actors, attired in exquisite costumes designed by Sally Jacobs under influences from the West, Persia, and Africa to suggest parallels with Brook's own cultural inquiries and pilgrimages during the years since the ICTR was established. The audience watched actors as many "birds," transformed as a result of the simplest props or changes in apparel: a duck suddenly emerged from turquoise silk loosely wrapped around a forearm held horizontally; a fan placed on a man's head yielded a VIP -- a Very Proud Peacock; a wide-eyed actor holding a tiny wooden grate before his face became a caged parrot; a bit of pale blue fringe served as the fluttering tail of a skittish dove; the gnarled end of a long branch was metamorphosed into an ostrich's head, crowning a poor creature that has walked across the desert; wings of silks and brocades held out on bamboo sticks in front of the actors represented most of the flock.

For the first time in Brook's career he made extensive use of masks in *The Conference of the Birds*, particularly Balinese masks, some ancient and others of recent design, all quite naturalistic. Brook describes the effect he sought with the Balinese masks:

> ... We found, having rehearsed with and without masks (which is why we put them on and off), that there were moments when the natural, ordinary reality of the actor is better than the mask; because you don't want all the time the exalted impression. It is like using adjectives; there are moments when a good style is naked and uses simple words, and there is a moment when without a glorious adjective the sentence can't make its point; and the mask is suddenly a glorious adjective that exalts the entire sentence.[16]

Other times Brook's ensemble demonstrated expertness of mime and gesture in evocation of the aviary through Japanese Bunraku theatrical techniques with the actors as both puppeteers and puppets. A proud falcon with a delicious French accent shaped convincing talons from a simple hand gesture; a head gracefully cocked or a shoulder deftly raised suggested the behavior of birds or defined a feature with subtle imagination – far more subtle than Trevor Nunn's felines in *Cats*.

The birds narrate and dramatize a number of stories about human folly and the vanity of human wishes, linking the species of homo sapiens all too well with the most featherbrained of the birds: the holy man whose chief concern is his beard and not his soul; the old man who conserves his tears as it they were gems parallels the nightingale, played stylishly by Natasha Parry, who cannot join the quest because she is too passionately committed to her roses.

Brook's painstakingly developmental approach to *The Conference of the Birds* may be glimpsed in the report he gave to Margaret Croyden for inclusion in the brief history of the ICTR, "The Center: A Narrative," which was distributed at the La Mama performances:

There are very few masterpieces in the world which have gone beyond subjective experience that really touches something that involves a real witness of man's essential experience. . . . CONFERENCE has always been a challenge because it goes beyond one's capacity to penetrate it completely. Nobody can completely take hold of it, so that as something to work on, it's inexhaustible. . . . Now in our early period we used fragments as bases of improvisations and so we never really touched the whole piece. On the last night in Brooklyn [at the Academy of Music during a 1973 ICTR tour] we did three different versions of CONFERENCE, with three different versions of CONFERENCE, with three different sets of people leading them. Yoshi Oida and Michele Collison did a show at eight P.M. and that one I call the rough theater. Natasha Parry and Bruce Myers did the mid-night CONFERENCE all by candlelight, which was exquisitely sensitive; and I call that holy theater; and then Liz Swados and Andreas Katsulas did the dawn show, which was entirely ritualistic and musical. After the three shows we talked, and I said to them that one day perhaps we would do the work again and we will incorporate all three versions into one. And so we left it – until this year [1980], when we did in fact attempt to incorporate all three.[17]

The force of Brook's imagining, the sheer theatrical power of observed vitality, and the confidence of its telling elevate *The Conference of the Birds* nearly to the desired synthesis of the rough and holy theatre which Peter Brook envisioned years ago in *The Empty Space*. The production further served as a compendium of the director's eclectic appropriations of theatrical styles and techniques from both the East and West which finally went beyond any one particular style. To Brook's credit everything here does not fit neatly together; the rough messiness preserves theatre's necessary strangeness.

While the visual appeal of the evenings at La Mama remain most memorable, Brook's likewise supplied considerable aural interest to complement the visual effects and haunting imagery, especially through the contribution of his talented percussionist, Toshi Tsuchitori whose subtle accompaniment to *Ubu*, ingenious effects to conjure up a Land Rover and the thousand natural sounds of Africa in *The Ik*, and lastly the evocative, senuous score for *The Conference of the Birds* enlivened the productions at La Mama. Few directors have

190

paid as much attention to music as an element of the theatrical event as has Peter Brook, and the results were particularly satisfying during the visit to the United States in 1980.

Near the end of *The Conference of the Birds*, Brook's company dispensed with their bird trappings and performed a little choreographed segment with only bamboo sticks – those staples as implements from the workshop years. Interestingly, the former wonder and excitement of the sensuous production were maintained now through the simplest, abstract means, for the presentation had fully enlisted the participation of the audience's own full-fledged imagination – pun intended -- by this time in the proceedings; and those perceptions completed the work of art. In this way *The Conference of the Birds* invited comparison with Brook's inspired legerdemain in *A Midsummer Night's Dream* .

The New York critics generally waxed enthusiastic -- if not doting – about Brook's ICTR visit to La Mama. Fairly typical of the press reaction was Mel Gussow's description of the visit in the *Times* as "the supreme theatrical event of the season."[18] To be sure the less centrist and establishment critics like John Simon and Erika Munk were somewhat less enamored. The latter summarized the evenings rather devastatingly: "Brook comes bearing the grand old 60's baggage; theatre as moral act, group creation, primitivism, ritualism, audience contact, astonishing gestures and utterances, big ideas, magic actors, minimal texts."[19]

Not everyone bought Brook's anthropological postulates of the psychological unity of humankind, though the director's high-mindedness freed of political ideology may have been ingratiating to the establishment press. While Brook celebrated the aesthetics and spiritual traditions of Third World countries, he avoided the ideological concomitant. Kenneth Bernard cryptically remarked, "anthropology is a clinical form of tourism as well as a quasi-scientific form of colonialism."[20] Robert Brustein took a similar stance with his suggestion of an element of unconscious but indulgent condescension at work in Brook's portrayal of Africa in the works displayed at La Mama. "Was it possible," Brustein asks, "that with these pieces Brook had created his own form of deadly theater which audiences now attended out of social rather than cultural piety?" i.e., a sophisticated audience congratulating itself on its privileged witnessing of the simple wisdom of " 'little people.' "[21] This condition may be more the problem of the Western audience than a reflection on the director. Certainly Brook's aesthetic is no longer, if it ever was, primarily informed by European and Western models. As a director Brook emphasizes the importance of theatre/performance, the dyad historically associated with Asian and African cultures to unite actors and audiences at the expense of the more typically Western dyad of drama/script which usually cedes primacy to writer and director.[22] On the basis of the work presented at La Mama, nothing appeared more classical than anything else in Brook's art terms, and the age of imperialism had truly passed with the emergence of the ICTR's global village. But Brook's theatrical experiment in this pursuit testified more to his humility than to his arrogance which might be more characteristic of other avant-garde directors. Despite his aspiration to spiritual insight, Brook's work with the ICTR seems more a therapeutic bridge across cultures for the benefit of all his participants, be they actors or members of the audience.

VI. A Parisian *Cherry Orchard* at the Bouffes du Nord (1981)

Lest Brook be accused of permanently substituting the intervention of performance against the authority of the text, the director has returned in recent years to interpretation of such standard "texts" as Chekhov's *The Cherry Orchard* and Bizet's opera, *Carmen.* Following a prolonged ten week-rehearsal period, Brook staged in the spring of 1981 *The Cherry Orchard*, not with the ICTR, but at his Parisian theatre, the Bouffes du Nord, in a French version written by Jean-Claude Carrière. The production made use of a bare set abetted by the cindery walls of the old building itself; the stage picture relieved of its barrenness only by Brook's ubiquitous Persian carpets which were spread on the floor and sometimes bunched up to form little mounds for sitting. Otherwise largely unfurnished until Act III and without suggestion of a literal orchard [or even a tree] anywhere in the playing area, Brook's production of Chekhov's play relied on the talents of his players to evoke place and mood. As with earlier productions which had been performed at the Bouffes du Nord, Brook employed the empty space to good dramatic effect. Julius Novick, writing in *The Village Voice*, observed of Brook's staging: "How rich and strange it is to see Chekhov's denizens of a decaying civilization go through their paces in the midst of that great, destroyed, reclaimed, ironic, multivalent space [of the Bouffes du Nord]."[23] The distillations of refinement through simplification on display during the ICTR visit to La Mama were taken one step further toward apotheosis and quintessence when similar cutting-back had been sensitively applied to staging of a great dramatic text from the realistic theatre which in production had often seemed excessively cluttered and busy.

If Brook temporarily returned to theatrical masterpieces with *The Cherry Orchard*, his perspective on this monument of realistic theatre – realism itself becoming avant-garde about this time in the twentieth-century – represents no great departure from his earlier experimental aesthetics as can be ascertained in his conversation about the production with critic Mel Gussow: " 'The reason *The Cherry Orchard* touches people in extraordinary ways is because, as in any great work, behind it is a myth. This is a poem about life and death and transition and change. Chekhov was writing it when he was dying. Knowing that he had a short time left, he felt a theme emerging: something loved has to be relinquished, disappointment has to be accepted. ' "[24] Thus the mythic element of Chekhov was foregrounded in Brook's production, but not to elimination of the quotidian details which make Chekhov's masterpiece a comic play about real life.

The tireless alumna of her husband's numerous experiments, Natasha Parry embodied Mme. Ranevsky as fully as possible, glamorous but solidly Russian as the actress's ancestry made possible [Peter Brook's mother-in-law was listed as advisor to translator Jean-Claude Carrière]. Michel Piccoli, best-known for his varied film roles over a twenty year period, was lured back to the stage to play Gayev, Mme. Ranevsky's brother who for once was played as a man of suavity and elegance as Chekhov imagined him to be. This character's dignity, notwithstanding the intimations of internal moral damage, gave evidence of Brook's respectful approach to the depth of insight in

Chekhov's play. Similarly, Brook's Firs, portrayed by the retired comic actor, Robert Murzeau, who said he waited sixty years to do Chekhov when the director and his assistant, Maurice Bénichou, asked him to join the ensemble, achieved a fullness of characterization rare in Chekhov stagings. This Firs invited and received pathos at the end of the production but not with the usual mawkish devices. His last words were whispered, somewhat as Paul Scofield's Lear whispered in Brook's earlier production of Shakespeare's masterpiece. The parallel may have been intentional, since Firs is the eldest who perhaps has suffered most and who ends as possibly the most dignified embodiment of the era which passes in the course of Chekhov's drama.

Dramatizing exactly and concretely the significance of "home," "departure," "decision and indecision," "loss and recovery," Brook predicated a special mythic wholeness in this production of *The Cherry Orchard* as almost a rebuke to the disintegration and aborted goals which have overtaken domestic values amid the frustrating and confusing complexities of modern life -- the essential sadness of which is symbolized in Chekhov's play, of course, by the breaking of the string. This time round Brook surprisingly conducted his search for spiritual and mythic meaning in the very core of bourgeois materialism, shown most physically in the sumptuous costumes of his "unfurnished" production. It has taken Peter Brook a long time to come to the realistic theatre and to the degree of quietness necessary for hearing a string break in the sky. Brook with his own Russian ancestry, his discipleship of Gurdjieff, and his Meyerholdian understanding of Chekhov's theatre as nearly musical form rather than as behavioral study had at last come home, albeit at a French address. There is hope that an English-language version of *The Cherry Orchard* will be staged in the near future under Brook's direction in London.

VII. Brook's Return to Opera: *La Tragédie de Carmen* (1981;1983)

Peter Brook's return to opera, an artistic form which he once declared dead following his ill-starred tenure at Covent Garden, took place in his own "poor" theatre, the Bouffes du Nord (1981), and not in a grand operatic house. The presentation was Brook's own radically scaled-down, re-arranged, revisionist "deconstruction" of Bizet's *Carmen*, now entitled *La Tragédie de Carmen* in the adaptation by Brook, Jean-Claude Carrière and the composer Marius Constant. These collaborators pared the standard *Carmen* to an eighty-minute version, of chamber opera intimacy, for what Brook hoped would be concentrated truth of an archetypal variety served up with lyric transparency. Seeing the musical drama as a clash between two ways of life, Brook's version emphasized the primitive Gypsy element in conflict with the more repressive Spanish values, and toward this end he restored some details from the original Mérimée novella which had been eliminated in the libretto for Bizet's opera.

The cast was composed of only six voices – four singers and two actors – and a small orchestra of fifteen members. In the Paris production, Brook alternated three Carmens and three Don Josés, often mixing up the partners for renewed freshness. In the New York production which reopened late in 1983 the long-dark Vivian Beaumont Theatre in Lincoln Center, Brook used five casts in a variety of combinations. Brook sought to make the essentially unnatural form of lyric drama as credible as possible, as if it were inevitable that most of the dialogue and dramatic action would be sung as living, direct theatre. His production was partially informed by the neo-realist movement in contemporary French and German theatre, as Jane Kramer, writing in *The New Yorker* implies without making the connection explicit with her choice of vocabulary dear to the hearts of the neo-realists: [Brook] "wanted to give his singers, as much as his audience, that experience of something daily, something ordinary and open-ended. It is amazing to see young singers relax under his tutelage [Brook always deplored the fierce competitive nature of operatic singers during his years at Covent Garden]."[25]

La Tragédie de Carmen was staged in close-up, originally in Brook's own 600-seat theatre to good effect, though somewhat less so in the immense Vivian Beaumont at Lincoln Center. However, even in the latter space, Brook was able to civilize a formerly unmanageable theatre by merely removing a few seats and making a thrust stage into the auditorium. In New York the orchestra was nearly hidden in the wings so that it would not be interposed between the audience and the dramatic action. Typically Brook found Shakespearean analogies for his version of *Carmen*. He compared the two non-singing characters, Lillas Pastia and Zungia, to Shakespearean characters who speak prose rather than verse. Further the director used the venerable Shakespearean device of doubling for some of the roles. Lastly, Brook compared *Carmen* to Shakespeare's *Antony and Cleopatra* with their shared plots of a clash of values from two quite different worlds and the similarity of the gypsy Carmen and the exotic Cleopatra. Yet the Renaissance quality of this production put one less in mind of Shakespeare, perhaps, than of his Spanish contemporary, Lope de Vega, and his well-known aphorism about the stage: "three boards, two actors, and a passion." The focus was intimate, often death-centered; the director who once won acclaim for crowd scenes now abandoned those scenes in *Carmen*.

Bizet's music, without grand choruses and other affective elements which Brook viewed as extraneous, became the agent of a rather lugubrious drama of sexual passion, betrayals, and homicides. The operative word *tragedy* seemed somewhat misapplied, but the death-laden *mise en scène* often suggestive of a bull-ring was sober and compelling; his intention to wrest this operatic material from the realm of operatic culture and transfer it to the realm of experience has parallels with other Brook efforts. In the collision of conventions and imagination, Brook succeeded in releasing the latter with his usual economy of means. Spain was evoked simply with burlap sacks, one of which becoming animated as Carmen herself, Brook's favorite pieces of stage-decor, pillows and carpets, actual campfires, and lots of dust and sand. The theatrical effects were strongly reminiscent of Brook's work on *The Ik*. Striking images of the production linger such as Carmen rolling an especially suggestive cigarette on her thigh or the drawing of a gypsy's magic circle in ochre around the sleeping lovers who enjoy a moment of peace before their doom; the violence of Carmen's kick delivered to the Spanish virility of an officer recalled similar moments in Brook productions all the way back to *Dark of the Moon*.

After extraordinary success in Paris and throughout western Europe, Brook's *La Tragédie de Carmen* met with a rather mixed response in the United States, partly as a result of uneven and sometimes unfortunately inadequate singing. Perhaps this production presented in Lincoln Center within the cultural space of both the Metropolitan Opera and New York City Opera would have fared better downtown at La Mama where Brook first intended it. Brook deplored the high cost of tickets uptown [the top price in Paris had been about $ 8.00], and he urged viewers to elect the cushion seats on stage or in the balcony for $ 10.00 as being the most desirable locations for viewing the production. For a number of American critics, as for their earlier European colleagues, and many members of the audience, Brook's *Carmen* proved a devastating demystification of nineteenth-century grand opera in favor of tragic reality.

At its weakest, *La Tragédie de Carmen* fell between two stools of opera and theatre; at its best, Brook's simple, sensuous, and passionate *Carmen* represented a perfect union of words and music, feeling and natural expression in most facets of its staging and in its original conception. It was a creative collaboration between a contemporary director and Bizet, truly crossing centuries, rather than an ego-centric "take-over" by a conceptual director in the manner, for example, of a Richard Foreman. Despite all of Brook's alterations of Bizet's opera, the director's abiding respect for the core of the material was vindicated.

As a stage director, Brook continues to favor the inclusive over the exclusive, cultivating a variety of styles instead of imprinting something totally autographic as signature to each production. With *The Cherry Orchard* and *La Tragédie de Carmen*, Brook has resumed being metteur en scène, an interpreter of established masterpieces of theatre, as opposed to spiritual mentor of an experimental or research-oriented theatre ensemble, though the activities of the latter role doubtlessly affected the performance of the former. The inspiration of great dramatic texts upon Brook's inventiveness has always been most satisfying, and it is pleasant to see him continuing to fulfill that promise once more before returning to experimental work with the ICTR.

197

VIII. The *Maha-Bharata* Project (1983-   )

The other side of Peter Brook's work inclines toward the mystical and visionary over the pragmatically theatrical, and his ongoing project which bears witness to this facet remains the Maha-Bharata Project with the regrouped ICTR, following a respite of a year or so, an ambitious endeavor which has been rather delayed in implementation. The plan calls for nothing less than a dramatization, running anywhere from three hours to twelve hours in performance, of the earlier of the two great Sanskrit epics of western India, *The Mahabharata*, the longest poem said ever to exist, perhaps eight times longer than the combined length of the Homeric *Iliad* and *Odyssey*. Brook sees this project as the establishment in the English language of a new dramatic text – one of major importance – "on themes of Shakespearean universality, which can be absorbed into the working repertories of theatre companies and groups everywhere," as the director's 1980 prospectus for the project expressed it. The raw material of the Sanskrit epic with its final reconciliation of conflicts and processes which brings together heaven and earth, war and peace, the origin of law, education, the meaning of justice, the role of the sacred, life, knowledge, and death offers Brook his most grandiose challenge in shaping a theatrical event out of great themes which are not conceived as the Western perspective traditionally has understood them. Brook has gone so far as to argue that anything not in *The Mahabharata* really does not exist! Not a religious poem in the Western sense, the epic nevertheless is embued with a feeling for the sacred at all times even in the midst of lewd, comic, even vulgar narrative with a wide-range of movement and absence of distinctions between angels and devils.

The theatrical traditions which Brook wants to explore with his company in preparation for *The Mahabharata* include, not surprisingly, Kathakali, the indigenous southwestern Indian dance-drama based on content from the Hindu epics, and Balinese dance, the latter which once upon a time revolutionized the theatre of Artaud. In addition, Brook plans field research in the sub-continent of India itself where the performers can work in the actual locations of the events dramatized. Obviously this effort constitutes Brook's most

198

ambitious attempt to date at cross-fertilization between culture, although *The Conference of the Birds* and *Meetings with Remarkable Men* suggest earlier milestones toward it.

Originally a finished version of a script, prepared once more by Jean-Claude Carrière in collaboration with Brook, was projected for initial public presentations early in 1983. That date has, of course, been postponed, and with delay the original budget projection of two and a half million dollars has been revised upward. Should Brook's project be viewed as an avant-garde experiment or as an act of hubris? The answer is probably both/and rather than either/or. There is something laughable in the notion that *The Mahabharata* must now be viewed as a pretext for its ultimate destination as a performance under the co-authorship and direction of Peter Brook. Yet in the long dialogue between Arjuna, the hero of the epic, and his charioteer Krishna, "The Blessed One," the avatar of Vishnu, often termed the jewel of the *Bhagavat Gita* ('Song of the Blessed Lord"), Brook finds the essence of Hinduism and the singly identity of all messiahs; in this Eastern confirmation of the supreme place of love in the relationship between man and God, we achieve the willingness to act without fear of the consequence of action – a truly blessed state for a man of the theatre. Brook is not unaware of the danger of confusing religion and theatre, as he explained during a forum on *Marat/Sade* back in 1966:

> ... then the theatre is a religion, and that means that people
> with their limited human experience, are setting themselves
> up in direct rivalry with Christ, Mohammed, and Buddha,
> claiming to know how to create a ritual that can deeply stir
> people. If you look at it closely one sees this as lunacy, hubris,
> homemade do-it-yourself religion. On the other hand one sees
> the difference between the emotional experience of theatre
> and the true religious experience.[26]

Perhaps in his subsequent exotic journeys, celebrations of theatrical holiness, and meetings with spiritual mentors, Brook somewhat forgot his own caution, but not really. Over the years Brook has enlarged his ability to discern spiritual sources of art and in theatrical terms to communicate something like the religious essences of art which are applicable to and complementary of human existence.

199

Those political, territorial, and religious factors which have traditionally separated the people of the world – Catholics against Protestants, Moslems fighting Jews, Hindus against Moslems, and numberless smaller conflicts – Brook works to overcome through theatrical art and understanding in touch with eternal and universal experiences grounded in myth and ritual. Herein lies Brook's contribution to postmodern inter-culturism through a broadened view of performance which extends beyond theatrical space. While Brook remains apolitical to a large extent insofar as he does not usually urge direct action as politics traditionally has been understood to do, he may contribute to the so-called politics of the imagination through performative acts which point toward subjunctive futures. In this sense religion replaces politics in the postmodern world, as Brook has been inclining for a number of years.

Though Brook has in recent years sought out exotic, non-Western texts toward these postmodern ends, a model is available within Western culture, as Brook appreciates, in the habitual design of Shakespeare's romances. In his own symbolic, postmodern Globe Playhouse Peter Brook works to restore the public ritual of communal drama. His performance texts almost always have literary sources and antecedents – often venerable in the extreme. The search continues for connections and linkages of words, rituals, images, and dreams to embrace the entire human race, living, dead, and to be born captured in performance. Brook combines the emancipated and the avant-garde with traditional and popular culture with the effect of making his audience feel advanced in their views but comfortable in their sensibility. Philosophically, Brook seems most like the postmodernists in his denial of any fundamental difference -- despite certain practical differences – between actor and audience with reference to the performance of their shared life's journey.

NOTES FOR CHAPTER SIX

1 Margaret Croyden, "Exploration of the Ugly: Brook's Work on *Oedipus*: An Interview with Colin Blakely," *The Drama Review*, 13 (Spring, 1969), 120-124.

2 Martin Esslin, "Oedipus Complex," *Plays and Players*, May, 1968, p. 24.

3 Andreas Freund, "Peter Brook Is Setting Up a Theatre Center in Paris," *New York Times*, June 5, 1970.

4 A. C. H. Smith, *Orghast at Persepolis: An International Experiment in Theatre Directed by Peter Brook and Written by Ted Hughes* (New York: The Viking Press, 1972), p. 58.

5 "A Talk with Peter Brook," The American Theatre, 1969-70 (New York: Charles Scribner's Sons, 1970), pp. 17-23.

6 Christopher Innes, *Holy Theatre: Ritual and the Avant Garde* (Cambridge: Cambridge University Press, 1981), p. 137.

7 Margaret Croyden, "The Achievement of Peter Brook," in *Lunatics, Lovers and Poets: The Contemporary Experimental Theatre* (New York: Dell, 1975), p. 266.

8 Quoted in *Orghast at Persepolis*, p. 243.

9 Andrew Porter, "In Triumph through Persepolis," *Theatre '72*, ed. Sheridan Morley (London: Hutchinson, 1972), pp. 161-170.

10 "Leaning on the Moment: A Conversation with Peter Brook," *Parabola: Myth and the Quest for Meaning*, 4 (May, 1979), 46-59.

11 International Message for World Theatre Day, March 5, 1969, for International Theatre Institute, Paris.

12 Michael Gibson, "Brook's Africa: An Interview," *The Drama Review* 17 (September, 1973), 37-51.

13 John Heilpern, *Conference of the Birds: A Story of Peter Brook in Africa* (Harmondsworth: Penguin Books, 1979), p. 299.

14 Peter Brook, "The Living Theatre of the Outback," *The* [London] *Sunday Times*, 17 August, 1970.

15 Victor Turner, "Dramatic Ritual/Ritual Drama: Performative and Reflexive Anthropology, *The Kenyon Review*, NS 1 (Summer, 1979), 80-93.

16 "Lie and Glorious Adjective: An Interview with Peter Brook," *Parabola: Myth and the Quest for Meaning*, 6 (Summer, 1981), 60-73.

17 Margaret Croyden, "The Center: A Narrative," May, 1980, n.p.

18 Mel Gussow, "La Mama: Three Evenings by Peter Brook," *The New York Times*, May 6, 1980.

19 Erika Munk, "Peter Brook: The Way's the Thing," *The Village Voice*, May 12, 1980.

20 Kenneth Bernard, "Some Observations of the Theater of Peter Brook," *Theater: A Magazine Published by the Yale School of Drama*, 12 (Fall/Winter, 1980), 72-78.

21 Robert Brustein, "The Quest of Peter Brook," *The New Republic*, June 28, 1980, pp. 27-29.

22 On these geographical and cultural distinctions, see Richard Schechner, "Drama, Script, Theatre and Performance," in *Essays on Performance Theory, 1970-76* (New York: Drama Book Specialists, 1977), pp. 36-62.

23 Julius Novick, "Gray Paree," *The Village Voice*, August 5, 1981.

24 Mel Gussow, "Peter Brook Returns to Chekhov's Vision," *The New York Times*, August 9, 1981.

25 Jane Kramer, "Letter from Europe; Paris, February 17," *The New Yorker*, March 1, 1982, pp. 121-127.

26 "Marat/Sade Forum: Peter Brook, Leslie Fiedler, Geraldine Lust, Norman Podhoretz, Ian Richardson, Gordon Rogoff," ed. Richard Schechner, *TDR*, 10 (Summer, 1966), 214-237.

Chapter Seven

CONCLUSION

Twentieth-century theatrical directors, at least those of a theoretical and experimental bent, may, with some stretching of the metaphor, be described as hedgehogs who wish to becomes foxes. Dissatisfied with their knowledge and practice of a few homely truths, they have sought -- often in the name of theory -- to generate from this knowledge either a whole litter of smaller truths or one great truth sufficient to transform the artistic universe. The hubris of the latter Peter Brook often shares, but his mixture of intuition, imagination, extensive experience, and common sense have usually spared him the worst presumption of the more extreme theorists of the "New Theatre," despite his eclectic susceptibility to the newest wave breaking over the old theatre. Not apparently burdened by the anxiety of influence, Brook has been quick to subsume the trends of the avant-garde to stimulate his own creativity and that of his actors, but, perhaps on the basis of his own place in world theatre, the results frequently display a mainstream character in his application of others' experiments. If as a young director Brook bridged the gap between the commercial and fringe theatre of London, as a world figure in the arts he has extended his talent for bridge-building to hitherto unrealized connections amounting to the syncretic. His primary inspiration in this pursuit was the man who invited him to Paris as head of the ICTR, Jean-Louis Barrault with the great French actor-director's conception of "total theatre."

The function of language in the theatre has persisted as one of Brook's abiding interests, and his experimentation within this context has been wide-ranging and extensive. For Brook the deepest rule is that every subject should have its own form. Language can never be separate from form, or form from the subject. To say something new, or something different from what already has been said in the theatre, requires a different language because old forms carry with them old ideas. In his more extreme experiments, as Christopher

Innes succinctly explains, Brook has reversed the "traditional priorities of communication, elevating the secondary elements of gesture, pitch, tone and the dynamics of sound or movement that give expressive values, over the primary element of intellectual meaning. The difficulty is that forms of language, verbal, vocal, emblematic or physical, communicate with any precision only to the extent that their symbols are known and shared." (*Holy Theatre: Ritual and the Avant Garde*, pp. 136-137) Brook holds to the almost mystical notion that the theatre rooted in immediacy and presenting a universal human encounter – especially when arrived at collectively with a multi-national company – pushes beyond all traditional language. "Brook's emphasis," according to Innes, "has been on integrating the individual actor in the group on the dubious premise that expressive forms created by a collective – however small -- will have the force and universality of archetypes. This exploration of non-semantic body language implies that, extending Barrault's concept, theatre should not imitate life but directly create experience." (*Holy Theatre*, p. 137)

Similar doubts about Brook's success with his linguistic experiments have been voiced by his former collaborator Charles Marowitz, author of a famous *New York Times* piece on Brook back in 1968 which summed up the director's career to that date plus forecast that "if the prodigy [Brook] who became the professional can assimilate all his influences and evolve into an artist of uncluttered individuality, the next 10 years may be golden for Brook and transforming for the theater."[1] At least in the area of language Marowitz thinks Brook has not fulfilled his earlier promise. "It's not finding a new language or action image," declares Marowitz, "but the challenge of reorganizing existing theatre language which Brook might well face."[2] Further, Marowitz is bothered that Brook seems determined to create a mystical theater operating by its own criteria beyond the possibilities of criticism. It must be recognized at the same time that when Brook presents one of the great dramatic texts, he shows himself usually a serious respecter of the language, and his actors strive to speak the words with cogency and clarity. Despite his own superb results in working with dramatic literature in notable productions, Brook continues to experiment on occasion as if he were re-inventing the theatre from scratch. This tendency may be the basis for Marowitz's most telling charge made against Brook in 1968 that the director works best with second-rate material, since in Marowitz's eyes Brook seeks conversion of the text to his own uses and private purposes at the expense of significant interpretation. That conversion often proved highly satisfactory when the strength of the original material was not particularly great. Actually the years with the ICTR and the group-generated improvisations on skeletal text material appear to confirm this charge more than we might like to admit. On the other hand, Brook's recent assay of Chekhov suggests a counter-movement for which we can be grateful. Marowitz always faulted Brook for the latter's failure to deal adequately with Stanislavski; the connection between Brook and Chekhov may yet rectify the neglect of Stanislavski as well.

Brook's genius emerges in his ability to compress, and the Mahabharata project suggests his most ambitious application yet of economy to superfluidity, paralleling his success in stripping language of the unnecessary, streamlining without loss of resonance.

Controversy persists over what category Brook should be placed in as a British director. Someone like the late Kenneth Tynan argued in 1977 that Brook was the last real master-director of the proscenium stage and a product of the English-speaking establishment theatre which Tynan insisted still badly needed him: "I don't think the world at large needs his thoughts, but I think the English theatre, in its upper and more establishment reaches, needs his flair."[3] However, a decade earlier than Tynan's pronouncement, Charles Marowitz considered Brook a "non-English talent obliged to flower in unconducive surroundings." ("From Prodigy to Professional") Certainly Brook has never been a director to stay either still or at home! Having caught the continental flu at an early age, Brook became attuned to the theoretical, anthropological, and structural thinking from France and Germany which placed the arts – including the theatrical arts -- in a wider and deeper context than the usual conception which prevailed in England. It was perhaps his perceived reductiveness and repetitiveness of the British theatre which brought Brook to Paris and from there to the world at large. British insularity and traditional English scepticism yield in Brook to the cultic, communal, and ritualized impulses toward the holy – the interpreter less an empiricist than an exegete of the sacred text.

The dimension missing in Brook's search for *communitas* is the political, a fact that separates him from the agit-prop theatre which sees evil as a consequence of societal wrongs to be corrected. "Brook sees evil," as Kenneth Bernard observes, "essentially as faulty vision to be cured by the proper 'journey' or 'search.'. . . He is close to the 'profile' of the Living Theater, which, although its ends are declared to be political, sees in the theatrical event 'the climax and centre of their search.' "("Some Observations of the Theater of Peter Brook") As Brook tries to refine the instincts of his actors – and by extension through them the audience as well – but does not tell them what to do, he seeks to melt ideological and political postures into personal sensibility through theatre's power to transform and elevate.[4] Without succumbing either to political ideology or avant-garde theatrical methodology, Brook's engagement with performance attempts to be spontaneous and strong, as it was when he began as a prodigy, and because of this response there occurs for actors and audience alike an experience of opening and enlargement through the event. Testimony of Brook's effect in this regard on the performer covers the gamut of actors who have worked with him from the stars of the British theatre to members of the ICTR; they acknowledge his elemental power to enlist the imagination of others in his own almost magical confrontation with the so-called "other" world of the theatre. Not a formula of any kind, Brook's means are derived from intuition, courage, and the accumulation of experience from a lifetime working with plays and players. And the last constituency to be so affected by Brook is, of course, the audience whose consciousness becomes a kind of drama through participation and observation, but the transaction here is more mystical than political, though less sacred than therapeutic. "Everything in the theatre," Brook explained in an interview with Daniel Labeille, *"everything in the theatre* [Italics are Brook's] is a meeting. There are different elements that meet so that the theatre becomes both a place and a point of meeting and every theatre phenomenon is a meeting between two, or three, or five things."[5] Journeys end in lovers' meeting if the theatrical preparation has been adequate, and the director's "formless hunch," as Brook calls it, profound and daring enough.

The "formless hunch" is Brook's principal contribution to the rehearsal process, but that too is seen with reference to a *meeting* between the hunch and the large mass of material accumulated in rehearsal. In the final stages of rehearsal Brook encourages the actor "to discard all that is superfluous, to edit and tighten." (" 'The Formless Hunch': An Interview with Peter Brook") Direction, consequently, becomes a matter of simplified apparatus and liberating, albeit deepened, perceptions worked out between Brook and the performer. In turn, a similar, though largely unconscious, transaction between the performer and the audience occurs. Such performances may come to closure, but the mind cannot really close them off. Their end-result is not settled being but rather unsettled becoming which explains why so many of Brook's productions remain in the memory of the theatre-goer long after the director is quite content to move on to another project, as Brook ceaselessly does.

Brook does not like to look back, but his admirers inevitably do in order to get a retrospective command of his achievement. The director commented on this aspect of himself in his interview with Labeille who was trying to get him to recall years later details of the production of *King Lear*:

> You see, in a sense I am very uninterested in the past, but totally uninterested, and as far as I'm concerned this really is what the whole of theatre is about. Things come and go and, in fact, all the work that we've been doing now, for instance with the Paris group for seven years, is based entirely on the uniqueness of the performance. So that, though we do play for a run, as well as other things, all our improvisations, the interesting things, are never repeated. (" 'The Formless Hunch' ")

While Brook does not say so in his interview with Labeille, his conception of the theatre as a meeting in the sense of a religious ceremony within a celebrant community – the Holy Theatre – requires the immediate, non-repeatable moment possible only with the living presence of actors and audience together in a single space -- empty except for their unique transaction. That the theatre's uniqueness presupposes mortality gives Brook's theatre its special poignancy and may explain why his work in film avoids the sense of stylistic continuity which an *auteur* is supposed to demonstrate – such continuity following in some sense from the repeatability of the film medium itself. For all of his non-English characteristics, Peter Brook proceeds as a stage director in the traditions of English empiricism, working on the piece at hand and not worrying too much about the theory. He has some notion – or formless hunch -- about what the piece is, or should be, and does his best to bring that notion to realization – which is not to say that when the production has been mounted, it bears an iron-clad resemblance to the idea of it he had in mind during rehearsals. Brook's perspective on the theatre is very close to the distillation provided by Jonathan Miller who noted: "The art of the director is the art of the ephemeral. But while it lasts it is an epiphany."[6] The theatrical moment gleams with meaning and beauty and then vanishes forever.

We have seen Brook serving the commercial theatre, subsidized showcase institutions like the Royal Shakespeare Company, and finally his own laboratory workshop with its performance wing; in all of these contexts Brook has been testing the nature and function of theatre. His career shows the overlapping of these categories, since on occasion he worked in all of them simultaneously. In recent years his preference has been for the laboratory conditions of the ICTR, but Brook's most engaging attribute may well be his pluralistic versatility. He avoids the snobbery of certain fundamental hierarchial oppositions with his celebration of the "Rough Theatre," thereby eliminating the received distinctions between so-called high and popular art.

Less ingratiating is the implicit assumption in some of Brook's field-experiences into non-Western cultures – part of his pursuit of "Holy Theatre" – that these "corporate" cultures demonstrate some kind of mystical superiority over the more strongly individualistic structures of Western civilization. Despite his ardent support for Western freedom and individual rights, Brook occasionally seems to indulge a nostalgia for the holiness he perceives in less advanced cultures where the long-evolved individualism of the Western heritage has not created the greater loneliness and sense of alienation which goes along with it. When his primitivist aesthetic appears to be the only path to holiness, Brook's anthropology takes on the character of romantic myth. Brook perhaps would like to overcome the condition of life for literate humanity which is constantly signifying, yet what is signified can only be interpreted as a function of how it is signified. Literacy's loss of plenitude and instinctive imagining may merit mourning.

While Brook may look like a post-modernist in his supposed revulsion against the means and materials of the Western world during his mystical absorptions in global rituals and myth, this devolution of his own culture passes when he returns to a Western avatar such as Shakespeare. A foolish consistency has never been one of Brook's failings; indeed to his great credit, Brook combats his own doubts and certitudes with equal energy. His headlong, spunky, and highly energized theatre – pluralistic, inter-cultural, eclectic -- makes actors and audiences want to come back for more, even if one never is sure just what to expect on a return visit. What endures is the special shared relationship in Brook's theatre between the watcher and the watched. Seldom has Brook been a director who fixes permanently or even capitalizes very much on the good things of earlier productions in later ones; he uses them, spends them, lets them go, and then counts on discovering or borrowing new devices. So far his capacity for seemingly infinite renewal has not failed him. The numerous journeys and meetings around the world may be necessary for this process to work. The result for Brook is that he does not leave the theatre as something ethnocentric.

We have come a long way with Peter Brook and his theatre. The violence and theatre of cruelty of an earlier decade have given way to something quite opposite. If once for Brook spectacle became a functional substitute for sacrament, his meetings with rich symbolic life in Sufi thought and Hindu epics – and assorted remarkable men – suggest a longing for the holy which may yet transcend the therapeutic substitute faith of self-fulfillment. On the basis of ever-expanded sharing in Brook's theatre arises the hope – if not of a return to the sacred or holy -- at least of an authentic therapy of commitment to communal purpose.[7]

Peter Brook may not be the greatest innovator or avant-garde theorist of post-World War II Western theatre, but he is the director at least for the English-speaking world who in our present critical, maybe even dissolving, stage of outworn theatre conventions, including the experimental, has the eclectic imagination to lead the actual theatre eventually to a stage of synthesis linking East and West. With Brook still at work in a variety of performing spaces, in light of his impressive track record of the past, he remains a key dynamic force in the evolution of the theatre as it will be at the end of the twentieth-century. His theatre like himself is heir to many cultures, religions, and imagery of the world but conformist to none. Having grown up artistically amid a climate of Western intellectual liberalism, Brook became a citizen of the world, and his theatre mirrors just such amplitude. The director we see now manifests a renewed concern for the quotidian as well as continued quest for the far-flung epiphany as if he were both Wallace Shawn and André Gregory combined from the popular cult film by Louis Malle, "My Dinner with André," (1981) perhaps tempered with just a little other-worldliness of E.T. That's eclectic!

NOTES FOR CHAPTER SEVEN

1 Charles Marowitz, "From Prodigy to Professional as Written, Directed and Acted by Peter Brook," *The New York Times Magazine*, November 24, 1968, pp. 62-63, 92-118.

2 Interview with Charles Marowitz, London, Oct. 22, 1980.

3 Kenneth Tynan, "Director as Misanthrope: on the Moral Neutrality of Peter Brook -- the wrong turning taken by a major British director," *Theatre Quarterly*, 7 (Spring, 1977), 20-28.

4 I am indebted for some of this description to conversation and question-answer in a public session with Jerzy Grotowski, Columbia University, New York, June 22, 1982.

5 Daniel Labeille, " 'The Formless Hunch': An Interview with Peter Brook," *Modern Drama*, 23 (September, 1980), 220-226.

6 Arthur Holmberg, "Jonathan Miller Bids Farewell to the Stage," *The New York Times*, May 29, 1983.

7 See in this regard, Philip Rieff, *The Triumph of the Therapeutic: Uses of Faith after Freud* (New York: Harper Torchbooks, 1968), p. 261.

SELECT BIBLIOGRAPHY

BERNARD, Kenneth. "Some Observations of the Theater of Peter Brook," *Theatre: A Magazine Published by the Yale School of Drama*, 12 (Fall/Winter, 1980), 72-78. A somewhat negative evaluation of Brook's recent activities predicated on the proposition that "anthropology is a clinical form of tourism as well as a quasi-scientific form of colonialism." Further, Bernard raises doubts about what he terms Brook's "eschatological methodology" with its excessive reliance on the intuitive and non-rational.

BERRY, Ralph. *On Directing Shakespeare: Interviews with Contemporary Directors*. London: Croom Helm; New York: Barnes & Noble, 1977, pp. 113-133. One of the best published interviews with Brook on his approach to Shakespeare. Berry's appendix on Brook's French production of *Timon of Athens* is likewise useful.

BROOK, Peter. *The Empty Space*. New York: Avon Books, 1969. The best account of Brook on Brook which has not been superseded by anything else from him in the years since its initial publication.

"Knowing What to Celebrate," [Interview with John Lahr], *Plays and Players*, 23 (March, 1976), 17-19. A brief but pithy interview which introduces some of Brook's principal assumptions behind a number of his major theatrical projects of the recent past and near future, from *The Ik* to provocative hints concerning the *Mahabharata* project.

"Leaning on the Moment: A Conversation with Peter Brook," *Parabola*, 4 (May, 1979), 46-59. A stimulating discussion of Brook's aims in theatre and film seen in the context of a journal which specializes in the study of myth and the mystical tradition.

"Lie and Glorious Adjective: An Interview with Peter Brook," *Parabola*, 6 (August, 1981), 60-73. In some sense a continuation of the preceding entry. This discussion with the director concerns primarily the transformative power of masks as derived from recent experiences such as *The Conference of the Birds*. Some intimations of directions to be taken in the *Mahabharata* project.

"Oh for Empty Seats," *The Encore Reader: A Chronicle of the New Drama*, ed. Charles Marowitz, Tom Milne, and Owen Hale. London: Methuen, 1965, pp. 68-74. The essay, first published in *Encore*, January, 1959, reveals Brook's penchant for emptiness as a stimulus to theatrical experiment and innovation in an idealized theatre independent of traditional economic considerations. Interestingly, Brook has managed to bring his ideal into reality with his Paris-based ICTR.

"Style in Shakespearean Production," *The Modern Theatre: Readings and Documents*, ed. Daniel Seltzer. Boston: Little, Brown, 1967, pp. 244-256.

An often-anthologized essay which appeared originally in the premiere volume of *Orpheus* (1948). Brook argues for latitude, even radical freedom, of interpretation in order that the reality of the dramatist's vision can be presented according to a style which will be appreciated and understood by contemporary audiences without doing injury to the Shakespearean text. An important manifesto against a museum-conception of Shakespearean production which Brook has fulfilled in his own notable stagings throughout his long career.

CROYDEN, Margaret. "The Achievement of Peter Brook," *Lunatics, Lovers, and Poets: The Contemporary Experimental Theatre.* New York: McGraw-Hill, 1974, pp. 229-285. A fine survey of Brook's career by an American enthusiast in a highly-regarded critical volume; Croyden ably shows the way Brook explores both the old and the new, striking blows equally against conventional, deadly theatre as well as what has become standardized in the avant-garde.

HAYMAN, Ronald. "Peter Brook," *Playback.* New York: Horizon Press, 1973, pp. 31-59. A quick retrospective of Brook's career enlivened with some relevant quotations from the director himself.

HEILPERN, John. *Conference of the Birds: The Story of Peter Brook in Africa.* London: Faber and Faber, 1977. Anything but a heart of darkness report of Brook and his Paris-based company's excursion into the African continent as seen through the perceptive eyes of a journalist who accompanied them.

INNES, Christopher. *Holy Theatre: Ritual and the Avant Garde.* Cambridge: Cambridge University Press, 1981, pp. 129-144. Sees Brook as a pragmatic director, influenced by Jean-Louis Barrault's conception of "total theatre," whose self-conscious and sometimes pretentious experiments often result in functional ends and valuable, if limited, purpose.

MAROWITZ, Charles. "From Prodigy to Professional as Written, Directed, and Acted by Peter Brook," *The New York Times Magazine*, November 24, 1968, pp. 62-63, 92-118. A succinct and perceptive summation of Brook's career to a point of significant change by a frequent collaborator in the decade of the sixties. It remains an excellent starting point for evaluation of the director.

"Lear Log," *Theatre at Work: Playwrights and Productions in the Modern British Theatre, a collections of interviews and essays*, ed. Charles Marowitz and Simon Trussler. London: Methuen, 1967, pp. 133-147. A valuable record of details about the rehearsal process for Brook's Royal Shakespeare Company production of *King Lear* by his assistant director who candidly demurs on some interpretive decisions made by the director.

"Notes on the Theatre of Cruelty," *Tulane Drama Review*, 11 (Winter, 1966), 152-172. Detailed notes by Brook's associate for the so-called "Theatre of Cruelty" season in London.

212

POLLACK, Daniel B. "Peter Brook: A Study of a Modern Elizabethan and His Search for New Theatrical Forms," Unpubl. Diss. New York University, 1972. A rich compendium of views and reviews of Brook's work to 1972 from a variety of published sources. The title is somewhat more provocative than the supporting evidence or the thesis of the study itself.

SCHECHNER, Richard. *The End of Humanism: Writings on Performance.* New York: Performing Arts Journal Publications, 1982. An impressive collection of essays by a distinguished American theorist, some of which may have application to Peter Brook considered as a post-modernist or an interculturist.

SELBOURNE, David. *The Making of A Midsummer Night's Dream.* London: Methuen, 1983. A detailed and lucid record of Brook's day-to-day methods and rehearsal strategies for one of his most acclaimed Royal Shakespeare Company productions. An indispensable book-length analysis of Brook at work.

SMITH, A. C. H. *Orghast at Persepolis.* New York: Viking, 1972. The first book-length of a single Brook enterprise, here his Iranian expedition, culminating in Orghast. A fascinating account of the beginning of Brook's chief experimental phase.

TREWIN, J. C. *Peter Brook: A Biography.* London: MacDonald, 1971. An amiable biography and appreciative assessment of Brook's career to approximately 1970 by a venerable observer of the British theatrical scene.

TURNER, Victor. *From Ritual to Theatre: The Human Seriousness of Play.* New York: Performing Arts Journal Publications, 1982. Seminal essays by a leading anthropologist, theorist whose ideas may be applied to some of Brook's recent theatrical experiments.

TYNAN, Kenneth. "Director as Misanthrope: On the Moral Neutrality of Peter Brook -- the wrong turning taken by a major British director [Interview given by Tynan with editors, Catherine Itzen and Simon Trussler], *Theatre Quarterly*, 7 (Spring, 1977), 20-28. Witty rebuke from a leading British man of the theatre about the experimental direction Brook has taken in Paris; Tynan thinks the British establishment theatre needs Brook, and in that context the director has often best acquitted himself.

213

218